A Sporting Chance

Books by Daniel P. Mannix

A Sporting Chance
Last Eagle
All Creatures Great and Small

WITH MALCOLM COWLEY
Black Cargoes

WITH JOHN A. HUNTER
Hunter
Tale of the African Frontier

WITH PETER RYHINER
Wildest Game

FOR YOUNG PEOPLE
The Outcasts

A SPORTING CHANCE
Unusual Methods of Hunting

by Daniel P. Mannix

E. P. Dutton & Co., Inc.
New York   1967

CONTENTS

ILLUSTRATIONS

7

INTRODUCTION

For the past twenty-five years, I've hunted with unusual devices. The East Whiteland Hunt still recalls with deep emotion the day my cheetah not only caught the hunted fox but also three of their best hounds. Bill Piper speaks feelingly of the time I hit a wildcat with a blowgun dart while Bill was standing under the tree just where the wildcat jumped. Arthur Miller could hardly do justice to the remarks of our local plumber when, called in to fix a stopped toilet, he found an infuriated rattlesnake caught in the drain. I'd been looking for that rattler for a week, and was glad to know where he was, but even after three years in the Navy I was shocked by the plumber's remarks. Plumbers aren't nearly so phlegmatic as people think; get them stirred up enough and it's amazing how eloquent they can be.

Next to a wife, hunting with unusual devices takes up more of a man's time than any other hobby. The *Encyclopædia Britannica* needs four pages to outline a brief description of how to train a falcon. After reading this description, P. G. Wodehouse remarked that as far as he could see the only things the hawk didn't have to learn were Sanskrit and the use of the trap drums. Dr. Newton Gaines, Chairman of Texas Christian University's Physics Department, got a boomerang as a toy and after discovering that the flying stick embodied the basic principles of the helicopter, discus, gyroscope, and inclined plane, wrote a treatise on the subject so complicated nobody except an Australian bushman could understand it—and the bushmen are so busy boomeranging passing wallabies they can't be bothered. And when it comes to hunting with hounds—well, Jorrocks summed up that situation when he said, "There's nothin' so queer as scent, 'cept a woman."

From all signs, the idea of giving your quarry a sporting chance is spreading through the entire hunting fraternity. So many states now have separate archery seasons that riflemen are demanding equal time. Falconry has become legal in state after state. Every clear body of water seems to be packed with scuba divers chasing fish with spears, and at Stone Mountain, Arkansas, a special tract has been set aside for crossbow hunting. So many people are keeping feral cats they've started a club with a magazine featuring such useful hints as what your legal rights are if your pet tiger eats the postman. For five years running, the beagle was the most popular of all dogs as people could use them to chase rabbits.

I'd suspect that there are several reasons for this revival of ancient sports aside from mankind's natural interest in the bizarre. The old techniques require more skill and are therefore more of a challenge. The easiest way to get fish is to throw a stick of dynamite into a lake, but most fishermen prefer fly casting. It's better for the fish, too, to say nothing of any stray scuba divers who may be in the vicinity. Also, the old methods bring a man closer to nature—which after all is the whole purpose of hunting. Hitting a rabbit with a shotgun teaches you nothing about the animal. Running him down with a pack of beagles makes you an expert on how a rabbit thinks, the tricks he uses to fool the hounds, and how he lives. It is also a salutary experience to discover that most rabbits have more brains than you have when not hopelessly outmatched by firearms. When game was abundant, a big bag was a hunter's main consideration. Now the sport is more important than the actual kill.

Hunting is a primitive instinct, and men hunt to escape from the mechanical world they've created. If you use a mechanical device for hunting, you're polluting the old with the new. It's like kissing a girl with an automatic computer; it's practical and sanitary but it doesn't taste the same.

I wasn't always a reactionary. When I left the armed services back in 1946, we all knew what the next war was going to be like. It would be a "push-button" war conducted by highly trained scientists who sat in laboratories watching complicated systems of dials. Today I've got a nephew in Vietnam. To prepare for his military duties, he spent three months learning how to strangle somebody with a two-foot length of piano wire. Many of our men are using hand-carved Montagnard cross-bows made by a remote hill tribe, to ambush the enemy. My old outfit, the Navy, is busy training porpoises to protect their divers from sharks. The last person to have a porpoise lifeguard was a Roman schoolboy living at the time of Augustus Caesar. Little things like that shake my faith in modern science. One of these days somebody will invent the stone ax-head, and revolutionize modern warfare.

We exterminated the primitive Indians because all the Indians did was hunt and fish. Then we built a mechanical world so we could make enough money to retire someday and to hunt and fish. There seems to be something wrong somewhere with this philosophy. Perhaps it's because as devices grew increasingly more complicated, they defeated their own purpose. The automobile was the perfect vehicle of escape so we could hit the open road and get away from it all. "Horse and buggy days" was a term of reproach. Now the roads are so crowded nobody can move and so many youngsters are interested in horses that Pennsylvania, the first state to introduce the modern superhighway, has started a course in horseshoeing at Penn State University.

There's a limit to what machines can do, even as machines. It wasn't simply chance that in the last war Sir Charles Portal, commander of the R.A.F., and Hermann Goering, commander of the Luftwaffe, were both enthusiastic falconers. They understood flight not only in terms of torque and the internal-combustion engine but also in terms of true flight—the almost mystic coordination between mind and motion. Scientists are turning increasingly to the study of animals to learn how human beings behave while there are still some animals left. When Harry F. Harlow, at the University of Wisconsin, wished to determine to what extent babies are dependent on mother's love, he conducted experiments with infant monkeys. He discovered that young monkeys when raised without their mothers became neurotic even though they were physically healthy. In their recent book *Genetics and the Social Behavior of the Dog*, Scott and Fuller draw inferences from their study on dogs that may affect human relationships.

To many people, a great difficulty with the old methods is that they are arts rather than sciences, and anyone using them must be an artist—or at least a highly trained craftsman. By the end of boot camp, any normally capable G.I. can be a reasonably good shot, but to be an archer requires years of practice. Yet an increasing number of people seem willing to make the effort to learn the old, almost forgotten skills.

Wild animals especially have always fascinated me, particularly the predators. The stoop of a falcon on its quarry, the careful stalk of an ocelot after a pheasant, the fishing skills of an otter—surely these are some of nature's high points. The naturalist can spend years in the field and never see a predator in action. The man who hunts with a trained animal can see it every day. The predator's killing skills are only one part of nature, but it is an important part, as man often discovers too late when he has exterminated the predator and then has to devise some way of controlling the predator's former prey. The predator is important in his own right not only as a thing of beauty—the world will be a poorer place when there are no eagles in America, cheetahs in Africa, or tigers in India—but also because when a species vanishes it can never be restored.

Twenty years ago a porpoise was simply a destroyer of valuable food fish. Today the government is conducting elaborate experiments to study their curious sonar means of locating prey underwater. Suppose man had succeeded in exterminating the porpoise as he did certain species of seals that seemed worthless at the time. A toad was an unpleasant-looking creature that gave you warts and that was to be killed on sight. Now the giant toad (*Bufo marinus*) is being bred by government agencies and imported to Formosa, New Guinea, and the Philippines to control everything from cutworms to rats. The price you pay for sugar and sweet potatoes depends on bufo's predatory skills. But only the very fortunate field naturalist or the pet keeper who can allow his pets to roam at large knows what a predator is capable of doing. A hunting animal kept in a cage is not a hunting animal at all; he is a prisoner unable to show his real abilities.

The Constitution guarantees our right to own firearms. This is a useful provision so we can snatch a shotgun off the wall and shoot a redskin or redcoat. I haven't seen either around lately, but if they do turn up it's a comfort to know we're ready for them. Bearing arms is part of our democratic heritage, and there's nothing more democratic than a shotgun: pull the trigger and you're bound to hit something, probably the hunter in the next field. Because anyone can use firearms without practice or without any knowledge of nature, the results are often interesting. Bill Green, who plays a prominent part in two of these stories, was riding a favorite horse near Fairlee, Vermont, when a shot rang out and the horse dropped under him. An excited hunter stuck his head out from over a ridge and shouted, "Did I get him?" "You sure did," said Bill. "Fine, I'll be right down," said the hunter. "Don't worry, I'll wait for you," Bill assured him. When the man arrived, Bill was sitting on the dead horse, and asked, "How do you want him—with or without the saddle?"

Incidents like this can't happen with primitive weapons. The hunter has to spend months learning not only how to use his weapon but also the habits of his quarry. He must not only be able positively to identify it but must also be close before he can release his arrow, dart, or bolt. I was in Wyoming some years back while a ranger was checking sportsmen's cars during the elk season. We saw one car coming with the trophy tied over the mudguard, but light kept flashing from the animal's hooves in a curious way. When the car got closer, we could see that the hunter had shot somebody's plow mule. The mule was shod, and the sun reflecting off the shoes had made the flashes. The ranger made no comment as he checked the driver's card authorizing him to shoot one elk, except to say, "Going to have the head mounted?" The ranger later remarked, "That sort of thing goes on so much you can't do anything about it." That hunter had never had to develop any of the skills or out-of-doors know-how essential to a man using the old methods.

The wholesale destruction made possible by firearms isn't always funny. Another ranger told me of a district thrown open to hunting for the first time. On the opening day of the season, cars were parked bumper to bumper around the doomed area. At dawn, the hunters moved in almost shoulder to shoulder. Then the shots began to ring out. The ranger counted an average of 38 shots per minute. When the massacre was over, he and his associates went in to inspect. "Nothing that breathed the breath of life had survived," he told me. Everything, including songbirds, had been killed.

Real hunters don't behave like this, of course, but as long as anyone can buy a gun and start blazing away, such tragedies will occur. Once we had so much wildlife we could afford this sort of thing. Today we can't. There are two solutions. One is the European system of big estates where the game is raised as a commercial crop and you pay a considerable sum to shoot. A keeper goes with you, and in addition to the entrance charge you pay for any bird or animal you hit. The other system would be for sportsmen, at least in certain areas, voluntarily to use less destructive weapons. Though they wouldn't come back with much of a bag, they would have learned a lot about real hunting; and the way things are going now, there won't be any bag for anyone pretty soon if we don't cut down on our destructive capabilities.

This would reduce the number of hunters but that is bound to happen anyway, as we are rapidly producing more hunters than game. For centuries it has been recognized in Europe that if a man wants to shoot grouse or partridge he must be prepared to pay a fee compatible with the cost of preserving the birds and maintaining the land where they live. For this reason, only the comparatively well-to-do hunt with firearms. The man of moderate means uses ferrets to bolt rabbits, terriers to dig badgers, or owns a single hound and joins with friends in similar circumstances to form a pack to hunt foxes or hares. This may seem unfair, but as the forests and open range disappear, some such arrangement is inevitable, or all game animals would be exterminated.

Perhaps it isn't as bad as it seems. Perhaps to some, learning how to make and use a boomerang is more interesting than using a high-powered rifle. Perhaps listening to the cry of hounds is as pleasurable as listening to the fusillade of shots when a rabbit runs down a line of hunters. Perhaps taking a walk in the country is more rewarding than sitting in a traffic jam breathing exhaust fumes. Once owning a rifle or a high-powered automobile meant power—they symbolized Progress. Today, automobile manufacturers are calling their cars after animals to induce the public to buy them.

We are constantly being told that the days of the "American dream," of the barefoot boy with his fishin' pole over his shoulder, his dog trotting at his heels, and his slingshot sticking out of his hip pocket, are over. We must accustom ourselves to living in steel-glass-asphalt catacombs or sub-urban developments. But surely we don't have to go out of our way to destroy what is left. Many mechanical devices for hunting are prohibited by law: punt guns, poison gas, recording calls to bring in wildfowl, baiting, salt licks, electric devices to attract fish, jack-lighting. I don't suggest more laws—we have enough as it is. But let's at least let youngsters know it is possible to hunt without elaborate mechanical means of murderous efficiency. Let's realize there was a time when the words "hunter" and "woodcrafter" were synonymous and when the chase rather than the kill was the prime interest of the sportsman.

A Sporting Chance

CHAPTER 1

The Feral Cats

Many centuries after man had domesticated the dog, the cat domesticated man. It must have been strictly the cat's idea, for although there are many ways a dog can benefit man, a cat is almost no good at all. The domestication probably happened in Egypt, where cats were regarded as sacred. The cat was willing to be worshiped as a god, and still is. He has never acknowledged man as a master. He associates with man only as long as man knows his place.

Dogs and cats are hereditary enemies, and dog lovers hate cat lovers. As far as dog lovers are concerned, the only person who'd keep a cat is an evilly disposed witch. This line of reasoning is easy to understand. Cats, not being animals that live in packs, have no loyalty. Even the way a cat pours herself around on noiseless pads gives you the creeps. A man can understand a dog fairly well, but no one can understand a cat; cats don't even understand themselves.

All this being more or less true, why keep a cat? The best answer is that cats have a curious fascination for many people. In 1962, a twenty-two-year-old novice from the Convent of the Good Shepherd in London took some children to see a circus. After the lion act, she left the convent and joined the circus as a lion tamer. In America, a trainer with the old Al. G. Barnes show asked a wide-eyed seventeen-year-old girl if she'd like to go in with some of his tigers. She innocently slipped into the barrel-barred cage while the trainer waited grinningly to catch the cute little blonde when she came dashing out. A Sumatra tiger glided toward her with that terribly suggestive crouching movement only a cat can make. The girl watched, paralyzed. Then she started toward the cat like a woman going to meet her lover. The tiger stood watching her. Then he slowly turned and bounded to his pedestal. The girl was Mabel Stark, and she's been working with tigers ever since.

Unless you understand what these two women felt, there's no use having a feral, or wild, cat. Even with a margay, the smallest of the feral cats, you have a pocket-sized model of the Egyptian god Bast running around the place. Any feral cat is a private ju-ju—which may be defined as a jungle spirit mainly devil but capable of condescending kindness. The bigger the feral cat, the more of the ju-ju she possesses.

The main pleasure you'll get from a feral cat is aesthetic. Nothing is such a marvelous example of grace combined with functional design. No dog can equal the elegant, smooth-flowing power of a cat. Often I used to watch Rani, our cheetah, lying full stretch on the bed, purring like the distant roll of deep drums, the ebony mustache marks from eye to cheek standing out against his tawny hide, the black tip of his incredibly long tail twitching slightly, and I'd think: When he dies, I might as well die too. I'll never see anything as grand again. Rani did die, and the house has never been the same.

A cat's style of hunting doesn't make him a good companion of the chase for man. Most cats hunt at night and stalk their prey. They do not hunt by scent and will not follow you for long distances. Also, they're highly unpredictable. Cats, however, have been trained as hunting companions. The Egyptians trained them as retrievers. The sportsman would paddle his canoe into the papyrus swamps with a domesticated wild cat sitting in the bow and a few boomerang-like throwing sticks beside him. When he knocked down a duck, the cat would run across the mudflats, worm his way through the reeds, and retrieve the duck. For this type of retrieving a cat might be better than a dog. Martial says that in Rome lions were trained to attack and kill wild cattle. The same lions would also catch hares and bring them uninjured to their masters. Martial says he saw this himself. I suppose it's possible. The Romans imported lions by the thousands and were able to pick out especially docile individuals. Then several men would be assigned to do nothing but work with that particular animal. No such situation exists today.

The question is always asked, "But are cats really intelligent?" When someone asks that question he means "Can a cat be trained to do what you want consistently?" The answer is that cats aren't intelligent by that definition. They are quick to learn if they want to learn; that is, if they can see some advantage to them in performing a certain act. If they can't see any purpose to the act, it's almost impossible to get them to do it. They have extremely retentive memories. If, for example, while hunting a cat succeeds in capturing quarry by some action, the cat will always duplicate that same action when hunting that type of quarry in the future. Once my pet ocelot, Tiba, found a rabbit crouching in its form by an angle of the fence, stalked and caught it. From then on, she never passes that spot without checking to see if there's another rabbit in the same place. For this reason, cats are far more creatures of habit than dogs. They develop marked habit patterns, and seldom depart from them.

An animal trainer once told me: "People who know nothing about animals believe that cats think like humans. People who know a little believe cats think like dogs. People who know a lot realize that cats think like cats." I've often heard people say delightedly, "My cat doesn't realize she's a cat—she thinks she's a human being." Some animals do think they're human if taken from their mothers when extremely young and raised by hand. They identify with the first moving object they see, especially if the object will feed them. That is why ducklings hatched by a hen will follow the hen and behave like chicks. A bottle-raised lamb is afraid of other sheep and insists on staying with human beings—she regards them as her "flock." Cats never do this no matter how raised. They don't regard themselves as human; they regard you as another cat. Cats will often attack you as they would another cat if you go near their food. A male cat will attack you if you go near his mate when she's in season as he would attack another male. A male feral cat will herd game toward his mate so that she, being quicker and more agile, can make the kill. After the kill, he drives her away until he's eaten what he wants. He'll also drive game to you, but after you've killed it he expects you to get out of the way until he's finished eating.

This is quite different from the way a dog behaves. The dog knows quite well that he has no right to the quarry until you give him permission to feed. As a result, any attack he launched would be without warning and with intent to kill. A cat, on the other hand, will signal you to get out of his way by growling, lashing his tail, and putting back his ears as he would to another cat. If you refuse to move, he comes forward slowly, lashing his tail against his sides while his growl increases in pitch and intensity. He is warning you to behave yourself much as you would warn an animal that has overstepped the bounds of decorum. Cats signal what they are going to do before they do it, unlike a wolf, which will turn and bite without warning.

All feral cats—no matter whether they are a six-hundred-pound Siberian tiger or a margay—are "untamable" in that they will not consistently obey orders, and "vicious" in that they will usually turn on you if you attempt to force them to do something against their will. It takes, then, a special sort of person to like feral cats. The household must be adapted to the cat, not the cat to the household. I am constantly getting letters that ask such questions as, "I want to keep a pet ocelot, but will he bite the children when they pull his tail?" Answer: "He sure will. Train the children to leave him alone or don't get a feral cat." Another standard question: "I'm getting a jaguarundi, but my wife will die when she sees it. I'm at work all day, so she'll have to take care of it while I'm gone, and she hates animals. What do you suggest?" Answer: "Get another wife."

The most popular feral cat seems to be the ocelot. Ocelots average about forty pounds, and are some fifty inches long, including the tail. They are found in Central and South America (where they are known by the descriptive title *tigrillo,* or "Little Tiger"), and occasionally turn up in the American Southwest. They resemble a sawed-off leopard, both physically and psychologically.

I've owned a female ocelot named Tiba for five years. Tiba was a gift, given me by Sergeant William Hobbs of the United States Marines at the suggestion of the local police. During the time that Hobbs owned her, Tiba slipped her collar one evening and went walking in a new housing development, where she found an eight-year-old Cub Scout dozing in his sleeping bag on the front lawn of his parents' home. The family had just moved out from the city, and the boy was thrilled at being able to sleep out of doors in the wilds of suburban Philadelphia, where, he felt sure, all sorts of wild animals abounded. Tiba, being cold, climbed into the bag with the boy. The child woke and tried to throw Tiba out, so she scratched him. In the rumpus that followed, the hysterical parents called the police, who decreed that Tiba must go. Because we live well out in the country, Sergeant Hobbs gave her to me.

When I first saw her, Tiba was draped across Hobbs's bed, dozing with half-closed eyes as cats will, and looked exactly like a small leopard—in fact, a big male ocelot is nearly half as big as a female leopard. I don't know of any animal that can recline as gracefully as a big cat, not even Brigitte Bardot on her towel. They seem to have no more bones than a fur neckpiece, yet the suggestion of power is always there. Tiba was in prime condition, and her pelt had that soft, living patina that made it glow with a life of its own like a rich Oriental rug that somehow has neon lights incorporated in its weave. Once a cat is dead, the coat loses this luster within an hour or so—just as the penetrating eyes glaze and become as meaningless as yellow oysters. Tiba had huge, perfectly round eyes that were fixed on me with the unwinking intensity of the floodlights used by police during the interrogation of criminals. When Mrs. Hobbs spoke to her, Tiba made a polite motion with her tail. A dog uses his tail as a British officer uses his swagger stick, while a cat uses hers as a lady uses a fan. Lovely and graceful as Tiba was, I could understand why whenever Sax Rohmer wanted to illustrate the sinister nature of the evil Fu Manchu, he compared the doctor to a great cat.

"My husband likes to roughhouse with Tiba, so he gets bitten up a little, but she never hurts me," Mrs. Hobbs explained. "She'll grab my hand in her mouth and worry it as a dog does a rat, but never breaks the skin."

I could understand this. When a feral cat is separated from her owner, she will scream or cry to attract his attention as she would in calling to her mate but when with him she makes no sound except purring or, if very angry, hissing or growling. In general, animals communicate with each other by a system of signs rather than vocal sounds. With cats this is often "tooth talk." When a cat wants you to take him for a walk, he will take your trouser cuff in his mouth and pull it gently in the direction he wants you to go. If he is hungry, he will take your hand in his mouth and chew on it gently. He will also do this when playing, but then generally rolls over at the same time and pats with his paws without extending the claws. If you get rough with him, he'll get correspondingly rough with you, although enjoying the game. If you scold him and slap his nose gently, he'll realize that he's hurting you, and relax. If a cat means business, you'll know it. He'll grab your hand fast with a growl, and clamp down.

A chain was snapped on Tiba's collar, and Sergeant Hobbs carried her to the car. On the way, Mrs. Hobbs gave me a detailed account of Tiba's diet. When there were no Cub Scouts around, Tiba got a pound and a half of raw meat (beef, not horse) with two ounces of a mixture consisting of 40 percent calcium powder, 30 percent skim milk, 25 percent Ledinac, and 5 percent iodized salt daily. Once a week she got half a pound of raw liver.

"Ma'am," I told Mrs. Hobbs, "my barn is crawling with giant rats; hordes of rabbits are eating our garden, and a brigade of woodchucks are devouring the pasture. As far as I am concerned, this fugitive from the temalacatl sacrificial stone can drag her spotted behind off the bed and earn her keep massacring these varmints—an occupation for which she is magnificently equipped both mentally and physically."

"Oh, Tiba will love that!" said Mrs. Hobbs happily. "She adores hunting, but we can't let her do it here. If the neighbors missed a dog or two, they might become unpleasant."

Actually, letting an animal eat quarry of any kind is a risk. You don't know what diseases or parasites they may pick up from the game. It's safer to feed them only carefully prepared, sterilized foods, but far less interesting for the animal. Also, they do derive benefits from the fur and feathers of their prey. Both contain oils that nourish the predator and help clean out his stomach.

I had intended Tiba as a house pet, which was all right with Tiba; the only trouble was that the house wasn't big enough for all of us. Tiba would have been the first to admit that, but she had definite ideas as to who was supposed to move out. True, we had a lot of nice furniture that was ideal for sharpening claws on, and we had also provided plenty of cushions full of interesting stuffing that, once removed, could be batted around in all directions to resemble a blizzard. But where we and Tiba definitely did not see eye to eye—or rather nose to nose—was in the matter of spraying. Tiba, like all feral cats I've met, was retromicturate, which, just in case you don't know the word, means that she urinated straight backward—none of this squatting down or lifting one leg. Tiba backed up against a wall, lifted her tail, and discharged a stream like a firehose. Ocelots use this technique for several reasons; in a wild state they mark their range so other ocelots won't trespass; the female does it to attract wandering males; and apparently when out hunting they also do it for the same reason a woodsman blazes a trail—so they can find their way back.

Because cats don't have a good sense of smell—at least compared to dogs—the urine must be very strongly scented to answer all these purposes. By the time Tiba had finished establishing ownership of our house, I can absolutely guarantee that there were no male ocelots within five hundred miles of the Mannix establishment—if there had been, we'd have heard from them. Tiba regarded our attempts to clean the walls as a personal affront to her contributions to our décor. She'd grab the cleaning rag out of your hands, chew the hell out of it and you, and then indignantly go back and spray the wall a second time. We finally had a large pen put up for her. It was fifteen feet square, of heavy wire mesh, with a shelf running across the back. During the winter we added a large doghouse stuffed with cedar shavings. Tiba stayed out in all weathers; although when it got very cold, say, around zero, we took her in for fear the tip of her long tail might freeze. Cats have poor circulation in the ends of their tails.

Tiba didn't seem to mind being caged, and quickly settled down. This is fairly unusual with an adult feral cat who has been with a family for a long time. The Hobbses had raised her from a kitten, and she was now five years old. Cats become greatly attached to a certain home and certain people, so attached that they often refuse to eat, and pine away when given to a new owner. I don't think this attachment can be entirely described as affection—although affection is certainly part of it. Cats do feel affection, even if they are not so demonstrative as dogs. It is also a matter of habit and devotion to a home range. The cat simply cannot adjust to a new environment. Tiba took the change easily because the Hobbses had been constantly moving, and Tiba had had no established home range. I handled her as Sergeant Hobbs had done, so she identified me with him, and I gave her live food in the form of rats and mice at once. Tiba was so fascinated by the chance to hunt, it got her mind off her homesickness.

The first few times I took Tiba walking I kept her on a lead. Feral cats must be broken to a lead when they are quite small; as far as I know it is almost impossible to train an adult. All cats fight a lead, and trying to jerk them along gives them an incurable hatred of it. If you jerk them a few times, you'll never get the lead on again. When the cat sees you coming with the lead, he'll throw himself on his back and fight with all four feet. In breaking them to the lead, a toy or food is used to distract their attention. If they continue to fight it, drop the lead and let the cat trail it. Of course, this is done in the house so the cat can't escape.

Luckily for me, Tiba was already lead broken, so she followed fairly well. No cat will follow like a dog; they go a few yards and then stop to look around or even lie down, but we made reasonably good progress. I always took her around the same route so she would learn it, and after she was at liberty she would tend to follow the same route. The first few times Tiba stopped at intervals to spray carefully any convenient tree to make sure of finding her way back to the safety of the cage—all wild animals regard a cage as a place of refuge rather than a prison—but once she learned the route she stopped bothering to leave markers.

I eventually found that the best time to take Tiba walking was in the early morning rather than in the late evening. The air was cool and fresh; there was dew on the grass that held scent; and more game was abroad. Tiba would drift like a spotted ghost, absolutely noiselessly through the thin white ground mist clinging to the grass. Often I would see her vanish into a patch of mist in a little hollow completely surrounded by clear open pasture, and wait for her to emerge. A few minutes later I'd hear the frantic screaming of a hysterical robin, and look up to see Tiba pouring herself out of the honeysuckle, her whiskers festooned with gossamer spiderwebs and small bright drops of dew glistening on her head. How she ever managed to cross the open space without my seeing her I could never understand.

The first game Tiba was able to catch was pigeons. A flock of pigeons often settled in our pasture to feed in the early morning, making a variegated blanket of blue, white, and brown, interspersed with strutting cocks and slim, coy hens avoiding their advances. Tiba quickly got to know where the flock usually alighted, and before we reached the place she'd move ahead, seeming to float above the ground as she passed through the tangle of pokeberries, thistles, and scrub locust that formed our hedgerow. Once she saw the flock, she'd freeze, sinking to the ground and remaining completely motionless, her round yellow eyes fixed unwinkingly on the birds. She had the patience of Fate, and often seemed more intent on staring the pigeons to death than on attacking. Occasionally she'd wait too long, and the pigeons would finish feeding and take off. When that happened, Tiba would watch them go, and then mince out to the field, sniffing the ground where they'd been with her face twisted into a curious snarl that seemed to help her powers of scent. Often she'd refuse to leave the field, and I'd have to lure her off with a rubber snake (her favorite toy) or by trailing a dead pigeon.

But more often Tiba would attack. She would gradually ooze her way through the bushes, never looking away from the birds but avoiding every twig and stalk like oil flowing around stones. When she reached the edge of the hedgerow she would stop again, waiting until some puffed-up cock in pursuit of a hen came close to her ambush. No matter how closely I watched Tiba, I never saw the beginning of her charge. She would suddenly be halfway between the hedgerow and her quarry as though fired out of a gun. If the special pair of birds she had been watching had wandered back into the flock, Tiba would ignore the nearer pigeons to follow her original quarry. Quick as she was, the pigeons were quick too, and always succeeded in taking off before she could reach them. Tiba learned to be prepared for this, and as the birds rose she would bound into the air after them, grabbing with her long forepaws, which seemed to extend like lazy tongs. Sometimes she would grab two at the same time, immediately killing them with two quick nips right and left, delivered so rapidly her head seemed merely to flicker.

I know of only one other ocelot owner who has tried hunting with his pet. Mr. Roger Claude of Salt Lake City, Utah, used his ocelot for pheasants. He wrote me:

"My ocelot was a dandy on pheasants in the snow and better than a goshawk with five feet for holding them. But she wasn't much for rabbits. She would try hard but didn't have enough wind if they really got going, and they usually did. I got a couple of hare with her. The procedure was this: I would carry her until we spotted the hare in its form. The hare would be thirty feet away, and as soon as it would move its ears or nose, she wanted 'down.' Since her claws were in full bloom, she got down. She would stalk the hare until a second before it would flush. She knew every time exactly when to rush. When she did connect I have never seen a hare killed and completely taken over so well. I finally had to get rid of her, as she was about as trustworthy as an eagle in a baby's crib."

Only two members of the cat family have been consistently trained to hunt by man: the caracal and the cheetah. The caracal is the African and Asian lynx (no relation, of course, to the Karakul sheep that provide the black, tightly curling wool). From time immemorial they have been trained in Persia and North Africa to catch partridge and other small game birds. Being longer-legged than an ocelot, they are even faster. I have been told that a caracal will often knock down half a dozen birds, striking right and left, before the flock can take to the air. Otherwise, their style of hunting is much like an ocelot's.

The grandest of all hunting cats is the cheetah. Hunting black buck with cheetahs was the great royal sport of India in the old days, and some of the rajahs had stables of thirty cheetahs, each with its own personal attendants. To see these magnificent gold-and-black animals the size of Great Danes, but built like greyhounds, being walked on silver chains by their brilliantly attired attendants must have been one of the great sights of the East. The cheetahs were all wild-caught as adults, for there have been less than half a dozen instances of their breeding in captivity, although one rajah enclosed a special park and stocked it with gazelles for his favorite pair in the hope that they would mate. Why they will not breed is a mystery. It cannot be due to nervousness, as cheetahs, alone of all the big cats, will become dog-tame, and even children can play with them safely.

The Indian black buck is a small antelope, standing less than two feet at the shoulder and weighing a little over fifty pounds, but they are very swift. Though cheetahs do not like to attack large quarry, they are the fastest of all mammals, reaching a speed of seventy miles per hour for a short burst. In Africa they live mainly on gazelles, so the black buck is a perfect quarry. The hunters start out in bullock wagons with the cheetahs riding on their charpoys (beds) in the rear. Because bullock carts are common, the black buck pay no attention to them, and this enables the hunters to get close to the game—an important consideration, for the cheetah is a sprinter, not a long-distance runner, and can run only for a quarter of a mile or so. The cheetahs are kept hooded, like falcons, so they will not make a bolt for the quarry too soon. When the cart has come as close as possible to the feeding antelope, a cheetah is unhooded and released. He makes a short stalk, and then charges. When he catches up with the buck, he either grabs it by the throat immediately or first knocks it over by jumping against the flank with stiff forelegs. Cheetahs kill with their teeth, not their claws. The claws on their paws are as blunt as a dog's and, also like a dog's, are nonretractable—or virtually so.

The cheetah's trainer "makes in" slowly with a long-handled spoon which he fills with blood from the buck's throat. "Making in"—approaching a trained wild animal on captured quarry—is always a delicate process as the animal's natural tendency is either to defend its kill or else to run off with it. He induces the cheetah to lap the blood while another man cautiously pulls the buck away. The cheetah is then hooded again and returned to the cart.

The oldest reference to hunting with cheetahs dates back to 865 B.C. when they were used by Hushing, a Persian king, although they were tamed by the Egyptians, and King Tutankhamen (about 1358 B.C.) had a bed with carved cheetahs as posts. After his trip to Jerusalem, Frederick II introduced cheetah hunting into Europe, and for the next few hundred years it was popular with sporting monarchs. Stradanus (1570) shows nobles hunting with cheetahs that rode behind them on horseback, the cheetahs sitting on flat-topped saddles strapped to the horses' croups. The quarry was hares. Hounds were used to find the hares, and then the cheetahs ran them down. Cheetahs rely almost entirely on vision when hunting, and do not attempt to track quarry.

I got Rani in 1947 from Warren Buck, the well-known animal dealer. Rani was about a year old, and fresh from Kenya. He was one of a consignment of five young cheetahs; but while the others crouched sullenly in a corner of their cage, Rani bounced around like a rubber ball, trying to hook passers-by through the feeding slot under the bars, or ricocheted off the sides and roof. Jule, my wife, said instantly, "That's the one for us." She was right, as she usually is. Rani wasn't vicious, simply full of pep and vinegar. He'd be much easier to tame than the sulky cats squatting in the shadows.

Rani cost us $900. We thought the animal was a female because the testicles hadn't dropped yet. Later, when we could handle him, we discovered our mistake, but the name Rani (a queen) stuck.

The first time I let Rani out, he jumped at me playfully and put his forefeet against my chest like a big dog. Though I was wearing a leather jacket that didn't give him a grip, suddenly two gashes appeared in the leather. Knowing that cheetahs have blunt claws, I couldn't imagine what had happened, but the next time I could see. Like all cats, Rani had dewclaws—two powerful, needle-sharp, half-moon claws, one on the inside of each foreleg. These claws usually remain hidden, but the cat can extend them at will almost at right angles to his legs. They enable him to hook onto large quarry and hold it until his teeth can come into play.

My first job was to teach Rani to come when called. I blew a whistle when feeding him, and after a few days whenever Rani heard the whistle he'd come running. Then I taught him to retrieve. Like a dog, Rani would chase a ball and carry it around in his mouth; so each time I'd offer him a piece of meat to drop the ball. Finally he learned to bring me the ball for meat. Then I tried to teach him to "heel." I was never very successful at this. Rani would follow for a while but then he'd get tired and lie down. Psychologically as well as physically, Rani was midway between a dog and a cat. Cats are very difficult to train to heel; they're too independent. Rani would heel until he got tired of it. Then he'd lie down and play with his long tail, chase rabbits, or just say "to heck with the whole deal."

Rani's refusal to heel for any long period was a great disadvantage when taking him hunting. When Rani was reasonably well trained in other respects, Jule and I went camping with him in the Southwest for four months, sleeping in a tent with Rani between us and taking him out after game during the day. As the cheetah came only a little above my knee, he couldn't see over the sagebrush as well as a man. Often I'd see a coyote or an antelope some distance off, but meanwhile Rani had wandered away and couldn't be found. But if he were with me, I could lift the cat up by the shoulders until he could see the quarry. Then the fun began.

Rani was death on jackrabbits. At first the rabbit usually didn't realize his danger and wouldn't go all out . . . pausing every thirty yards or so to make a high bound to see what sort of thing was after him. But when he realized that Rani was burning up the ground between them, the rabbit would really start moving. Though a big Texas jack can go like a rocket, a cheetah can go like a spotted flash of light. When the cheetah reached him, the rabbit would try to dodge. A rabbit can outdodge a single greyhound but he can't outdodge a cheetah. On the turns, the cheetah's long tail acts as a counterweight for his body, and Rani could spin around within his own length even when going at top speed. After the first few hunts, Rani never tried to seize the jack with his jaws. He'd reach out and knock the rabbit off balance with his foot before making a grab for him.

Not that Rani always won. Once I saw a fine big jack with coal-black tips to his ears watching us from behind a little clump of sage. I lifted Rani, but until the rabbit moved, Rani couldn't see him. Rani could see a moving ground squirrel on the slope of a hill a quarter of a mile away, but he couldn't identify a mule deer at a hundred yards as long as the animal stood still. Rani stared intently out over the sage with his big yellow eyes, and then the rabbit made the mistake of sitting up. That was enough for Rani. He dropped to the ground and quietly circled the clump of sage. He wanted to get as close to the rabbit as possible before starting his rush.

The rabbit was watching Rani through the brush, and when the cat got within twenty feet of him he started to run. Rani turned loose his terrible rush. He overtook the rabbit as though the jack were standing still, but the rabbit turned and cleared a little arroyo with a single bound. Rani went head first into the arroyo. I thought that he'd broken his neck, but he appeared on the other side still going strong. The hare had a lead now, but once again Rani overtook him. It looked like an easy kill, but the hare knew what he was doing. He ducked under a barbed-wire fence. Rani hit the wire full on, and doubled up from the impact. I had to carry him back to the car, and it was a week before he could run. I never ran him again in wire country.

Although cheetahs are not killers in the sense that leopards or even mountain lions are, I did once see Rani take a prong-horned antelope. A herd of antelope were feeding on some open flats covered with tall buffalo grass. I had Rani out after jacks, but when he saw the antelope he stopped transfixed. Then he began his stalk. A hunting cheetah does not crawl on his belly like a hunting house cat; he stands almost erect, and moves forward so slowly that it is almost impossible to detect the motion. I believe that it took Rani a full minute to lift one leg and put it down again. If one of the herd raised his head, Rani would stand rigid with one foot in the air until the antelope resumed feeding. The stalk must have lasted nearly an hour, and during that time Rani was only a few yards closer to the herd, but from the cheetah's point of view every foot he gained was of enormous advantage when he unleashed his sudden charge.

Then one of the herd saw the cat. He raised his head and stood watching Rani, who had instantly frozen into immobility. For what seemed an interminable time the two animals stood motionless, watching each other. At last the antelope resumed grazing; but he must have been watching out of the corner of his eye, for the moment that Rani moved again the buck wheeled and began to trot away. The rest of the herd promptly followed him.

Rani charged. One moment, he had been standing as still as a cheetah carved from stone. The next instant, he was halfway to the herd, his body a yellow blur among the purple sage. When a cheetah runs, he goes in a series of great bounds, all four legs clear of the ground at the same moment, somewhat like a running hare. The antelope broke into their famous bounding gallop that no North American animal can equal, but before they could hit their full stride Rani was up with them. Racing alongside the last of the herd, the cat struck the antelope on the flank with both feet, trying to roll him over. The antelope staggered but kept going. Again Rani overtook him, and this time the antelope stumbled and went down on his knees. In an instant, Rani had him by the throat. There was a wild flailing of hooves and then it was over.

Rani coursed several antelopes at other times, but the animals were either able to shake him off or kicked so savagely that the cheetah was unable to throw them off balance. At last, Rani gave up. They were too big for him to handle except by a fluke.

Rani was no coward, and could put up a terrific fight if necessary; but, like all predators with which I've worked, his basic interest was to obtain food, not to get into fights. His hunting instinct was strong; he would chase anything that was moving. We were camped by a stream in southern Utah, and I took Rani for a run in the hills. Rani was ahead, looking hopefully for jack rabbits, when a man on a motorcycle appeared, speeding along a dirt road. Rani stared at this apparition for a moment, and then apparently decided it was some new kind of antelope. In spite of my shouts, he took off after the cyclist.

Though the rider couldn't see me, he caught a fleeting vision of Rani bursting through the sage after him. Rani charging was a terrible sight. The cheetah's big golden eyes were fixed on his prey with an awful determination; his long tail streamed out behind him; and he went like the wind. After one horrified glance, the man turned on more gas and shot away at forty-five miles an hour, obviously confident that he would leave his nemesis far in the rear.

He didn't know cheetahs. Without the slightest strain, Rani increased his stride and easily pulled up alongside the terrified man. Rani jumped at the rear wheel of the motorcycle with stiff forelegs, exactly as he had jumped at the flank of the antelope. Fortunately, the spinning wheel daunted him. He fell back at the last second. The motorcycle disappeared over a low hill, the driver leaning forward like a jockey on the homestretch. Rani stood panting in the road until I rushed up and collared him.

Jule was worried that we'd get into trouble over this incident, but I told her to forget it. "When that fellow tries to tell people what he saw, no one will ever believe him," I assured her.

When we reached California, we met Bee Adkins, a professional predator hunter who had a famous pack of hounds. Bee lived in a little cabin near Perris, about 150 miles southeast of Los Angeles. His home was sheltered on three sides by cliffs, and from his front doorstep a grand view of open country swept away to the distant blue mountains on the horizon. When we arrived, his hounds scented Rani while the cat was still in the car and started barking "treed" hopefully. Rani was quietly preparing to climb through the window and commit wholesale mayhem when Bee appeared and snapped a single order. Instantly the noise stopped. Not having similar control over Rani, I decided to keep him on a chain except when we took him into the desert for exercise.

Bee was a quiet man who looked like an old-time farmer, but in his youth he had been a famous gun hand and traveled over most of northern Mexico and the American Southwest hunting predators—both animal and human. My original idea had been to allow Bee's hounds to locate a coyote and then turn Rani loose, but when I explained this plan to Bee he didn't think much of it.

"I don't believe that cat of yours cares much whether he eats a coyote or a dog," Bee remarked. "Those hounds of mine are valuable, and I'd like to get one or two back. I know of several places I'm pretty sure we can find a coyote, and you can run that cat right out of your car at him."

Bee told me that some sixty miles away, near the town of Victorville, a rancher had complained that coyotes were ruining his watermelon field. The coyotes would come in at evening and wander through the patch, taking a bite out of every melon they saw. Bee told me that one coyote often ruined a hundred pounds of watermelon in a night. "As long as coyotes stay out in the desert and hunt rabbits and gophers, we don't bother them," he explained. "But when they come into farming country we've got to clear them out."

We left before dawn the next morning in my station wagon, with Bee acting as guide. Rani was sitting in the front seat between us, instead of riding in his usual place in the back, as I wanted to be able to release him at a moment's notice. We reached the ranch at dawn, and I drove slowly until we came to the melon patch. It covered several acres. The black forms of the melons showed dimly in the thin, early light, but there was nothing moving. I circled the patch slowly, switching off my headlights.

Then Bee said casually: "There are two coyotes lying out there watching us. They're sulling." Bee meant the coyotes were crouched down motionless, waiting for us to go away. "You'd better let the cat out."

Jule opened the car door, and Rani sprang into the patch. The cheetah couldn't see the coyotes until they moved; but I hissed to him, my usual signal that game was about, and the cat stiffened. He walked slowly across the plowed land, stretching himself as high as possible to see across the patch.

Suddenly both coyotes bolted for the brush, going in opposite directions. Rani took after the biggest. The coyote ducked into the greasewood with Rani hard on its tail, the cat bounding high in the air to keep his quarry in sight. We ran as fast as we could, although running through the soft earth of the patch was like trying to run through sand.

As Rani began to gain on the predator, the cat stopped taking his "spy hops" and barreled straight through the greasewood. The coyote hit a steep slope and went down it at full speed. Rani was only a few feet behind him now. I could tell that the cheetah was holding back until his quarry reached level ground. Rani disliked leaping on game while running downhill because if he missed his spring he was likely to take a bad spill.

At the bottom of the hill was a flooded wash full of floating brush. Some of it had formed a crude dam, and the coyote bolted across the dam like a cat on a fence. Rani's nose was almost rubbing the predator's tail when suddenly the coyote flung itself off the dam onto a sandbank and doubled back. Rani tried to follow, but one of the cat's legs went into a hole on the dam and he plunged into the water.

The current swept the cheetah downstream, spinning him around like a canoe out of control. Rani disliked water, but every time he came around his big eyes were still fixed on the coyote and he continued to swim doggedly after the predator, with complete disregard for his own predicament.

The coyote was smart. It had stayed in the shallow water. Now, half swimming, half wading, it reached the bank and rushed past us up the hill, back toward the melon patch. Rani hit the shore far downstream and started after it again. By cutting in at an angle, Rani managed to catch up with the coyote as it reached the top of the hill.

Reaching out with one of his long front legs, Rani hit the speeding coyote on the flank. The coyote went down. I thought it had had it; but the coyote, using the force of the fall to gain momentum, rolled completely over and came back on its feet like a circus tumbler. Snarling, it came for the cat—head down, crest raised, and lips curled back. Then it charged the cheetah, slashing at the cat's face.

Rani rose on his hind legs like a rearing stallion and struck two swinging blows with his front paws as rapidly as a boxer drumming a punching bag. The movements were so graceful that the cheetah looked like an overgrown kitten tapping at a ball of wool, but at each blow a puff of dust leaped from the coyote's tawny fur. Rani leaped across the coyote, striking down with his forelegs as he went. Rolling on its back, the coyote followed the cat, biting at the cheetah's belly. I could hear the predator's jaws ring together as it snapped and missed.

Rani spun around and cuffed the coyote with lightning left and right blows, using his dewclaws. The coyote swung his head back and forth, snatching at the cheetah's paws while still lying on its back. When I came up, the coyote's head was still moving in rhythm to the blows, but not through any volition on the part of the coyote. He was dead with a broken neck. Rani was simply delivering a few last cracks to make sure his adversary was finished.

Rani lived with us until he was fifteen. He never became vicious, slept on our bed at night, and loved to play with any of the local children who might drop in. He was perfectly housebroken and would walk to the door every morning, giving a curious little birdlike chirp to be let out. A few minutes later, he'd be back to lie in front of the fire in the living room, purring like a diesel engine warming up.

Rani never completely recovered from the back injury he'd received hitting the barbed wire after the jack rabbit. As he grew older, it troubled him more and more. We called in first veterinarians and then orthopedic surgeons, but there was nothing they could do. Rani finally had to be put down.

A friend of mine asked me why I hadn't had a rug made from the hide. I didn't for the same reason that if a child dies you don't have a lampshade made from his skin. I have never gotten another cheetah. There could never be another Rani.

CHAPTER 2

The Blowgun—
Silent Killer

"The most mysterious and awe-inspiring weapon in the world is the blowgun," wrote William Farabee in *The Central Caribs*. Mr. Farabee is right. Absolutely noiseless, deadly accurate up to forty yards, and more fatal than a rifle if poisoned darts are used, the blowgun is an extremely dangerous weapon. Mystery writers from Conan Doyle to Sax Rohmer have had sinister Orientals committing murders with blowguns, but their descriptions of the weapon are usually all wrong. There is no poison that can be used on blowgun darts that won't take at least fifteen minutes to kill the average man. On the other hand, blowgun darts have far more penetration and range than writers realize. Light wooden darts can be sent two hundred feet, and a steel dart will go through a one-half-inch plywood board as though the wood were cardboard.

My first hunt with a blowgun came about by accident. I was in Florida, visiting an old friend, John Hamlet, who had just returned from the Philippines, where he had spent several years trapping monkeys for the National Foundation of Infantile Paralysis. One evening the game warden dropped in to look over the collection of native weapons John had brought back with him. I happened to mention that I'd always been interested in blowguns.

"A farmer has been complaining about a wildcat killing his chickens," said the warden. "If you had a blowgun, this would be a good chance to try it."

"How about using mine?" suggested John. He walked over to a closet and pulled out a Philippine blowgun with a quiver of darts.

The gun was bamboo, and six feet long. There were two types of darts in the quiver. The ones intended for small game had large heads and a series of miniature barbs carved along the sides that must have cost some Filipino plenty of time and trouble. These darts were not poisoned, the dart killing like a miniature arrow. The poisoned darts, intended for bigger game, were lighter and had a small head, whittled out of the dart itself.

"This outfit was made by the Zubanoan Indians who live in the mountains of Mindanao," John told me, handling the poisoned darts with more care than a mother handling a newborn baby. "They're a peaceful, gentle people, and they'd have been exterminated centuries ago by the warlike tribes if it wasn't for these guns. Not even a tough Moro wants to come up against a poisoned blowgun dart."

Under John's tutelage, I went out to the back yard and practiced with the gun, using the nonpoisoned darts and a bale of straw as a target. The trick was to give one quick, hard puff; if you blew steadily the dart didn't fly with the right velocity, and tended to wabble in its flight. Up to seventy-five feet the gun was very accurate. Beyond that, the darts began to drop and you had to aim high. After a little practice, I could hit a grapefruit three times out of five at seventy-five feet, the dart going right through the fruit. At 150 feet I could hit the bale of straw, and the dart would bury itself three inches. John told me that the Zubanoans used to get monkeys for him with the gun. They were so expert that they could hit a monkey in the tail with a poisoned dart and then, when the animal dropped, they'd cut off the tail before he could get the full effects of the poison.

With this outfit, I decided to try for the wildcat. The game warden told me that the cat was operating at a farm near Bonita Springs. I drove down there the next morning and enlisted the help of Bill Piper, who runs the famous Everglades Wonder Gardens. Bill is an all-around woodsman, and knows the Big Cypress area (the northeastern section of the Everglades) as well as any man. Bill had hounds, and he promised to take me out the next morning so we could see what the blowgun could do.

We started off before dawn in Bill's jeep, with two of his hounds in the back. Bill followed an old trail that twisted like a looped white ribbon among the tall thin pines burned black by forest fires. We reached the farm a little before noon, and the farmer lent us a couple of horses so we could follow the hounds through the swamp. The day was so hot that the hounds couldn't stay on the burning sand, and kept under the shade of the palmettos. Scenting was almost impossible, and Bill cut the swamp for tracks without any luck. We had started back to the farm late that afternoon, following the fence line on our tired horses, when something bolted out of the yellow grass under the hooves of Bill's horse. It was gone so fast that all I saw was a gray flash, but Bill shouted, "That's the cat! Here, boys, here!"

The hounds hadn't seen the cat, but they trotted up politely. A few seconds later, I heard them scream with excitement as they hit the hot scent. Bill kicked his horse ahead, pointing out the trail. The hounds picked it up and took off through the scrub, yelling every time they got a fresh whiff, each trying to outrun the other. Bill raced after them, leaning low on his horse to miss the trees. I followed as best I could. The blow-gun kept catching on branches, and the horse was slipping on the mud and tripping over cypress boles, so I didn't make very good time. In ten minutes I'd lost sight of Bill and was even having trouble keeping within earshot of the hounds.

I heard the short, hard chopping bark that meant the cat had treed, and pushed on as fast as my horse would go. But before I came up, the barking changed to yells and then to howls. The cat had jumped from the tree, and a fight was going on in the palmettos. I could catch an occasional glimpse of the hounds' backs and thrashing tails. Then the cat broke loose and streaked off again. The hounds followed, yelling eagerly, but, it seemed to me, being careful not to close the distance too much.

I followed Bill's form through the cypress as well as I could. Then I lost him and had to rely on his horse's tracks. At last I heard the hounds again barking "treed." When I came up, Bill had dismounted and the hounds were standing at the foot of a tree, barking hopefully. One of them had a long red gash in his ear.

"Don't get too close," Bill warned. "He may jump again."

The cat was on a limb about twenty feet from the ground. He was watching the dogs, but when I dismounted he raised his big ruffed face and studied me for an instant. Then he moved out along the limb, obviously preparing to jump over the dogs' heads.

"Don't use poison," Bill warned me as I reached into the quiver for a dart. "The dogs will be on him as soon as he comes out of the tree, and I don't want to run the chance of having them scratch themselves on a poisoned dart."

I took one of the big barbed darts. It was twenty-two inches long and the barbs were a half inch wide, although the shaft itself was no thicker than a knitting needle. The dart should have the killing power of a .22 bullet. Because I was about seventy feet from the tree, I decided that the big dart might drop slightly, so I aimed just over the cat's shoulder and gave a quick puff. The dart went exactly where I'd aimed . . . about an inch over the wildcat's back. I found later that these big darts were so carefully trimmed and balanced that they flew exactly the same as the smaller ones in spite of their size. I slid in another barbed dart and fired again.

The cat jumped straight up into the air. Then he spun around and bit out the dart with one chop of his jaws. I had two more darts between my fingers, and I fired them almost as fast as you could work the bolt of a rifle. The cat plummeted out of the tree, but I could tell from the way he fell that he was dead before he reached the ground. Both darts had entered the body over their barbs—that is, had gone in about two inches deep. I believe the poisoned darts with their narrower, sharper heads would have gone completely through.

I began to think that a blowgun might be an ideal weapon for small game around my Pennsylvania farm. Even without poison, a dart should be adequate to knock over a rabbit, squirrel, rat, or even a woodchuck. So when I got back I started to do some experimenting.

The basic principle of a blowgun is very simple: it works exactly like a kid's peashooter. The darts used may be anything from three inches long to a couple of feet—although the lighter they are, the farther they'll fly. At the end of the dart, where the feathering would be on an arrow, there is a "stopper" of some sort. This stopper must fit snugly inside the barrel of the gun, but not so snugly that it makes the dart stick. A twist of cotton is generally used as a stopper, and it stays firmer if covered with a varnish of some sort. The fit of the stopper is important, as it is the force of the blower's breath against it that shoots out the dart with such amazing force. Sir Charles Brooke, a British police officer in Malaya, tells of seeing natives drive a dart three inches deep into the side of a deer at one hundred yards, although I was never able to send a dart more than two hundred feet with any gun I made or obtained.

In theory, the longer a blowgun is, the greater range and accuracy it possesses—somewhat on the principle of a long-barreled Kentucky rifle. The puff of breath you give corresponds to the amount of powder in the rifle. The dart should leave the muzzle of the gun at the instant that the full force of your puff is expended; otherwise the extra length of the gun is simply wasted space, holding back the dart by friction without adding anything to its speed and range. The Jivaro Indians, living in Ecuador, sometimes use blowguns seventeen feet long, and are said to be able to hit a hummingbird at fifty yards. Maybe so, but to use a gun that long they must have lungs like a blacksmith's bellows.

I obtained a twelve-foot Jivaro gun; but, apart from not having enough breath to work the damn' thing properly, I found it had other disadvantages. Trying to carry the gun through underbrush was like trying to tote a flagpole. Also, when I put it to my lips, the long gun would vibrate no matter how steady I tried to hold it, and the end would sag as does the end of a fishing pole held out straight at arm's length. The Jivaro blowgun maker had evidently realized these disadvantages, for he'd tried to overcome them. The gun had been deliberately made thick and heavy to cut down on its tendency to vibrate. Then, instead of simply using a hollow reed, the Jivaro had made the gun out of a sapling, split longitudinally down its length, and had hollowed out two corresponding grooves down the center of each section. He had then glued the sections back together with gum and lashed them in place. This had enabled him to polish the central grooves in a manner impossible when simply using a hollow reed. The procedure had another advantage as well. The grooves had been cut in such a way that when the gun was put together, the hole through the center ran on a bias—that is, the hole did not go straight through the gun but ran on a slight diagonal. By holding the gun in a certain position, the upward-slanting diagonal counteracted the sagging of the tip.

Of course, you had to know how the diagonal ran in order to hold the gun correctly, so the Jivaro had fastened two jaguar teeth near the mouthpiece to mark the top of the gun. (At first, I'd thought these teeth were intended for rear sights.)

The darts for the gun were about one and a half inches long, and as thin as matchsticks, with points as sharp as a porcupine's quill. They were made from the inner rib of a palm leaf, and were surprisingly tough. About an inch behind the poisoned head, a notch had been cut in the wood so the dart would break off in the flesh, leaving the poisoned head in the wound. This prevented the wound from bleeding and also prevented a monkey or a man from pulling out the dart after being struck. One of the small Jivaro quivers holds two hundred of these slender darts if they don't have their cotton stoppers. The Jivaro takes along a gourd full of cotton, and twists a bit of the cotton around the end of a dart just before shooting it so he can carry more darts in the quiver. He also has the jawbone of a pirana tied to the quiver to notch the dart above the poison head. If this were done ahead of time, the head might break off as the dart was pulled from the tightly packed quiver.

The Jivaro blowgun was too much of a gun for me, and I switched to a bamboo gun made by the Cherokee Indians of North Carolina. This gun was eight feet long, and the darts were one and a half feet, the stoppers being made of thistledown. The darts were fairly heavy, but they'd fly straight for about sixty feet. The Cherokee apparently try to stun their quarry rather than impale them, for the darts were made of soft wood, blunted at the ends. I made some darts of my own, using hickory, and sharpened the points.

There was an old chuck who'd dug under the fence and made a hole at the edge of our lawn that raised heck with the grasscutter. The next time I saw him out, I got the Cherokee gun and crawled up behind some box-wood. My first dart missed him, but the chuck, instead of taking alarm, ran over to the dart to see what it was. Then he stood up on his hind legs, which was a big mistake on his part. My next dart went through him. He bolted for the hole, and I thought that I'd lost him; but when I came up, his legs were still sticking out. The dart had prevented him from getting down the burrow just as an arrow would.

I got two other chucks in the course of the summer. A blowgun has it all over a bow and arrow for woodchuck hunting, and in some respects over a gun, as a hit chuck can't dive down his hole. Unlike an archer, a blowgunner doesn't have to stand or kneel. He can lie flat on his belly with his lips to the mouthpiece of the gun and wait until his quarry gets into position. Unfortunately, the range of a blowgun using such heavy darts is limited, and the slightest breath of air affects the flight of the dart.

Although I never had the chance to use one, I also examined some of the Malayan blowguns, generally considered to be the finest in the world. During the last war the Dyaks in the Brunei area, near the Palawan Islands, used these guns on the Japanese sentries with murderous effect. The guns were about eight feet long, made of a single straight length of wood, and the central hole had been bored by a metal drill. I was told that the blowgun maker twirled the drill between his palms, at the same time guiding it with his bare toes. As with the Jivaro guns, the hole was run through on a slight bias to allow for the sag at the tip. Some of these guns had white bone sights for night work, and others had spearheads lashed to the ends to serve as bayonets for close work. An American officer who fought the Dyaks during the Philippine Insurrection wrote, "Whether advancing or retreating, they kept up a continual fire, holding four darts between their fingers for immediate use, with others stuck around their quivers."

There are only two places in the world where the blowgun is used as a real weapon: the Malay archipelago and South America. In both areas, plants supplying a poison suitable for the darts exist. The blowgun was known to the ancient Aztecs (some magnificent blowguns inlayed with gold and precious stones are in the Palacio Nacional in Mexico City), and even the Iroquois Indians used it to some extent. Blowguns are also used in Indo-China and parts of India. (They are unknown in Africa, although there is an almost universal belief that the guns are used by the Pygmies of the Ituri forest. I don't know how this rumor started, but it isn't true.) But once away from the "poison belt," the gun is regarded as something useful only for knocking over small game—about as effective as a slingshot. Within the "poison belt" it is the principal weapon of the native tribes. Putting poison on the darts converts the blowgun from a toy into a deadly weapon.

The base of all blowgun poisons is some type of strychnine, usually derived from the seeds of trees belonging to the Loganiaceae family in the South Pacific or else from the curare vine of South America. Whereas most strychnines produce convulsions and a stiffening of the muscles, curare acts in the opposite manner. It relaxes the "end plates" between the nerves and the muscles, thus making it impossible for the lungs and heart to function, and the victim dies of asphyxiation. The sap of the vine is boiled until it becomes a thick, gluey mass, and then the heads of the darts are dipped in it. Often other ingredients are thrown in, such as poisonous spiders, the venom glands of snakes, and certain magical herbs. These items do no good and only dilute the real poison.

When the conquistadors invaded South America and met Indians using blowguns, they were terrified of the tiny darts that produced death within an hour and for which there was no antidote. They tortured the Indians to find the secret, but the Indians died silent. It was not until

1595 that Sir Walter Raleigh brought the first samples of "urari" to Europe. In 1889, Dr. White brought some curare-tipped darts to London as a curiosity. The doctor's servant accidentally pricked his finger with one, and nearly died.

My first chance to use a blowgun on big game came when I got a letter from Bee Adkins, who'd taken Rani and me out after coyotes. He invited me to take a hunting trip with him to old Mexico. Bee was taking six of his hounds, and we'd be camping out for three weeks in the wild country near Alamos, a little town in the northwestern part of Mexico some 300 miles southeast of Nogales.

By then I had another blowgun, a commercial job five feet long, made of half-inch tubing, and shooting steel darts with brightly colored golf tees on the ends to act as stoppers. This light, easily handled gun could stand up under rough treatment and you could aim and shoot with it as easily as with a rifle. It was accurate up to seventy-five feet, and the steel darts had far more penetration than any of the wooden darts I'd been using.

I'd got this gun originally to deal with pigeons in our barn, messing on the hay and farm machinery. At night you could see dozens of them sitting on the beams, but if you fired at them with a gun you blew holes in the roof. I figured that a blowgun would be the perfect answer. There were also rats in the chicken house. Often there would be three or four lined up at the feeding troughs filling themselves. I didn't like to use traps or poison in the chicken house, and if you fired at them you generally wrecked the feeding troughs. Here, again, I figured that a blowgun would do the trick.

I had to use heavier darts than those supplied by the company to knock the quarry down. The light steel darts would go through the quarry but he'd run off with them. I used one-sixteenth-inch metal rods with blunt heads. I also used them on squirrels. Maybe an Indian can hit a running rabbit or a flying bird with a blowgun, but I certainly can't. Squirrels will sit on a limb and cuss you out, which makes them a good target. Because the gun is noiseless and the squirrel doesn't realize that the tiny darts flying past are dangerous, he'll sit there and let you get in half a dozen shots.

Just the same, I had trouble. Even with the blunted heads, steel darts would often go right through a squirrel and pin him to a limb. Then I had to climb to get him. Also, if any of the darts hit the tree, they'd stick there and it took a pair of pliers to get them loose. So I finally switched to wooden darts for squirrels. These would go through the squirrel but not stick in wood.

For big game in Mexico, I knew I'd need poison. I preferred to use curare, which has the great advantage that you can eat an animal killed by a curare-poisoned dart. Curare is deadly only if it enters the bloodstream, whereas with strychnine the hunter must quickly cut away the flesh around the dart, to prevent the spread of the poison, if he intends to eat his kill.

My first job was to get hold of some curare. Armed with a letter from *True* magazine, who were interested in the experiment, I managed to get two hundred cubic centimeters of curare from the Squibb Laboratory in New Brunswick, New Jersey. It was quite a job, as pure curare isn't the kind of stuff they like to hand out to casual visitors.

I had the steel darts grooved so that they'd hold more of the curare, which incidentally looks much like sugar with a slight yellowish tinge. I coated the darts with a quickly absorbing vegetable grease to make the curare adhere. Medically, curare is used in the treatment of shock cases and also as an anesthetic, as in small amounts it relaxes the patient without causing ill effects. A dose of about twenty cc is fatal, so less than half of one cc is generally used in medical work.

I met Bee in Tucson, and we headed for Mexico in a jeep with the dogs in the rear. We reached Alamos late the next afternoon, and here Bee picked up some Indians as guides. Making camp a few miles from the town, we started out the next morning with the dogs.

By about ten o'clock, it began to grow hot. We didn't find any streams, and the hounds were suffering worse than we were. By noon we hit a pool at the foot of some cliffs, and the dogs threw themselves into the water and lay there gasping, with only their noses above the surface. Bee had a job getting them to leave the precious fluid.

Late that afternoon we hit an arroyo densely overgrown with mesquite. Bee said to me: "You take up a stand at the far end and I'll send the dogs in. We may get something up."

It took me a long time to get to the other end of the arroyo, for fighting my way through the mesquite was a slow, sweaty job. Bee sent the dogs in before I'd reached my position, but in the intense heat they worked slowly. I sat down on a rock, put a poisoned dart into the gun, and laid out two others beside me. Handling these poisoned darts was a very different proposition from working with the ordinary ones. They were needle-sharp and heavily coated with the curare. My hands were scratched with cactus and thorns, and I had to be careful that the curare didn't come into contact with an open wound. Also, when loading the dart into the gun, some of the curare got scraped off on the rubber mouthpiece. Although curare isn't supposed to be poisonous if taken internally, I wiped it off with some leaves. I was very glad that I hadn't tried using any of the strychnine poisons, or I wouldn't have dared to put the gun to my lips.

There was a fairly clear stretch in front of me, which was lucky, as even the tiniest twig or leaf will deflect one of the light darts. There was no wind, which was also a good thing, although less important with the steel darts than with the wooden ones.

There was a rustle in the bush, and a deer trotted out and went past me up a game trail some twenty yards away. He didn't seem particularly bothered, and the hounds hadn't as yet given tongue. I raised the blowgun quietly and gave a puff. With the long wooden darts I'd been used to using, I could follow their flight as you can with an arrow and tell if I were overshooting or undershooting, but with these little four-and-a-half-inch darts, only a sixteenth of an inch thick, all I could see was one quick flash of the colored stopper as it darted away in the direction of the deer. The deer paid no attention but kept on going.

I grabbed up another dart and slammed it into the gun without worrying about getting the curare on my cuts. I fired again, aiming somewhat lower. I aimed too low, for I could see the dart knock up dead leaves under the deer's body. This time the deer stopped and turned to look at me. I already had the last dart in the gun and, aiming carefully, gave a quick puff. The deer gave a bound and vanished into the cover, but whether he was hit or only frightened I couldn't tell.

I shouted to Bee and went over to look for the darts. I found the one that had hit under the deer's body at once. There was no sign of the other two, but that meant nothing, as in the brush it would be impossible to find the little things except by a miracle of luck.

Bee had brought up the hounds. He took the last of our water and, pouring it into his hat, bathed the hounds' muzzles in it. "They won't be able to trail far in this heat," he told me.

"They won't have to," I assured him. "If I hit, we should find the buck within a few hundred yards."

Unlike strychnine, curare is a painless poison. The victim has a sensation of sleepiness, and finally dozes off. Indians often use curare poisoned

darts on monkeys high in trees. A monkey hit by a bullet or by a strychnine poisoned dart will grab the nearest branch and continue to cling to
it even after death. With curare, the monkey simply goes to sleep and
eventually falls to earth.

Bee put the hounds on the trail, and they started off slowly. We were
in cactus country, and although the old hounds managed to avoid it, Bee
had two young dogs who kept getting stuck with the prickly buds. Still,
they kept on trailing. The scent was very uncertain. On the shade side of
an arroyo or in mesquite cover, the hounds would suddenly give tongue
and start running. Then we'd hit a stretch of open desert where Bee was
doing the tracking and the hounds following along behind. There was no
blood spoor as with a rifle wound, and without the hounds it would have
been hopeless. We'd gone about a quarter of a mile, and I'd begun to
think that I'd missed, when we found the dead deer lying under some
little scrub pines. Bee called off the hounds immediately, afraid that they
might grab the body and prick themselves on a poisoned dart.

It took us five minutes to find the first dart and nearly half an hour to
locate the second. Both had been driven clear up to their heads in the
deer's body, and the brown fur covered the little golf tees. One was in the
shoulder and the other in the flank. The deer had not jumped the first
time he was hit. Either he didn't feel it or thought he'd run against a
cactus spine. The darts aren't much thicker than a hypodermic needle,
and the dart in the flank had struck him a glancing blow, going in sideways under the skin, never more than half an inch under the hide.

Actually, the deer had suffered far less than if he'd been hit by a rifle
bullet. After running a time, he'd simply felt sleepy and lain down to
rest. Later, I read an account of Indians using blowgun darts on a young
tapir. The animal continued rooting in the mud after being hit by four
darts. Apparently the prick of the darts is so slight that the quarry hardly
notices it any more than he would the bite of a large horsefly.

Constructing a blowgun can be as simple or as complicated as you want
to make it. A good, serviceable gun can be made from a length of half-
inch brass or aluminum pipe with a disk of hard rubber fitted over one
end as a mouthpiece. A mouthpiece is necessary, for the operator must
have something against which to press his lips in order to get the maximum force into his blow. A foresight can be made from a piece of copper
wire twisted near the muzzle. No rear sight is necessary.

I made some good darts from steel knitting needles cut in half, with
round wooden plugs as stoppers. The darts should be kept as sharp as

possible to get maximum penetration, and a small pocket whetstone is a useful item. If the darts are brightly colored, they're easier to find in underbrush.

If you want a more elaborate outfit, your troubles really commence. In the first place, a gun over eight feet cannot, I believe, be made of metal tubing. The tubing will either sag too much when the gun is held to the lips or be too heavy to use. A long gun must be made of wood and the central hole slanted to overcome the sag. For extreme range, metal darts are too heavy, and begin to drop too sharply to make accurate shooting possible. For shooting at over forty yards, I don't believe the Jivaro darts can be improved upon, although they are so light that they can be used only on a dead calm day or in the depth of a forest where the trees cut off the wind.

The relationship between the length of the gun, the weight and length of the darts, and your own breath have to be worked out by practice. The better pair of lungs you have, the longer gun you can use. Light darts must be poisoned to make them really effective. While I was in England, the curator of the Ashmolean Museum at Oxford told me that in his opinion the deadliest poison comes from the Upas tree (*Antiaris toxicaria*), which is used by the Borneo natives to poison their darts. I'll take his word for it. In my opinion, a blowgun is a weapon sufficiently interesting to be used for its own sake without messing around with little-known poisons.

CHAPTER 3

Falconry—
the Sport of Flight

During the Middle Ages, falconry achieved a popularity never approached by any other sport before or since. In Europe it was a mania, a way of life, almost a religious ecstasy. A distraught monk wrote of the nobles: "They hunt everywhere, at religious festivals, between battles, between church services; they even hunt in their sleep." Hawks were allotted by rank, and you could instantly tell a man's position in life by the species of hawk he was carrying. In the Orient the sport was even more popular. Marco Polo says the Great Khan had 20,000 falcons, each with its own falconer. The rare white gyrfalcon of the North was considered to be the most valuable object in the world, and worth a king's ransom.

No one knows how old falconry may be. Sir Henry Layard found a frieze at Khorsabad showing men with birds on their fists who may have been falconers, but as the frieze has now vanished it is impossible to say. However, there is a relief in the Louvre, dating from about 900 B.C., showing a falcon wearing the trappings of a trained bird. The sport probably originated in the Middle East and was introduced to Europe by the Vikings after one of their Mediterranean raids. It immediately became popular, and remained the great sport of the nobility until the hawk was superseded by the fowling piece during the early eighteenth century. Even so, falconry has never entirely died out, and is becoming so popular in America today that both falconers and conservationists are concerned lest the growing demand for trained birds place too heavy a strain on the rapidly diminishing hawk population.

There's considerable confusion as to what is meant by a "falcon." The raptors—birds of prey—are usually divided into eagles, hawks, owls, and vultures. All can be trained to hunt by man. I myself hunted iguanas in Mexico with a golden eagle, Tequila, and Aguila, an American bald eagle. Aguila is now thirty years old and in fine shape, the life span of an eagle being probably well over fifty years. As I obtained Aguila in 1939, before the wise federal law protecting these birds, I have been allowed to keep her; she could not possibly survive in the wild, and when put in a zoo cage beats herself against the bars, as she is used to being flown daily and kept on a block like a trained falcon. A number of other falconers have trained eagles, especially that wonderful Englishman Captain C. W. R. Knight, whose yearly lectures on his birds were an exciting event to anyone interested in hawking. However, the eagles are too large and slow-flying to be used on ordinary game, although on the open plains of the West they can be used on jack rabbit and even coyote.

Owls can also be trained—they can see perfectly well in daylight, by the way—and the great horned owl makes a powerful if slow hunter. But the owl's method of hunting is to fly through the woods at night and pounce silently on any small creature she sees or hears. Owls have acute hearing, and can see in darkness so complete that most other animals are blind. Because their flight is noiseless, the owl's presence is not suspected until too late, and these night birds do not require speed to capture their quarry. In the daytime their quarry can generally escape, and as few falconers like to hunt in the middle of the night, owls do not make good hunting birds. Vultures eat only carrion, and although I once had a pet Turkey vulture named Susie who could spot even a dead mouse while soaring a quarter of a mile high in the sky, hunting for carrion can hardly be considered a sport. As a result, for falconry only trained hawks are used.

Hawks are divided into several families such as the kites, buteos, harriers, ospreys, falcons, and accipiters. The ospreys are fisheaters; the kites are too highly specialized (the Everglade kite eats nothing but one species of fresh-water snail); and the harriers live largely on frogs, small snakes, and mice. The big, soaring buteos are the commonest of all hawks and are found all over the country. Some of the best known are the red-tailed and red-shouldered, Swainson's and rough-legged. Although powerful birds, they are so slow that falconers seldom use them, though a good buteo can be death on rabbits. That leaves the falcons and the accipiters.

The falcons as a family are distinguished from all other hawks by three characteristics: long, thin swallow-like wings, brown eyes, and a *V*-shaped protuberance on the upper beak. In this country there are six species of falcons, ranging in size from the noble white gyrfalcon, who is only an occasional winter visitor, to the tiny kestrel, or sparrow hawk, little bigger than a robin, who lives mainly on insects but shows as much style capturing a grasshopper as its big relative the gyrfalcon does taking a swan.

By far the best known of all the falcons is the peregrine, a bird with a body length of about twenty inches and a wingspread of forty-five inches. This is the bird generally used in falconry. A peregrine can fly ninety miles an hour in straightaway flight, and in her "stoop" (corresponding to a plane's power dive) goes over two hundred miles per hour—some say over three hundred mph. This stoop is peculiar to the falcons; no other raptors employ it. Typically, a falcon will take only flying birds. She rises above her quarry, turns over, and comes down head first in her stoop. As she passes the quarry she delivers a blow with her short curved hind talons. If the blow goes home, the quarry leaps in the air as though hit by both barrels of a shotgun, and then falls stone dead. When it strikes the ground, the falcon alights on it. If the bird is still alive, she kills it by snapping the neck with her beak, using the *V*-shaped notch for leverages.

Accipiters are the only other family of hawks generally used in falconry. They have short, rounded wings to enable them to fly fast in forests (the French call them the "rowers"), very long tails they use as rudders when dodging around tree trunks, and for the first three or four years of their lives yellow eyes that gradually turn orange and finally blood red as the bird reaches full maturity. The best known of the accipiters is the goshawk. The goshawk is considerably bigger than a peregrine (twenty-six inches long, with a wingspread of forty-eight inches). The commonest accipiter is the Cooper's hawk (found only on this continent), who is a somewhat smaller edition of the big goshawk. There is also the little sharp-shinned hawk, about the size of a pigeon, who can catch small birds.

Accipiters do not fly high nor do they stoop. They are flown "at the bolt," that is, directly from the falconer's fist at the quarry. They make a sudden dash at the game and bind (seize) directly to it. In the Middle

Camping in the Southwest: Jule Mannix with the Mannixes' hunting cheetah, Rani, and a hooded falcon

Rani stalking a coyote

Rabbit hunting with Tiba, the ocelot

Hunting a wildcat with a blowgun

FACING PAGE: Blowgun hunting
for deer

Daniel P. Mannix
holds the wildcat
brought down with
a blowgun after it
was treed by
Bill Piper's hounds

Blowgun and darts
from the Philippines.
The barbed center
dart is for knocking
over small game;
the other two are
poisoned and are used
for hunting deer

FACING PAGE: The
peregrine is generally
used in falconry

Dan Mannix catching a wild peregrine falcon on the beach, using a pigeon lure and "head-set"

Falcon taking a pheasant

A swift hunter is the shy **Cooper's** hawk

ABOVE LEFT: The Wacamba of Kenya, East Africa, are probably the world's greatest native archers. ABOVE RIGHT: The poisoned arrows ready for the hunt. BELOW: Wacamba making poison for arrows

Ages they were employed by the yeomanry as practical meat-getters, as a goshawk will take anything she's flown at, from a goose to a mouse. Their favorite game is rabbits. Most game birds can outfly them unless the accipiter binds to her quarry as it's rising and hasn't had time to build up speed.

The first question everyone interested in falconry asks is "Where can I get a hawk?" There are a few other questions you'll have to ask yourself first. Do you have a place to keep it? Hawks must be kept in a mews—a hawk house corresponding to a kennel for dogs or a stable for horses. The mews must be at least ten feet square, and preferably larger. It must have a perch where the hawk sits at night, and a sand or sawdust floor that can be easily cleaned. When the hawk is molting, she is allowed to fly free in the mews. Trained hawks positively cannot be kept in a cage; they'd beat themselves to pieces against the bars in a few minutes. Keeping a hawk in the house is utterly impractical unless you have an entire room you're prepared to turn over to the bird.

During the day the hawk is put on an outside block to "weather": get some sun, bathe and preen herself. She is restrained by leather straps around her legs, called "jesses." These jesses always remain on the bird's legs even when she flies; they are the badge of a trained hawk as a collar is the badge of a domestic dog. The ends of the jesses are fastened to one end of a figure-eight-shaped swivel. A leash is passed through the other end and tied to the block. Someone must always be around to keep an eye on the bird in case of dogs, children, or a sudden change in the weather. Because hawks cannot be left in the sun too long, the block has to be moved into the shadow occasionally. Hawk watching seems traditionally to be woman's work; wives do it for husbands who have to go to work and mothers for sons at school, but before you get a hawk make sure you have the right sort of wife or mother available. Hard as it is to believe, there are some women who just don't like hawks.

Lastly, you must have a supply of pigeons readily available. Hawks need fur or feathers to clean out their crops, and the warm blood of a freshly killed bird helps them digest their food. Also, if you've flown a hawk who refuses to come back, the only way to lure her in is with a live pigeon—and at one time or another all hawks are reluctant to return.

For these reasons, it is impossible to keep hawks in a city. Even in the suburbs, trying to keep a hawk in a housing development is difficult; there are too many children and dogs around to harry the bird. Falconers have to live out in the country.

If you meet all these requirements, you can start worrying about where to get a hawk.

Hawks are either taken from the nest as fledglings (such birds are called eyasses) or trapped when adults (if not in mature plumage, they're "passagers"; otherwise they're "haggards"). Eyasses are much tamer than wild-caught birds but never make as good hunters, lacking experience. Peregrines and the western prairie falcon nest on the sides of cliffs, while the smaller falcons, such as merlins (often called pigeon hawks) and kestrels, nest in trees. All the accipiters build nests of sticks in high trees.

Twenty years ago, there were thirty-odd peregrine eyries in Pennsylvania, and every spring a group of enthusiasts would travel from one eyrie to another, counting the number of eyasses and checking on the parent birds, most of whom we knew by sight. Today, not one of those eyries remains, and the peregrine is fast ceasing to be a nesting species on the eastern seaboard. Gunners killed a number, but the real deathblow almost certainly came from the widespread use of insecticides. Small birds ate the poisoned insects, and when the falcons ate the birds they received a cumulative dose of the poison that either killed them or rendered them sterile. The accipiters have not been so hard hit, as they live largely on small mammals that are not insectivorous.

If you want to get an eyass, you have to be enough of a naturalist to find a hawk's nest in the spring. Hawks are never sold by dealers (or at least shouldn't be), so you have to get your own bird.

Even if eyass falcons could still be obtained, nearly every falconer would prefer to use an adult bird. The adults are not only much better hunters; raising a young bird is a terrific job. The eyass must be fed freshly killed birds several times a day, and getting a reluctant young hawk to eat is an art in itself. In Europe, trapping adult falcons was so difficult that a haggard was considered to be an almost priceless possession. The Mollen family in Holland, whose ancestors used to trap hawks for medieval nobles, have spent five hundred years perfecting the art. They worked out a system by which trained decoy pigeons lure a hawk down and pass her on from one to another of them until the falcon finally strikes a pigeon on the ground, and a curved net called a "bow net" is jerked over her. The pigeons work in cooperation with a small bird called a shrike that sits beside them and whistles signals to the trapper. There is also a lure hawk mixed up in the business, and judging from the things the lure hawk is expected to perform I gather he must be a Ph.D. In addition, an eagle owl, much like our great horned owl, is often used. Like the rest of this zoo, he is also carefully trained. His job is to fly back and forth across an open space at regular intervals. Falcons hate owls, and the presence of the owl keeps the hawk's mind off the bow net.

A friend and I got a copy of the plans the Mollens use for laying out this flying circus. The plans looked a little like the blueprints for a new type long-range bomber, but mainly like nothing else ever seen in the world before. If you can imagine a diesel engine, each part of which is afraid of all the other parts and is trying to get away from them, you have some idea of what we were up against. It was fun in a way, but not the sort of fun I ever want to have again.

We even, heaven help us, tried trapping with this zoological United Nations we had assembled. Cape May Point in New Jersey is on the flyway of migrating hawks, and in those days falcons were not protected. At the end of a week we had caught the various members of our band of pigeons ten times, the owl twice, and the lure hawk once. The only wild life we caught during this experiment was each other. Throughout all our preparations a magnificent peregrine falcon sat on the stub of a dead pine, watching us with intelligent interest. When we had finished, she flew down, looked over our nets and lines, and then flew away, shaking her head sadly.

Since then, falconers have discovered several islands lying off the coast of Virginia that are stopping places for peregrines migrating south from Canada. These birds are mostly first-year passagers, not so set in their ways as haggards but with far more flying experience than eyasses—in other words, perfect for falconry. The question was how to trap them without trying to duplicate the elaborate Mollen setup. By trial and error, the falconers finally evolved a technique called "digging in."

As it's impossible to tell where on the island the migrating falcons may be, the falconers race up and down the coasts in jeeps, leaping over sand dunes and roaring through surf as they watch for the birds. One man sits on the hood, hanging on as best he can, and when the jeep is below a flying hawk, he throws up a live pigeon. The falcon dives out of the sky, seizes the pigeon, and drops to the beach to eat her kill. Instantly the falconers fling themselves out of the jeep and start burying one of the party up to his neck in the sand. A bushel basket is flung over his head and another pigeon thrust into his hands. Then the falconers jump in their jeep and rush off, leaving their friend looking like part of the beach.

The jeep circles around and by slowly approaching the hawk induces her to leave her kill without frightening her too greatly. The dead pigeon is then picked up and the jeep drives off. The falcon sees the second pigeon in the buried falconer's hand. Sometimes the bird comes right in. More often, she takes an hour or so to make up her mind. When she does finally take the pigeon, the falconer grabs her and then waits for his friends to come back and dig him out.

I remember one autumn when we were lucky enough to hit the beach during a big flight. In two days, six of us had caught more than fifty birds. There were three jeeps and two other cars with the air pressure in their tires reduced to ten pounds to give them traction on the sand. One Maryland falconer was run over three times by cars driven by overeager falconers while he was dug in on different hawks. Fortunately, the soft sand prevented his being hurt. I was dug in on one bird in such a hurry that the toes of my shoes were left sticking out through the sand. A magnificent falcon lit on the toe of my right boot and sat there for an hour and a half, preening her feathers and ignoring the pigeon in my hand. It was October, and the sand was very cold and damp. When the bird finally came in and my friends dug me out, I had the beginnings of a fine case of bronchitis.

That night we took over an old ammunition shack abandoned by the Coast Guard after the last war, and rigged up a makeshift mews. Only two or three birds were kept. The rest were eventually turned loose, the falconers first putting bands around the birds' legs so that if they were trapped later on the Fish and Wildlife Service would have some record of the birds' migratory habits. Every strip of leather that we had brought was pressed into service to make jesses and leashes. One night there were seventy-five peregrines in that shack at the same time. I never expect to see anything like it again. Yet if you get a contrary wind or stormy weather, you can spend a fortnight on the islands and never see a bird. I've had that happen, too.

Newly caught hawks are controlled by means of a "hood," a little leather cap that fits down over the bird's head and completely blinds her. By some curious trick of hawk psychology, a blinded bird becomes perfectly quiet. "Manning" (taming) a hawk is a very delicate process. The hawk can never be punished. The falconer carries the hooded hawk on his gloved fist for several hours each day, talking to her and occasionally stroking her with a feather. The hawk must be quickly persuaded to eat through the hood, for as a result of the shock of being captured she may go on a hunger strike. A famous Dutch falconer who had hunted with his hawks all over Europe and Asia was once asked what he considered his greatest triumph in hawking. "I can get a quarter of a crop more food down a newly caught hawk than any other man alive," he answered proudly.

When the bird will eat readily through the hood, the falconer unhoods her and tries to get the bird to feed from his fist bareheaded. When the bird becomes used to seeing the man, the real training begins. The falconer persuades the bird to jump to his fist for food, and then flies her a short distance in the open, keeping a strong, light line, called a "creance," fastened to the jesses just in case the hawk should get any ideas. Finally comes the crucial day when the hawk is permitted to fly free. Not infrequently this is the last time the falconer ever sees the bird that has cost him so much time and trouble. But if she's been correctly manned, she'll return to the lure.

The lure is a feathered leather bag with a long string attached so the falconer can swing it above his head and make it imitate the movements of a wild bird. Bits of pigeon are tied to the lure by drawstrings, and the falcon dives at the swinging lure as though it were a live bird. Eventually the falconer allows the hawk to catch the lure and feed from it on the ground. Not only does the lure bring the falcon back; stooping at it gives her much needed exercise as well. Accipiters won't stoop to the lure, and the only way of exercising them is flying them at live game.

Falcons are usually flown over bird dogs who get the game up for them. Most of our hunting dogs were originally bred to work with hawks rather than with guns, so they take naturally to it. I remember one afternoon's hawking near Valley Forge, Pennsylvania, with a friend who was flying an intermew passage falcon (a bird captured as a passager in her brown, immature plumage who had molted through in the mews into her blue-and-white adult colors). He was flying her over a pointer named Sally. Both bird and dog knew each other perfectly.

We climbed a low hill overlooking a cornfield now in stubble with a few hollows full of honeysuckle—perfect pheasant cover. My friend took off the bird's swivel and leash, holding her up so she could look over the lay of the land. The bird was a female. With all hawks, the female is roughly a third larger than the male, and correspondingly stronger and faster, so females are generally used. In fact, in falconry parlance only the female can properly be called "a falcon." The male is a tiercel.

This bird's name was Lady. She opened her wings and drifted off my friend's fist, glided a few feet, and then suddenly went skimming over the tall grasses like a thrown boomerang. Sally, the pointer, stopped panting over her pink tongue and sat up, whining to be sent into cover. The falcon made a circuit of the field, the tips of her long wings almost touching the frostbitten tops of the sumac bushes in the hedgerows. She came back so low and so fast that we both ducked, although Lady could judge her distance to an inch. Then the falcon began to rise over the field in a series of great ringing circles, taking advantage of every air current to lift her higher.

My friend followed her with a pair of field glasses while the pointer eyed the cover longingly. The falcon went up until she looked no bigger than a butterfly. When she had reached her pitch, her "place of pride" as the old falconers would say, she began to ride the air currents with outstretched wings.

"All right, Sally, go find 'em!" my friend called, and the pointer tore into the field, seemingly rushing in half a dozen directions at once. The field was empty, and she dived through the hedgerow and vanished in a meadow of tall bunch grass.

"Lady can still see her," said my friend, watching the bird through his glasses. Lady was following the dog's movements from field to field, banking into the late afternoon breeze as she quartered back and forth, turning her head to watch the pointer.

We followed Sally as well as we could. Sally had trouble finding any pheasants, and the falcon "waiting on" high overhead began to find it difficult to stay in position as the breeze grew stronger and she was carried downwind. Several times my friend had to show her the lure to bring her back into place. Suddenly Lady came down in a long, hissing stoop, missing the dog's head by inches. Sally gave an astonished yelp, and the falcon shot up again, slowly mounting to her pitch.

"She does that when she gets impatient with Sally," my friend explained. "She decided Sally was just fooling around, and wanted to teach her a lesson."

After this little exhibition of temper, the hawk and dog seemed to work better together. Lady hung over the pointer as the dog worked field after field, and occasionally Sally would stop as though waiting for her to get into position again. We followed at a distance.

Abruptly the rustle of Sally's progress through the grass stopped. We moved up silently and found the dog frozen at point. Lady had drifted too far downwind, and we had to wait until she came up. As the falcon came towering over us in perfect position, my friend shouted and we rushed forward. A single cock pheasant roared up.

With her wings folded tight to her body, Lady came tearing down. At the speed she was going it would have been suicide for her to grab the pheasant. She was going so fast she seemed to drop in a series of great bounds, and the bells fastened to her legs—all trained birds carry bells so they can be traced in cover—stopped ringing and began to whistle as the wind poured over their lips. As she shot past the cock, she delivered the falcon's terrible raking blow with her hind talons. A puff of feathers flew up, and the pheasant staggered. The hawk shot up, but before she could strike again the cock turned and dived almost vertically into a hedge-row.

My friend shouted to Sally to go in. The pointer rushed along the hedgerow, and we could see the pheasant running ahead of her. At the end of the row, the cock took to the air once more, my friend yelling like a banshee to attract Lady's attention.

But Lady had got discouraged and was sitting comfortably on the limb of a dead tree some distance off. By the time she saw the cock, he'd achieved a long lead. Even so, Lady took out after him, and both birds, flying all out, vanished toward a distant ridge. Although it was easy enough to see them against the light sky, when the ridge formed a dark background they were invisible.

"This flight is going to end in the next county," my friend prophesied grimly. In the old days, falconers were always mounted so they could keep the birds in sight, but we had to trust to our feet. By the time we reached the summit of the ridge, there was no sign of either bird.

My friend cut straight across open country, swinging the lure and call-ing. I walked along the edge of some woods, moving quietly and listening for the tinkle of Lady's bells.

When the sun began to set, I gave up and started back for the ridge. As I passed the woods a second time, I noticed a large brownish-white patch on the ground, and walked over to investigate. There sat Lady on the dead cock. The falcon had carefully plucked her kill and was sitting surrounded by a circle of feathers. Though she was full gorged, she was still listlessly pulling on a piece of meat like a little boy at Thanksgiving who knows that he can't hold any more but is still in there fighting. I was afraid to "make in," knowing that if I frightened Lady my friend would probably never see her again, as she was much too full to pay any attention to the lure. So I stood and shouted until my friend heard me. He crawled up to Lady on his stomach and slowly took hold of the jesses.

Duck hawking is probably the most exciting of all falconry. Ducks are fast, tricky, and if they reach water—"take to the splash," as the old falconers called it—are sure to get away. It takes a good falcon to catch any sort of duck.

One afternoon I took a haggard peregrine I called Comet out after crows. We came over the crest of a little rise and saw below us three teal in a small puddle made by a recent rain. This was too good a chance to miss, and I put Comet into the air. She made her point over the puddle, knowing I'd jump the ducks for her. The teal had other ideas. They saw the falcon, and refused to leave the water. Ducks can be successfully hawked at only in small, shallow pools. In ponds or lakes nothing will induce them to take off with a hawk in the air. Even in the puddle, these three birds were so determined I had to wade in after them. Finally one leaped up.

Comet turned over and came down in a perfect stoop, but as she struck, the teal closed one wing and rolled with the blow. Comet made a wild snatch as she went by and managed to bind to the duck so that both birds fell in a tangle to the ground. I was sure Comet had him, but the teal shook himself free and took to the air again. After a moment's hesitation, Comet followed him in a long tail chase. The teal had such a long start that I expected to see both of them disappear over the horizon. Just before they went out of sight, I saw the teal drop beyond some trees, Comet following him to the ground.

When I got to the spot, Comet was sitting on the bank of a stream, looking around for her quarry. After nearly half an hour, I located the teal hiding under a tangle of roots upstream from the hawk. As soon as he knew his hiding place had been found, the teal dived and came up in midstream. Lying motionless on the water with his wings partly spread, the teal floated past the watching hawk. Comet, like most animals, could not readily identify a motionless object as being alive. She allowed the teal to float past her, and as soon as the smart teal was around a bend he shook himself and flew off.

Flying the accipiters is so different from working with the falcons that technically it's not considered falconry at all, but "ostringing." Most ostringers prefer the goshawk above all accipiters, but personally I've always been interested in the Cooper's hawk. Although the Cooper's is somewhat smaller than the goshawk, he is quicker and far more easily obtainable. No matter where you live in North America, there's a good chance that a pair of Cooper's hawks are nesting within a few miles of your home. There's an even better chance that you will never see the birds or their nest. The nest is well hidden, and there are no telltale feathers around it. Some distance off is the "feeding tree" where the hawks take their prey. While one bird broods the eggs, the other hunts. The kill is carried to the "feeding tree," and the hunter gives a low call. The brooding bird makes sure that there are no trespassers, and then flies to the "feeding tree," where the hunter and mate share their quarry.

Although there is no one species of hawk that is a "chicken hawk," the Cooper's is probably more apt to take the farmer's chickens than any other species. He lives near farming country, will attack anything he can kill, and specializes in ground quarry. They are astonishingly bold, and have even flown through an open window and grabbed a chicken being plucked by a farmer's wife. In raiding a chicken yard, the hawk does not soar over the yard and betray his presence to the chickens and the farm. He waits in the nearest cover, studying the chickens until he has finally selected a victim. Then he flies silently toward the yard, keeping the chicken house or barn between him and the flock until he is close enough to turn loose his final rush. Nearly always he is able to kill and carry off his prey before the farmer, hearing the frantic cackling of the flock, manages to arrive with his shotgun. Usually it's some perfectly harmless buteo the farmer later shoots as "the chicken hawk." A game warden once gave me an almost infallible way of identifying a Cooper's hawk in the field. "If you can get your sights on a hawk, it isn't a Cooper's."

The owner of a pheasant farm, knowing I was interested in hawks, once presented me with a fine female Cooper's. She had followed a hysterical cock pheasant into a pen, and the keeper had run up and grabbed her before she could escape. As the owner of the farm handed me the bird, tied in a sack, he said, "I don't care what you do with this damn' thing as long as you don't let it go."

She was a beauty. She had a three-foot wingspread and a torpedo-shaped body. She was a fully matured bird; her back feathers were a brilliant slate blue; her white breast was crossed with orange-red stripes that ran from side to side; and her eyes were ruby red. During the first year of its life, a Cooper's is brown with yellow eyes, and the breast stripes run longitudinally; but after the first molt, the hawk develops adult plumage, and the colors become more and more brilliant with each molt for the next four or five years. This bird seemed to be about four years old.

As a tribute to her sweet disposition, I named her Apache. All accipiters are difficult to man. Unlike the lordly falcons, who accept captivity with dignity, accipiters are intractable, temperamental, unpredictable, and generally mean. They alternate between moods of hysterical fury and black despondency; in other words, they are manic-depressives. At the top of their emotional cycle they will attack any quarry. In Afghanistan, goshawks have been trained to seize a gazelle by the forehead and hold on until the hunters arrive. At their low point, accipiters scream with terror at the sight of a mouse. Oriental falconers call the upswing of the cycle "yarak," and keeping an accipiter in yarak is the main problem of the ostringer.

Of all the accipitrine hawks, the Cooper's is the most prone to these up-and-down moods and the hardest to get into yarak when in the sulks. Oriental falconers frequently use drugs to bring the birds out of their downswing, and before I got Apache manned I could have used a few drugs myself. Still, by giving her plenty of "castings" (fur or feathers to clean out the crop) I managed to keep her in fairly good yarak.

Although I spent hours trying to get Apache down from trees in which she was sulking, when she was in real yarak she lived up to the name I'd given her. Once she followed a rabbit so far down a woodchuck hole that I had to dig her out. At another time a starling took refuge in a roll of barbed wire. Apache, after running back and forth trying to find a way among the barbs, wormed under the tangle and, turning on her back, reached up a long leg and grabbed the starling from underneath. Then there was the time she fastened to a mallard; not until the duck had dived did the hawk give up, half drowned.

I had a cocker spaniel named Flush, and the hawk learned to work with the dog as a team—after Apache realized that she was supposed to catch what Flush put up, and not the spaniel. But once the hawk learned, she lost all interest in me and concentrated on Flush.

A Cooper's has trouble holding a full-grown rabbit, which weighs half again as much as she does and can put up a tough fight. Apache made several mistakes before she learned the trick of handling them.

She got her first real chance when a neighboring farmer complained that rabbits were eating his young corn. Apache, Flush, and I started out, with Flush ranging ahead through the cover edging the field, and Apache, bent low on my fist, watching the dog with intent, scarlet eyes.

She was so high in yarak that when I kicked over a clod of earth the hawk jumped from my fist and grabbed it.

I was holding Apache tightly by the jesses to make sure she didn't take off after any more clods when the hawk seemed to go mad. She struggled so wildly to escape that, even though I saw no quarry, I let her go. I had forgotten the incredibly keen eyesight of a hawk—eight times sharper than that of a human being. Apache shot off over the foot-high corn with two quick, hard flaps and a glide, two more flaps and a glide, her attention concentrated on something in the field below.

Flush raced after the hawk, barking excitedly, although I knew that he could see no more than I. Then I caught a glimpse of a gray form among the green shoots. A rabbit had been eating the corn and had started to steal away when it saw the spaniel. Apache, with her telescopic vision, had seen it when neither Flush nor I had any idea of its presence.

Apache swerved in full flight, her tail opening like a fan as she banked into the wind and plunged into the corn. There was a miniature explosion, and the rabbit burst out of the corn and headed for the safety of the hedgerow with the hawk clinging to its back like a cowboy riding a bucking bronco. Apache was unable to stop the rabbit, but just as it reached the briers the hawk threw out her wings to act as brakes, and flung herself backward. The trick nearly worked, but the rabbit was too strong. It plunged into the brambles with Apache holding on with one foot and grabbing wildly at the ground with the other. She was knocked wings-over-tail by the bushes, and the rabbit vanished, leaving Apache sprawled on the ground, panting and furious.

The hawk learned by her mistakes. The next day I took her out again, and Flush put up a rabbit that refused to leave the safety of the briers. Apache flew slowly over the patch, following every turn and twist of the quarry. There was an open spot in the middle of the patch where a tree had fallen, and whenever the rabbit approached this clearing Apache's wingbeat would increase as she prepared to swoop down, but each time the rabbit turned back.

Apache became so frustrated that I thought she might land in the patch and try to run the rabbit down. Cooper's hawks have very long legs and can run surprisingly fast, though not fast enough to catch a rabbit. Apache had another idea. Suddenly she turned sideways and came shooting down among the brambles like a falling knifeblade. I thought that this would be a repetition of the previous day's maneuver and that even if Apache succeeded in seizing the rabbit it would knock her off among the brambles. But no sound came from the patch except Flush's exciting barking. When I forced my way through the briers, I found that Apache had seized the rabbit by the head like a cowboy bulldogging a steer. Her talons had gone into its brain, killing it almost instantly.

Accipiters always kill with their talons, never with the beak. Their grip is unbelievably strong, and their talons are longer than a wildcat's claws and as sharply pointed. Once she had learned the trick of "bulldogging," Apache was death on rabbits, but her favorite quarry was pheasants, even though she seldom caught one.

Once, while she was having a fit of the sulks, Apache flew to the roof of an old springhouse and refused to come down. I started across the field toward her and accidentally put up a cock pheasant. I doubt that even a rabbit would have interested Apache at that moment, but she couldn't refuse a pheasant. She took off after the bird and overhauled him as though he had been standing still, as she had the height of the spring-house to give impetus to her swoop. The cock folded his wings and dropped into the high grass, but the hawk bound to him while the bird was still a few feet from the ground. Both birds rolled over and over, the cock kicking and striking the hawk with his wings while Apache hung on with her talons. When the cock stopped struggling I reached down to put him in the game bag; but as I bent over he came to life and exploded out of my hands, leaving his tail in Apache's talons. Before I could pick up the hawk, Apache flew off—not after the pheasant, but back to the springhouse roof. She was so mad at me she refused to come down, and spent the night there. It was not until noon the next day that she con-sented to return for a fat pigeon.

Once she was manned, Apache never tried to hurt me or any other human being. My two children could even pick up the bird without Apache's showing any resentment. Well-meaning people warned: "You'd better be careful; that hawk will go for the children's eyes someday." Even a newly caught hawk never attempts to strike at your eyes; he tries only to protect himself by biting or clawing at your hands. Apache never attempted to hurt the children. Sometimes when a child took the bird on her bare hands, Apache, trying to steady herself, would dig her talons into the skin; but when the child yelled "Ouch!" Apache would shift her grip.

Like all hawks, Apache would not retrieve game. Most people believe that trained falcons will fly back to their masters with their quarry like a bird dog retrieving. Hawks kill for their own benefit, not for their owner's. The falconer must see where the hawk has come down with her quarry and "make in" slowly, substituting a piece of meat for the quarry so the bird does not realize she is being robbed.

Falconry is a universal sport; there is hardly a country in the world where it is not practiced to some extent. In many of the Arab countries, falconry is practiced as a tradition, and virtually every sheik has a falcon or two as a matter of prestige. In India, although the great falconry establishments of the rajahs, with hundreds of hawks waited upon by hordes of hereditary falconers, have gone, the sport is still carried on by individual enthusiasts. While in India, I had the pleasure of corresponding with Brigadier A. S. Bedi of Poona, who is an ardent and expert falconer. In Russia, there is one of the great fur hunters of Kazakhstan still left—Musabai Zhankulov. These men hunted foxes, and occasionally wolves, with golden eagles. Zhankulov is now seventy-five and Sarbas, his eagle, seventeen, but they still hunt together, averaging one hundred foxes a year.

In France there is the Association Nationale des Fauconniers et Autoursiers. I met M. Abel Boyer, then the secretary, in Paris. The favorite game bird for falcons in France seems to be the partridge, as these comparatively small birds are usually found in open fields, well away from cover, and flush easily. In England, the Old Falconry Club is still very active. I went out with Mr. Norman Knight some years ago, hawking rabbits in Surrey with his goshawk. In less than an hour, the bird had taken nine rabbits with the help of two terriers to bolt the bunnies from hedgerows. Later, I saw Mr. Knight fly his bird at moorhens during a snowstorm. The snow was so thick we could not see the bird, and had to follow her by the sound of her bells. She got three moorhens in twenty minutes before the American present nearly froze to death and we returned for a hot toddy. Still later, I went rook hawking on Salisbury Plain with Jack Mavrogordato, perhaps the greatest expert on short-winged hawks in the world today. Jack was "hacking" two young English sparrowhawks (allowing them to fly free to build up their strength and hunting ability). They came from an artificial nest in a tree by his house. He showed me the trophies of a year's hunting with a trained adult sparrowhawk. I think he had taken over two hundred small birds and mammals with her. For rooks, he was using a saker, an Oriental falcon similar to the peregrine. Jack spent several years in the Sudan, and still keeps up his connections with African hawkers. Rooks, which resemble small crows, are expert if somewhat slow fliers, and depend on outmaneuvering the falcon. The flight is a study in aeronautical acrobatics.

Many falconers believe that nothing can compare with grouse hawking on the Scottish moors. Grouse are not only extremely fast but expert dodgers, and a flight of several miles is commonplace. Dogs are almost a necessity, as the grouse "lie up" in the heather so well that it is almost impossible to flush them except with a number of beaters or a really good spaniel. The best-known British grouse hawker is Geoffrey Pollard, who flies from Altnabreac, Caithness County. The few falconers lucky enough to have gone with him spend the rest of their lives talking about the experience.

Although a few dealers do sell hawks, both falconers and conservationists consider this sort of commercialization of falconry a highly dangerous practice. Many states have laws against either the sale or importation of the raptors. Falconers believe that anyone sufficiently interested in the sport should go to the trouble of obtaining his own bird. The raptors are having a hard-enough time to survive as it is without any additional strain being put on their numbers by commercial trapping. Shooting hawks has always been considered a praiseworthy pastime. Now most game commissioners permit only the shooting of "bad" hawks. But what is a bad hawk? Sportsmen and chicken farmers hate the accipiters, but fruit farmers and grain raisers cherish them. The accipiters keep down the rabbits and mice that girdle young trees and eat crops. Scientists estimate that a pair of Cooper's hawks are worth more than $200 a year to a truck gardener or a grain farmer. Sportsmen claim the peregrine kills large numbers of ducks, and refer to it as the "duck hawk," but I saw an enraged farmer nearly throw a falconer off a cliff when he tried to take an eyass from a peregrine's eyrie. The farmer explained that the peregrines were keeping down the pigeons that ruined hundreds of dollars' worth of hay in his barn.

I believe that all our forms of wildlife have been so greatly reduced that any sort of wholesale trapping or slaughter is unjustified. They should be preserved as part of our national heritage. Besides, no one knows when they may become useful. Flocks of starlings and sea gulls have caused a series of major crashes on runways when the birds are sucked up by the turboprop engines. In Boston, an Eastern Electra crashed, with sixty-three dead, as a result of starlings. After many experiments, Canada has found the best method of keeping the runways clear is by the use of trained falcons. The oldest flying technique in the world is now aiding the newest.

CHAPTER 4

Hunting With
the Bow and Arrow

The bow is the most useful all-around weapon ever devised by primitive man. It can kill an elephant or bring down a wood pigeon. Historically, the use of the bow might be said to be the turning point between the primitive and civilized man. In expert hands, the bow is so efficient a weapon that it is even being used by the United States Army under certain special conditions.

Originally the bow was intended only as a hunting weapon. Later, it was adopted for warfare; but there is a great difference between the hunting bow and the military bow. The hunting bow is a short, light weapon with a limited range and comparatively little power. Even in open woodland it is rare that an archer has a clear shot at game fifty yards away. The smallest twig will deflect an arrow, so the archer must be right on top of his quarry to get a successful shot. Hunting with a bow is 80 percent stalking and 20 percent bowmanship. The penetration power of an arrow discharged from even a light bow is astonishingly great. The American Indians, who used extremely light bows only some three feet long and with a pull of perhaps forty pounds, and stone arrowheads, could put an arrow completely through a buffalo. As the bow hunter must be close to his quarry to get a clear shot, and wants merely to transfix it with his shaft, the great range and incredible penetrating power of the English longbow of the Middle Ages, which was basically a military weapon, would be a waste in hunting. The hunter is not trying to bring down a mailed knight in open country at two hundred yards.

Anyone interested in archery should realize this distinction. Virtually every amateur archer insists on a bow with a pull of one hundred pounds, and wants it to be as big as possible, like the six-foot longbows used by the famous English archers at Crécy and Agincourt. Only an experienced archer could even string such a device, and few men could keep it bent while taking aim. Simply carrying such a bow through dense cover is a major headache. A five-foot bow with a fifty-pound pull is a much more serviceable hunting weapon. There is no use getting a powerful bow except for long-distance shooting in archery competition.

Nearly all primitive people use small, light bows. There are a few exceptions. In the South Pacific, fishermen shoot harpoon-like arrows from powerful bows to hit fish far underwater. In South America, some tribes have bows so powerful that the archer lies on his back, braces his feet against the bow and pulls back with both hands. These bows are used to shoot monkeys from the tops of tall trees. But except for such special purposes, the shorter and lighter the bow, the better it is for the average hunter.

The early bows were all "self-bows," that is, made from one piece of material—generally wood, although horn was sometimes employed (Pandarus in the *Iliad* used a bow made from ibex horn sixteen palms long.) Later the composite bow was introduced, made of wood with a horn backing and lashed with sinew. In general, such bows are more powerful, have more elasticity, and last better than the wooden self-bow.

Although the composite bow was carried to a high degree of perfection by the Turks, Europeans stuck to the wooden self-bow; and as a result the bow was little used in warfare, for the arrows could do no damage against armor. The great longbow was also a self-bow, but because of its length and special design it was extremely powerful. First developed in Wales, its construction was kept a closely guarded secret. Then, in 1323, Edward II went to Nottingham, where he paid a sum of money to a certain "Robyn Hod." This is all we know about that famous character except legend. When the king returned to London, he was able to equip a corps of archers with longbows. They were used at Bannockburn, but Edward made the mistake of first throwing his knights against the Scottish spearmen. The horses were impaled on the spears, and when the king at last used his bowmen, Bruce was able to outflank them with his cavalry. Thirteen years later, Edward III profited by the lesson to use the bowmen first as Crécy, with results that changed the course of history.

Today, only a few archers use self-bows, and they are usually either old-timers or men who prefer the traditional bow for sentimental reasons. Most modern bows are made of wood and fiberglass laminated. They have a better cast (flatter trajectory), greater accuracy, and more power, although a really fine yew bow in the hands of an expert bowman cannot be surpassed. Modern bows are usually recurved; the tips of the bow curve away from the archer when he holds the bow in shooting position. A recurved bow generally has more elasticity than a "straight" bow.

Although to us archery is only a sport, the bow is still the primary weapon of many people in Africa and parts of Asia. They use bows and arrows as highly practical lethal devices, and under certain conditions they are more effective than firearms—especially if the arrows are poisoned. As this is "real archery," conducted by highly skilled professionals as a trade rather than as a recreation, I think it is worthwhile to study their techniques, especially as there is an unpleasant possibility that someday our troops may be up against these primitive archers even as they are already fighting primitive tribes in Southeast Asia. European troops have encountered bowmen in the Congo, often with disastrous results.

Probably the greatest native archers in the world today are the Wacamba of Kenya, East Africa. These men use poison arrows that are so deadly that there is good reason to fear they may exterminate the large game animals of Kenya within the next few years. Originally the Wacamba killed only for food, but the demand for ivory and rhino horns, used in powdered form as an aphrodisiac throughout the Orient, has turned them into commercial hunters. Now that Kenya is independent, there is almost no control on their activities.

While I was in Kenya, I met several Wacamba bowmen and watched them shoot. Their bows, of a dark mahogany color, are made from a tree called the "mutuba." Their bows are almost straight and have very little curve even when strung. There are no notches to hold the bowstring. Instead, strips of rawhide are wrapped around the bow to keep the string from slipping. The string is tied in place with an elaborate knot that must be untied whenever the bow is unstrung. The Wacamba do not use notches on their bows because they claim that a bow should be strung at different tensions, depending upon weather conditions. Of course, this cannot be done if the bowstring is always slipped into the same notch. After stringing his bow, an archer holds it to his ear and twangs the string. He can tell by the tone of the bow if the string should be tied more tightly or slightly relaxed.

The arrows are beautifully made, fletched with vulture feathers, and somewhat longer than an ordinary shaft. The feathers are glued in place with tree gum, and for greater security are also lashed on with sinew as fine as the finest silk thread. The sinew is passed between each individual barb of the feather's webbing, the native fletcher doing the job so cleverly that the web is not disturbed. The shaft is made of a light, hollow reed.

The most ingenious part of the arrow is the head, made of hand-hammered iron and about twice the size of an ordinary broadhead. It has a stem about as thick as a knitting needle and some six inches in length. An inch or so of this stem is inserted in the hollow end of the reed shaft and held in place with gum. A wad of the gumlike poison is wrapped on the remaining five inches of the stem. No poison is put on the head itself, as the thin head cannot hold enough to kill large quarry.

The hunters always wrap the poisoned stems of the arrowheads with bandages of soft antelope hide to preserve the poison. It deteriorates rapidly if wet or exposed to the sun.

The Wacamba have a curious system for testing the strength of their poison. Before setting out on a hunt, the hunter will slash the upper part of his arm and let a trickle of blood run down to his hand. When the blood has reached the wrist, the hunter touches the blood with the poisoned stem of the arrow. Instantly the blood begins to turn black as the poison climbs steadily up the man's arm. Just before it reaches the open cut, the hunter wipes off the blood. The man can tell by the speed with which the poison mounts the trickle of blood just how potent it is.

The hunters go out in groups of seven or eight men. Their equipment consists of bows and arrows, knives, an adze for removing elephant tusks, and a fire stick for starting a fire. When they come to a drinking hole, they withdraw into the bush, string their bows, and build a small fire to warm the poison on their arrows and make it more potent. A few climb trees; others lie beneath shelving rocks; still others crouch under bushes. Sometimes during the evening a herd comes to drink. Then the poachers loose their arrows.

If the men are lucky, they will hit ten or fifteen elephants before the herd stampedes into the bush. The next morning, the hunters cut out the tusks of the dead elephants near the ambush. The elephants that have received only slight wounds will run for miles, but eventually the poison does its work on them. After allowing a day or so to elapse, the hunters climb trees and watch for the circling vultures that guide them to the rest of their kills. Such wholesale slaughter would be impossible with fire-arms.

John Hunter, who had lived most of his long life in Kenya and knew the Wacamba well, was able to make arrangements with a local poison-maker for me to witness the poisonmaking. I followed the head poison-maker and his two assistants several miles into the thick jungle that grew along an ancient lava belt. The poison tree was surrounded by a ring of dead bees and sunbirds that had made the mistake of drinking nectar from the tree's beautiful purple flowers. The poison plant resembled a large bush with thick stems as big as a man's thigh. I collected some branches and later had the plant identified as the mruchu tree (*Aocan-thera friesiorum*). The poisonous properties of this plant are well known to botanists, but the method by which the natives prepare the poison sap has largely been kept a secret. I believe I am the only person ever to photograph the process.

The poisonmaker and his assistants first impaled two pieces of cactus and a red flower on a stick that they stuck upright under the tree as a charm. Then they collected armfuls of the leaves, bark, and branches. Finally, they dug up some of the roots and added them to the pile. There wasn't much left of the tree by the time they'd finished, and the poison-makers are slowly destroying the mruchu.

Returning to the village, the poisonmaker boiled the collection in an old gasoline tin, stirring it with a bit of wild sisal. After several hours of boiling, he poured off the dark-colored water. This water was then re-heated in a flat iron dish until the water boiled off, leaving the residue of pitchlike poison. The whole process took about six hours. The entire mass of foliage and wood, a load for the three men, was thus reduced to a mass of poison weighing about half a pound. Hunters pay the poison-makers about $10 a pound for it.

Obviously a poisoned arrow is far more effective as a killing device than the ordinary shaft; even a slight cut from it will bring death. As the use of poisoned arrows is naturally illegal in this country, just how effec-tive is the standard broadhead arrow on big game, such as deer? This has become a very controversial question.

Archery has grown so in popularity that today most states have an archery season before the regular hunting season for bowmen. There are over seven million archers in America; Pennsylvania has the most bow hunters, followed by Michigan and California. With such an increase in bow hunters, some groups have complained that hunting with the bow and arrow is unnecessarily cruel to large game animals. A deer struck by an arrow, so the argument goes, often escapes to die slowly of its wounds. Arrows simply don't have the killing power of a rifle bullet, and therefore should be outlawed.

The difference between the effectiveness of a bullet and an arrow is important to archers. No arrow has the smashing impact of a hollow-nosed bullet, as the force of the powder charge behind the bullet is far greater than the power of any bow. A bullet fired from a heavy-gauge rifle will knock a deer down; it's like hitting him with a stone from a powerful sling.

On the other hand, the killing power of a big broadhead—especially the new broadheads that have four cutting edges—is considerably greater than that of a bullet. As the head passes through the animal's body, it cuts a path two inches wide. If the arrow hits a deer anywhere in the chest cavity it collapses both lungs, and death is almost instantaneous. If he is hit elsewhere, the deer will eventually die—far more certainly than if he were hit by a bullet in the same spot—but he will run a great distance before he dies of internal bleeding. On the other hand, the impact of a bullet is so great that the deer will usually be thrown down by the force of the blow, and before he can rise may be dispatched by a second shot.

An arrow, therefore, has no "stopping" power. If you fire at a charging lion with a heavy enough rifle, you can knock him head over heels. The lion, however, is not necessarily dead. As many a hunter has found to his cost, the lion will often recover from the shock in a minute or so, jump to his feet, and kill the man. If no vital part has been hit, he may even live to become a gun-wise, dangerous animal. If the hunter used an arrow, he could not possibly stop the lion's charge, but the lion would be doomed. The big cat could not possibly recover from the cutting effect of the broadhead, although it might take him an hour or so to die. The arrow, then, is eventually more fatal than anything short of an expanding or exploding bullet, but the effects are delayed. This is what causes the confusion when the relative effectiveness of the two weapons is discussed.

Some years ago, I went hunting mountain lion with Edwin Drexel, a professional archer who was then teaching the sport at the Episcopal Academy in Overbrook, Pennsylvania. As guide, we had Bill Green, a famous hunter who with his pack of Green Mountain hounds had hunted everything from grizzly bear in Canada to jaguar in Brazil. The American mountain lion weighs up to two hundred pounds, and the question was whether one could be brought down with a bow and arrows. Drex was using a seventy-eight-pound osage orange bow, four feet six inches long. It was a self-bow, standard equipment in those days, and with the exception of yew, osage orange is probably the best of all woods for bows. Drex had made the bow himself.

The hunt took place in Joe's Valley, 150 miles south of Salt Lake City. It was midwinter, and the temperature dropped to thirty degrees below zero at night and not much above that during the day. We slept in a cabin that had a lean-to where our horses were stabled, their long manes continually furred with hoarfrost. Bill's five hounds lived outside in barrels sunk in the snow and half filled with hay. For drinking water we melted buckets of snow on the cabin's potbellied stove. Shortly after we arrived, it snowed steadily for three days, and there was nothing to do but wait the storm out.

On the evening of the third day, Bill went out to ride the hills, and came back letting in a rush of fiercely cold air and the news that he'd seen a star.

"The storm's beginning to break," he said, kicking the snow off his high-heeled boots. "We ought to be able to pick up some fresh tracks tomorrow. That cat'll probably kill tonight or tomorrow morning."

We were more than ready. Drex had whetted the edges of his blue-steel broadheads (diamondheads were still unknown) until he could shave the fine hairs on the back of his hand with them. He even had a whetstone in his quiver so he could hone the heads if some were blunted in the hunt and had to be used over. The penetration of an arrow depends largely on having the head razor sharp.

The mists were still thick in the valley the next morning as we rode out. Bill rode first, breaking trail. We followed in single file, each horse stepping carefully in the hoofprints of the lead horse to save himself the effort of breaking through the snow. The hounds trotted along at the end, also carefully stepping in the horses' prints. An untrained observer might have thought a single rider had passed through.

We started up the side of a gradual rise that led to the great hills above us. We could see the tops of the peaks rising above the rolling mist like islands. We rode through some ice-plated brush that snapped like swizzle sticks under the horses' hooves. The cedar forests were just ahead, the emerald trees encrusted with gleaming snow. Above them rose the red rock peaks backdropped by a deep blue sky. Bill leaned back in his saddle so he could see up the steep slope.

"Something's been spooking those deer," he called, pointing over his horse's ears. Far above us black shapes were drifting over the snow. A herd of mule deer was trying to reach the protection of the cedars. The deer were so far away they looked like a covey of grouse scuttling for cover. Another herd broke through the trees below us. The leading buck caught his horns in a low branch and had to fight a moment to free himself.

"There's an old male lion lives in this valley, and I believe he's after them," said Bill. Our horses plodded forward across the glistening, unbroken snow. I could see Drex trying to string his bow by putting the tip into his stirrup.

We were still far from the top of the ridge when we struck an old "scratch" under a pine. A scratch is a pile of pine needles a lion collects to mark his range as a warning to other lions. The hounds gathered around, whimpering a little.

Bill said: "I'll take the dogs and go ahead. If you hear them begin to speak on a fresh trail, come ahead fast."

The wind had cleared away the snow to form a little island of bare earth and needles under the tree. We rode over and tied up our horses. The pine needles were actually dry, and we sat down gratefully. By now the sun was high in the utterly cloudless blue sky. We broke off the lower branches of the pine so we could stand. I started a fire with the deadwood. It burned without a wisp of smoke.

An hour later Bill reappeared among the cedars. He rode up, his horse wet and panting from the climb. The hounds limped over and lay down by the fire, panting.

"There're lion tracks up there, but there's snow in them," said Bill, easing himself out of the saddle into the snow. "Must be a couple of days old. Of course, he may be up a tree, but I sure thought he'd start moving last night or this morning. I can't figure how he got down off that ridge without leaving tracks on the slope."

We looked down the great trough of the valley, the snow shining like silver cream in the sun. Somewhere in the vivid green patches of the cedar forests was the big male. Bill crouched down on his hams beside us, studying the valley.

"We'd better cut that saddle for tracks," he said pointing to a U-shaped notch between two peaks. "I rode around here a couple of times during the storm, and maybe he saw me and left the valley."

We started along the slope for the saddle. After an hour's tracking we crossed some old tracks Bill had made the day before during a lull in the snow. Suddenly one of the hounds woke into life and gave a long, sobbing cry. Instantly the rest bustled up around him, tails going like flails. In a moment they were casting up and down Bill's old trail, giving the eager little whimpering cry of a vague scent. Then they all began to speak together.

"They've gone nuts and started trailing you," suggested Drex.

Bill pulled his horse out of the tracks and forced the mustang through the deep snow for a few feet. "Look at that," he pointed. "That lion's been walking in my tracks. He must have followed me down off the ridge yesterday, stepping in the horse's hoofmarks like the dogs do. That's why we haven't seen any lion tracks on the slopes."

Drex strung his bow. "Let's go!" he said briefly.

Bill was studying the trail. He had twisted himself around in the saddle with one leg wrapped around the horn and the other tucked somewhere under the tie strings.

"That cat must have followed my trail along the ridge," he said finally, shouting to be heard above the hounds. "We can cut across a little higher up and meet him."

Bill forced the hounds to leave the trail, and we started up the slope by a route I wouldn't have believed anything but a sleepwalking mountain goat would have tried. We crawled up the seventy-degree slope on our tired horses in a series of long crisscrosses, riding fifty feet in order to go up ten. In some places the horses walked along rock ledges two feet wide with a deep drop of four hundred feet on the other side.

"Kick your feet out of the stirrups so you can jump clear if your horse should start to fall," Bill called back. "We may hit a fresh kill on top of this range."

"One more spot like that last, and he'll find a fresh kill all right," panted Drex. "It'll be me." We crept around the edge of another rock perched on the brink of the precipice, the horses feeling with their hooves on the frozen rock. Then we were on a comparatively gentle slope near the top of the ridge.

The hot sun had eaten away the snow here, and we rode easily over the bare pine needles. The hounds, tired of walking single file behind the horses, went frolicking among the trees, and Bill had trouble keeping them together. "We'll hit the snow again," he told us. "The dogs can't trail on this bare ground anyhow. The sun kills the scent."

We did come on snow in a few minutes, but it was only a few inches deep. There was light crust, and the hounds slipped and skated as they struck it. "Get ready, because if the dogs hit a hot scent they'll go right away," shouted Bill from the rear.

Suddenly we came on the twisted form of a dead deer under a tree on one of the little pine-needle islands. The deer was just freezing. Tracks like the tracks of a monstrous house cat showed in the drift snow under the ledges. At once the hounds gave tongue.

Bill was examining the tracks. "That's the old male," he shouted. The hounds were casting around in frantic circles, noses to the snow, their sterns wriggling desperately. "Those tracks have melted out some so they look bigger than they are, but he must weigh close to 180 pounds."

Drex lashed in place the bracer that protects the archer's forearm from the bite of the released bowstring. "I'm going to change the bowstring. This one got wet in the snow and a little frayed where branches rubbed it."

"You don't have much time." Bill swung into the saddle. The hounds had hit the trail and were pouring through the cedars, yelping in their spasmodic full cry. "I'm going to stay with the dogs."

I waited for Drex. In spite of the excitement he worked fast and surely. Then we kicked our horses on after Bill and the pack. In a few minutes we saw them again. They had reached the end of the timber, and the hounds plunged down the side of a cliff, yelling fiercely. Bill followed them, his horse rearing and sliding up to his haunches in the deep snow. We followed them down the almost sheer side of the canyon. Drex was ahead of me, clinging to the reins with one hand and to his bow with the other. The arrows in his quiver rattled like shot.

The cry of the hounds grew fainter. "Musta found a dead spot in the trail," I gasped. Drex didn't answer me. The horses kept falling into little pockets under the snow, and we were busy trying to keep their heads up. Occasionally a single hound would speak eagerly, a lone, excited cry. Then his comrades would join in, but almost at once the sound would stop again.

Suddenly the cliff fell away almost perpendicularly. From the marks in the snow I could tell Bill and the hounds had gone down. We followed, my knees shaking so I could hardly grip my horse. The cliff face was cut by washouts, and the horses half jumped, half hopped over them.

The wind shifted, and we could hear the hounds in steady cry again. Then the noise broke. The steady baying of the pack changed to a savage, chopping bark.

"They've treed!" gasped Drex.

The barking of the frantic hounds grew louder and then seemed to fade away again as the wind shifted. At last we caught up with them. We could see the lion cornered on a ledge of rock. He stood with his head twisted to one side, snarling at the hounds. First one and then another of them would make a short rush at him, and the big cat would strike out with a talon-tipped paw. The hounds were mad with excitement, and the roar of their barking echoed in the valley below us.

Bill had dismounted and was trying to work his way closer to the hounds. Suddenly the lion turned and bounded away along the face of the cliff. The dogs followed, slipping and falling on the icy rock until I was certain some of them would end up in the valley one hundred feet below.

Bill bent down and watched the animals out of sight. Then he waved to us and remounted. We followed him around the edge of the cliff. We could hear the hounds barking "treed" again among the cedars. "He's taken to the bark this time!" Bill shouted back to us.

A moment later we saw the hounds, their forefeet against the trunk of a big cedar. Bill swung off his horse and ran toward them, his chaps sloshing about in the deep snow. "There he is!" he shouted above the noise of the hounds.

On one of the upper branches of the cedars crouched the huge, tawny cat, the black tip of his tail twitching slowly. He was almost completely hidden by the fringed boughs, but his whiskered mask showed in the green frame. Bill grabbed our reins and tied up the horses so they couldn't break away if the cat jumped out of the tree and started fighting.

Drex plunged through the snow almost up to his waist. He struggled up the hill to get a good stance, holding his bow above his head.

"I can't hit him in a vital spot," he shouted. "The limbs cover him up. Shall I take a chance?"

"No!" Bill called. "If you wound him, he'll kill the dogs and us too before he drops."

"I'll make him move." Drex wrapped his coat around one of his arrows and jerked off the steel broadhead. "I'll hit him with a blunt arrow."

"You'd better have a broadhead ready to notch in case he jumps," I shouted.

Beside me, Bill was muttering: "Jeez, I don't like this. I don't like it at all."

Drex stuck a broadhead into the snow beside him and then notched the blunt arrow and settled himself. Bill and I stepped back. Bill tried to order the hounds clear, but they couldn't hear him over their own racket. Drex raised the bow and loosed the shaft. The lion roared.

"Look out, here he comes!" yelled Bill. We could see one branch after another quiver and shake, each one closer to the ground. Then came a flash of yellow, and the great bulk of the lion appeared clear against the sky on a lower limb.

"There! Don't miss!" I shouted. Drex pulled his shooting tab in place with his teeth and snatched up the broadhead. He held the bow at full draw for a moment. The lion was moving his head back and forth, judging his distance for a leap over the hysterical hounds. I heard the bow sing, and the arrow seemed to drift up toward the lion. For an instant it showed clear against the sky, and then as it reached the lion the shaft seemed to vanish.

"You missed!" howled Bill. "Shoot, shoot!"

Again the bow gave its deep, harplike note. A second arrow leaped at the lion. It vanished up to the feathers in the cat's side. I saw the white cock feather suddenly turn red with squirting blood. The lion whirled and bit off the shaft with one chop.

Drex released another arrow. At the same instant the lion dropped his head, apparently instinctively to guard his chest. The arrow struck the skull and stood out like a plume. One blow of the big paw swept the shaft away. Then the lion sprang out of the tree. For a moment he seemed to hang in the air above us. Then he struck the snow ten feet in front of Drex. Instantly the hounds had him.

"Shoot, for God's sake, shoot!" yelled Bill. Drex stood with a notched arrow, but in the smother of hounds and lion it was impossible to make a shot. Then the tangle cleared. The dead or dying lion lay stretched at full length. The dogs were holding him by the head and feet. Drex stepped up and put in two more arrows at almost stabbing distance.

Bill rushed over to examine the hounds. One hound was badly cut around the neck and lips. He was the only one hurt. The rest continued to worry the dead lion savagely.

When we drew the lion, we found that the first shaft had gone completely through the big cat's body and glanced off a bone, and the head of the arrow was actually protruding from the lion's back. The injured hound had cut himself on the edge of the broadhead while he was fighting the dying lion.

After a little discussion with one of the horses, we got the lion on his back and started back. Bill was acting as a predatory control agent at the time, and was paid to kill a specific number of lions each year because of the damage they do to deer yarded up in the deep snow. He needed the hide to prove he was making his quota.

Bill was silent all the way back to camp. When we got the lion hung up by the cabin together with two others Bill had shot, he finally spoke.

"Boys, that's my last bow-and-arrow hunt," he said seriously. "It's too dangerous. Suppose one of my dogs cut himself really badly on those damn' arrowheads? No, sir, it's a great sport, but it isn't worth the risk."

Incredible as it sounds, the 19th Special Forces Group are using archers in jungle warfare. The arrows are equipped with an explosive warhead to blow up fuel drums and trucks. They are effective up to about two hundred yards. The exact design of the arrows is classified, so after some thirty thousand years of constant use, the bow and arrow is now officially a Top Secret weapon.

The advantage of this ancient weapon in modern guerrilla warfare is that the bow is noiseless. A bowman can put twenty arrows into a truck convoy without the defenders knowing what is causing the explosions or where the attack originates. The bows used have a pull of fifty pounds, but even so they have a greater penetration than most standard firearms. In tests conducted by the Special Forces, two men fired at a box filled with gravel, using a .30 caliber Springfield and a .45 Colt Service automatic from ten yards away. The bullets did not go through the box, but an arrow shot from a fifty-pound Mamba Hi-Speed bow did. Experiments are now being conducted to equip arrows with illuminating flares.

So the oldest of weapons has become one of the most modern.

CHAPTER 5

The Crossbow—Deadliest of Primitive Weapons

In the year 1199, Richard I of England rode out to inspect the fortifications of the Castle Chaluz in Normandy, which his troops were besieging. The king was in full armor, but even so he took care to stay out of bowshot of the fortress. Suddenly the king's retainers saw him reel in the saddle and fall heavily to the ground. Rushing to the fallen monarch, they found a short steel bolt buried in the king's neck. Even at that extreme range, the bolt had gone through the heavy armor as though it were cardboard. The king died a few days later.

Richard the Lion-Hearted had been killed by a new weapon of such terrifying potentialities that the French Lateran had tried to have its use forbidden except against infidels. This weapon was the crossbow. The crossbow was introduced into Europe about the beginning of the twelfth century by the Sicilians, who got it from the Middle Eastern tribes, who may have got it from the Chinese. Other authorities believe that the bow was a modification of the old Roman catapult and may have been used by the Roman legions. If so, its use had been forgotten for nearly a thousand years before the crossbow was suddenly revived as the only weapon (before the use of gunpowder) that could penetrate plate mail.

A crossbow resembles a short, extremely powerful self-bow mounted crossways at the end of a rifle stock. The archer "cocks" the bow by pulling the bowstring back until it catches in a release on the rear of the stock. The bow is discharged by a trigger under the stock, exactly as a gun is fired. The crossbow has several advantages over the longbow. It is very simple to aim and operate; it is tremendously powerful (crossbows discharging a bolt with a bodkin head can penetrate 19-gauge bulletproof steel), and a man can use it from any position—standing, kneeling, or lying down. It has only one real disadvantage: a comparatively long time is required to cock the bow after each shot.

During the Middle Ages, crossbows were made in all sorts of shapes, sizes, and designs. Some were so powerful that an archer had to use a windlass to cock them. These bows had a pull of some 1,200 pounds and could shoot nearly half a mile. Others were so small that a man could carry one hidden in his sleeve, like the old derringer of the West. Still others, called slurbows, were equipped with a gunbarrel, and fired bullets. There was a shotgun type, called the "prodd," that flung a mass of small stones. Some of the bows were equipped with peep sights, wind gage, and elevation adjustors. In Italy, I saw one with an ingenious hair-trigger device that made it unnecessary to jerk the trigger to release the mechanism, a fault of many crossbows. The Chinese developed the repeating crossbow, cocked by a lever arrangement. A hundred such bows could throw a thousand bolts in fifteen seconds against advancing troops. The Chinese used them against the Japanese in 1895, probably the last time in history when crossbows were used on a large scale as a military weapon, although, during the last war, Australian scouts were said to have used homemade crossbows to pick off Japanese sentries because the bows made no noise, and in Vietnam both sides are using crossbows as practical combat weapons.

The great power of a crossbow lies in its construction. A longbow man has to bend his bow and hold it bent while he aims. It takes a very powerful man to use a longbow with a one-hundred-pound pull. A crossbowman, by putting one foot in an iron stirrup in the end of the bow and pulling the string back with the full force of his shoulder muscles, can cock a two-hundred-pound crossbow.

In the last few years, American archery enthusiasts have rediscovered the almost forgotten crossbow. In 1950, the National Company of Crossbowmen was formed as a branch of the National Archery Association. The group has about four hundred members. Near Mountain View, Arkansas, on Route 66, the local Lions Club proclaimed a section of the Ozark Forest as "The Land of the Crossbow," installed moving targets for crossbow enthusiasts, and are planning to build a medieval castle as a hotel for visiting archers. George Stevens, former national crossbow champion who also has the distinction of having invented a repeating crossbow that surpasses the old Chinese model by shooting five regulation bolts in four seconds, gives regular exhibitions there. There are also regular competitions held by crossbowmen, usually in conjunction with standard archery meets. For a long time crossbow supporters had considerable trouble having their sport recognized by longbow men, as most archers consider the crossbow as a sort of bastard instrument that is neither a true bow nor a true gun. However, the crossbowmen are now more or less reluctantly accepted by most archery groups.

As for accuracy, a good crossbowman can hit a twenty-four-inch bull's-eye at one hundred yards fairly consistently. Mr. Paul Eytel, former national champion, can hit an apple at forty yards. This comes close to William Tell's famous stunt of shooting an apple off his son's head at sixty yards. Eytel uses a Dural bow (aluminum alloy) with a pull of seventy pounds and bolts made of aluminum tubing fourteen inches long.

Colonel F. Pierce of Coronado, California, holds the long-distance record. Using a laminated crossbow of wood and plastic, he has sent a bolt over six hundred yards.

Mr. Robert Yates of Daytona, Florida, is an experienced crossbow hunter. He wrote me of one deer hunt:

"I had killed one rattlesnake and had a nice string of squirrels I knocked out of oak trees with blunts when I saw two yearlings [deer] coming toward me. I froze and then heard another deer running. He was a buck, and stopped broadside to me next to the little ones. I had a broadhead in place and was ready. When he turned his head to look at me, I quickly aimed behind the front shoulder and let fly at twenty yards. I heard the peculiar 'chuck' of the bolt striking flesh, and with a leap he disappeared. I knew I had my deer so I sat down to wait while the broadhead did its work. The yearlings showed no alarm and continued to graze. After forty-five minutes, I decided I had waited long enough, and after pulling my bloody bolt out of a dead limb twenty feet beyond where the deer had stood, I began my search. The buck had dropped only about two hundred yards from where I hit him."

I got my first crossbow from Earl Powell, who lived in Vernon, California, and did trick archery sequences for the motion pictures. Earl made his own bows in all sizes and shapes. Some of them were beautiful devices, combining the graceful lines of a violin with the terrible potentiality of a high-powered rifle. One was made to pull four hundred pounds, and could be cocked only with a goat's-foot lever. The stock was made of figured Circassian walnut, and the bow itself of Osage orange backed with rawhide. All the metal fittings were handmade.

Cocking such a bow took quite an effort even with the lever, but once it was cocked the archer could take his time about aiming and releasing the bolt. Earl told me that he occasionally got orders for crossbows that were made to throw a charge of oo buckshot. There are also crossbows equipped with a barrel like a rifle, the inside of the barrel being grooved to spin the bullet for greater accuracy. These crossbow-rifles are silent, and fairly accurate up to one hundred feet or so.

Earl also showed me some bows he had made for the Nevada Fish and Game Commission to mark deer in order to study the animals' range and habits. A sponge soaked with dye is fastened to the end of a blunt bolt and fired at the deer. As the crossbow is so simple to use, any game warden can mark his own deer easily.

While Earl was showing me his bows, I wondered if it would be possible to go bear hunting with a crossbow. I remembered Bill Green and his famous hounds. Bill was living near Orford, New Hampshire, where his pack had established a record for bear. If the first bolt missed, I wanted to be sure there was a good pack of hounds around to slow up the bear until the bow could be recocked.

I got a practical hunting crossbow that Earl recommended, with a Springfield stock, open sights, and a two-inch Osage orange bow that pulled about 120 pounds. The heavy bow could be taken out of the stock and a light lemonwood bow substituted for target practice. With a heavy bow, even a blunt target bolt could go through a twisted-straw target and hit a tree trunk fifty feet farther on. For the hunt, I got a couple of dozen cedar bolts with steel broadheads. Earl told me to grind the edges of the broadheads down on a whetstone until I could shave with them. "Having your broadheads sharp more than doubles their killing power," Earl told me.

When I returned East, I telephoned Bill Green.

"A bear is a different proposition from a mountain lion," Bill told me. "In 1943, I was with the sheriff when he found the body of a hunter named Carl Herrick who'd taken a shot at a bear, and missed. There'd been a fight—the snow was packed down and there was plenty of blood and tracks. The bear had crushed in the man's left lung and chewed up his face and head. He'd been missing for three days when we found the body. I've had a couple of close calls with bears myself. Once, after a long run, the dogs treed a bear and I was trying to keep him up the tree until the hunter I was guiding could get there. The bear started down, and once a bear decides to do something there's no way to stop him. I fell in the snow, and the bear took a swing at me with his paw. His claws ripped open my boot as neatly as a brush hook could. The dogs ran in and held him until I could get in a shot, but I still have the scar."

"At twenty yards I can put a bolt through an oil drum with this bow," I said. "Could we get that close?"

"When the dogs bay him, you can get to within twenty feet. The question is, Will a bolt stop him when he charges?"

This is always the great problem with primitive weapons: stopping power. I asked Bill if he wanted to take the chance.

"There's a bear that's been stripping apple trees on a farm near here, and the farmer has been after me to get him. The bear dens up in a swamp during the day and then comes into the farm at night to feed. The farmer's dog took after him a couple of nights ago, and the bear chased the dog under the front porch and scared the tar out of the family. The farmer came out with a shotgun, but he didn't want to try following the bear at night. If you fly out here with the bow, we can take the dogs out and maybe pick up some fresh tracks."

I put in another telephone call to a friend of mine in Pennsylvania, Jim Butt. Jim was a deputy game warden and a crack shot. He was looking for a weapon that he could use in thickly settled country to knock over vermin but that wouldn't carry as far as a rifle bullet. Jim was interested in the idea of using a crossbow, and agreed to come along while I took the pictures.

I flew to Philadelphia and picked up Jim. After a little practice with the bow, he could hit a circle a foot in diameter at fifty feet four out of five times. It would have taken him years to develop similar accuracy with a longbow. After driving all day, we arrived in Orford, New Hampshire, a few hours after dark.

Mrs. Green had prepared a big venison dinner for us. Bill's house looks like a sportsman's museum. On the walls he has the hides of a mountain lion that must stretch nine feet, a cinnamon bear from California that looked to me like a near record, and a gigantic cattle-killing black bear that he took with his hounds in Vermont. He uses jaguar skins for rugs. In ten years Bill and his pack had killed 351 bears, and traveled from Alaska to the Matta Grosso after game ranging from grizzlies to jaguar.

Between the hides on the walls, he had pictures of some of his famous hounds: Ranger, who was killed in a fight with a Canadian grizzly, and King, who was in on over fifty mountain-lion hunts.

Bill wanted to see what the crossbow could do, so after we'd finished eating, we went out into the yard. Jim switched on the headlights of the car so we could see, and Bill rigged up a crude target made of a wooden box filled with hay. Jim stood off about fifty feet and released a bolt. I expected to see the shaft appear in the side of the box, but nothing happened.

"You missed," said Bill briefly.

Jim released another bolt. This time the box rocked slightly. When we went over to examine it, we found the first bolt had gone completely through it and was sticking in the side of the barn twenty feet behind the target. We had to cut the broadhead out of the wood with an ax. The feathers of the second bolt had become fouled in the hay and the broadhead had gone out the side of the box and was sticking up in the half-frozen ground.

"You can kill a bear with that thing if you hit him in the right place," Bill admitted.

Bill routed us out of bed at five o'clock the next morning. There was a heavy fog, about the consistency of woodsmoke. Bill said the fog was both good and bad. "It'll be hard to follow the dogs in it, but the bear won't travel far. I've cut his tracks a couple of times, and he generally beds up pretty deep in the swamp, but with this fog I don't think we'll have any trouble finding him with the dogs. He knows nothing can see him in the mist, and that gives him a feeling of safety."

"How big is he?" asked Jim.

"He's an old boar. I wouldn't want to try this stunt on too small a bear. A small bear can't tree; the dogs won't let him. As soon as he tries to climb, they'll grab him by the rump and drag him down. I don't want you shooting at a bear while he's on the ground fighting with the dogs. You might hit one of them."

Mrs. Green had cooked us a gigantic breakfast of venison steaks with pots of hot coffee. We ate heartily because we knew that if the hounds happened to hit the fresh trail of a "traveler" bear that was passing through the district on his way to the distant mountain ranges, we might have a three-day run. Once Bill lets the hounds start out on a track he stays with them, no matter how long a run it may be. On one occasion Bill lost the hounds over a mountain ridge and was two days finding them. He was searching the woods for tracks when he heard a sighing noise a few yards away. There were the hounds with the bear they'd kept treed for twenty-four hours; they were so exhausted from barking that they could only gasp. They'd made beds for themselves in the black growth, and in their efforts to reach the bear had torn off every square inch of bark on the trunk as high as they could reach.

As soon as breakfast was over, we stepped out into the sharp chill of a New Hampshire autumn morning. The kennels were only a few feet from the house. When the hounds saw Bill they broke into long, moaning cries of eagerness. Bill and his assistant, Loren Andrews, let out the six hounds that were going with us. They poured out of the open pen door like water out of a millrace, leaping madly about and wetting on the bushes in their excitement, their thin, curved tails working like overcharged pistons.

I'd never seen a pack of big-game hounds without a few "catch-dogs": tough fighting Airedales or bull terriers that will close with a raging bear or cougar after the hounds have run him down, and hold the animal at bay until the men come up. Bill explained that when he first began hunting he had a pack made up of "specialists": one hound with a good nose for cold-trailing, another with a strong voice so Bill could locate the pack, a good treeing dog, and several mean catch-dogs. "The trouble was that the dogs got so used to dividing up the work among them that if something happened to one of my specialists the others wouldn't work without him. If the catch-dogs got mauled, the hounds wouldn't hold the quarry. If the cold-trailer got sick, the other dogs didn't know how to puzzle out an old track. I got tired of running a brain trust, and decided to breed an all-purpose hound."

Jim cocked the bow to make sure it was working all right, and fired a target bolt into the ground. A crossbow should never be discharged without a bolt in place. The released string gave off a vicious twang. Jim had left the bow strung, for a crossbow, unlike a longbow, does not need to be unstrung when not in use unless the bow is to be left for long periods. Bill shook his head. "I sure hope that thing works all right or I'll have some dead dogs when that bear bays," he muttered.

Loren Andrew and Bill loaded the hounds into a pick-up truck that Bill had fitted out with special compartments, two dogs fitting into each compartment. The fog was spotty: heavy in the hollows and thin on high ground. As we went over the crest of a hill, the mist disappeared entirely for a moment, and I could see the thin light of dawn beginning in the east.

After half an hour's drive we left the paved highway and turned off on a dirt road that burrowed through the high stands of green hemlock. Loren stopped the truck and let out the hounds. They exploded from their compartments. Bill swung down to meet them, snapping orders like a top sergeant. The hounds cowed when he spoke to them but continued their nervous quest along the road for scent. Bill came back to us.

"O.K., this is where we start walking. That farm I was telling you about is on the ridge above us. We'll cut through the woods here and maybe hit some fresh signs."

We were glad to walk. I was cramped from the cold, and got stiffly out of the car. We started off through the forest. Although it was autumn and most of the leaves were off the hardwoods, the spruce and hemlock stands were as green as in midsummer. This forest ran clear to the Canadian border, and was so dense that a man could have stood fifty feet away and watched us without our seeing him. We walked on a soft wet mulch of autumn leaves and moss. Occasionally we'd come on a little clearing where the weak, watery autumn sun could reach the forest floor, but under the trees it was dark and green.

Hunting in these forests is a highly technical job requiring an experienced woodsman and first-class hounds. As we walked behind the hounds, Loren and Bill were automatically checking signs. If one of them was doubtful about a track, he'd speak to the other in a low voice. If they couldn't decide, Bill would bring in the hounds to check the spot. Both men would crouch on their hams, watching and listening to the hounds examine the sign. Then Bill would straighten up, "Yep, about two days old, I guess," and we'd go on.

The trees began to thin out, and we came on an old stone wall, green with moss. "The farm begins here," said Bill. He pointed to a place on the wall. "That's where the bear's been crossing. See how the blackberry vines are pushed around? Here's one of his claw marks on the stone. He hasn't gone through here for the last couple of nights, though. There're leaves lying there now."

We crossed the wall and went into the orchard. Even Jim and I could see the places where the bear had been stripping the apple trees. He had stood on his hind legs, grabbed a handful of branches, and torn them down by main strength. He had bitten through limbs four inches in diameter to get at the fruit. We saw one place where the bear had flattened a small tree, apparently for sport. The branches were spread out like a smashed umbrella.

The hounds had been casting around the orchard. Two of them began to whimper, their noses pressed to the damp grass. The rest of the pack hurried over, whining expectantly. Bill went over to them, taking care not to step on any signs. He pushed the dogs aside. "How do you expect me to look at that track while you got your noses in it?" he complained. He pressed the sides of the track with his finger, but the hounds crowded his finger out of the track with their eager noses. Bill crouched and listened to them talk.

"That track was made the night before last," he said finally, still watching the hounds. "The bear didn't come in here last night like I hoped he would. The scent's pretty cold by now, but I guess we might as well follow it out. What do you think, Loren?"

Loren was also watching the hounds, and didn't answer for a minute. "I guess we might as well. Maybe he cut his old track somewheres when he came out last night. Then we can pick up the fresh signs."

Bill spoke to the hounds and then started off on the old line. They had trouble owning (finding) it, and moved slowly. We followed them across the orchard. Suddenly Bill knelt down by a pile of fresh dung and he broke it open with a stick. The dung was spotted with apple seeds.

"This is where he came in last night," said Bill. The hounds were still on the old line. Bill turned to us. "Now, the minute I bring the dogs up, they'll start right away on this fresh track. Remember, when we catch up to the bear and he turns on you, don't start running right away. Wait until he's about three feet away, and then jump sideways. Most of the bear hunting around here is in thick cover, with the bear and dogs fighting all around you. You think you hear the bear coming. First thing you know, you've run right into him. Even when the bear is headed right for you, the chances are that he isn't charging; he's only trying to get away from the dogs. But you've got to remember, too, that no matter how busy the bear may be fighting the dogs, he's never so busy that he doesn't notice the men."

Jim took a carpenter's square out of his pocket and checked to make sure the bowstring crossed the stock at right angles. The bow fitted in a metal socket in the front of the stock and was held in place by aluminum lugs. Jim thought the bow might have got slightly twisted in the socket while he was carrying it through the heavy underbrush. This would cause the crossbow to throw somewhat to either the right or left, depending on which way the bow was twisted. Jim loosened the lugs, lined the bow up with the carpenter's square, and then screwed the socket plate firmly in place again.

"All set," he reported.

"Scout! Blue! Chief!" shouted Bill. The hounds loped up expectantly. While they were still ten feet away, they let out a howl of pure madness. They swung around, breaking into full cry as the fresh hot scent hit their nostrils. "Here, boys, here!" yelled Bill. He had been examining the tracks and knew which way the bear had gone. Sometimes, in the first frenzied excitement of hitting a red-hot trail, the dogs may backtrack and waste precious time. Each hound took a quick sniff of the dung before rushing off on the trail, probably to implant the scent of this particular bear well in his mind. During the run the hounds might cross the scent of another bear, and they didn't want to run the chance of confusing the trails.

We all started running, Jim holding the crossbow in front of him to make sure it didn't catch on branches. The pack poured through the woods like quicksilver through a handful of twigs. We followed as best we could, crawling under hemlocks, struggling through windfalls, tearing our way among vines. We hit a deep gully and slid down on our tails, our heels tearing deep furrows in the soft loam. Jim had to stop and tie the bolts in his quiver together with a piece of vine to keep them from jumping out.

Suddenly the hounds broke into the most ungodly clamoring I've ever heard. Their voices ran up the scale like a hysterical woman's, and through the racket we could hear the growls and savage yaps of combat.

"They've jumped him!" yelled Loren. He began running in earnest, and Jim and I toiled after him. The noise was coming nearer, and in a few minutes we could hear the crash of bushes and dead limbs as the fighting animals raged through the timber. We were running downhill through a growth of small evergreens, not much higher than a man's head, that made a cover as thick as a box hedge. I saw now what Bill had meant when he said you might run into the bear without knowing it. The animals were running in a circle, the bear stopping to fight with the hounds whenever they got too close. At one instant the sound came from straight ahead. The next moment it was on the left or right. Bill yelled to see if we were coming, and Loren whooped in answer.

Ahead of us the growth suddenly thinned out. There was a fairly open slope, studded with little groups of evergreens. I saw the hounds standing there, barking wildly, but no sign of the bear. Bill was in an open spot; he beckoned us to hurry. As I came toward him, there was a quick crackling under a group of evergreens, and a brown shape rushed out. In the thick cover it was impossible to judge size, and the animal looked almost like one of the hounds. It crashed by me, and I saw Jim coming toward us, waist-deep in black growth, holding the bow over his head. Loren and I shouted to him, but he couldn't hear us above the racket of the hounds. We could see that the bear was headed straight for him.

The bear wasn't fifteen feet from Jim when the animal suddenly broke out of the cover and went right at him. Jim took one astonished look and started running to his left. At the same moment the bear turned and began running in the same direction. They almost collided. Jim turned and jumped over some low bushes in a way that would have done credit to a deer. I was standing there wondering if Jim was all right when there was an explosion in the black growth behind me and the bear burst out a few feet away. He was gone again before I could move.

Jim came up to me. He was holding a broadhead bolt in place on the stock with his thumb. "Say, you know this damn' business is dangerous," he said seriously.

Bill shouted, "Come on, the dogs are holding him!"

The bear had got under a hemlock and was facing the pack. The hounds stood with legs apart, their weight evenly distributed, ready to jump if the bear made a rush. The bear was waving his head back and forth with a curious snakelike motion as he studied the positions of the hounds. Occasionally he would snap his jaws with a crack like a giant slapping two planks together. Spittle hung down from his lips. One of the hounds darted in, and the bear made a lunge for him. Instantly the other hounds charged, growling and snapping. The bear swung at them with his great paws like a boxer. I noticed that he kept his claws cupped inward so if he made connections he could jerk the hound within reach of his jaws.

Jim went down on one knee and raised the bow. He aimed along the bolt for the bear's chest, but with the hounds leaping in front of him a shot was impossible. The bear was resting, letting the hounds wear themselves out barking and jumping. Then for an instant the pack opened out, and Jim squeezed the crossbow's trigger.

The bolt vanished in the bear's chest, feathers and all. Instantly the bear roared and charged. At once the hounds were on him. The bear rolled like a wrestler, pinning Blue under him. I heard the hound scream with pain. Then Chief and Scout were on the bear's flanks, worrying and growling, trying to pull him off their friend. The bear spun around and grabbed Red. The hound went down fighting with the bear on top of him. I saw the bear grab the hound by the neck and shake him. Jim had recocked the bow, but with the hounds throwing themselves on the bear he didn't dare release another bolt. The bear was holding Red down with his paws, trying to get the hound's head in his mouth. Red had the bear by the upper lip, and was hanging on. The rest of the pack were tearing fiercely at the bear's thick hide, getting mouthfuls of hair but not doing any damage. Suddenly the bear shook the whole pack off as though they were kittens, gave a toss of his head that flung Red into the black growth, and tore away through the evergreens with the hounds screaming after him.

I forced my way through the evergreens. I could hear the hounds some distance off, and hoped the bear wouldn't turn and come back through the cover toward me. I couldn't see a foot ahead in the green tangle.

The yelling of the pack changed to a furious yapping and then switched to a spasmodic barking. "He's treed!" I heard Loren yell. Then I came out of the evergreens onto the edge of a gully. At the bottom were the hounds, leaping around the foot of an oak that grew up as straight as a telephone pole, without a single branch on it for fifty feet. The bear was shinnying up the tree exactly as a man would have done. When he got below the first branch, he grabbed the limb in his jaws and hung on a moment to rest his paws.

From where I stood on the bank, he was almost on a level with me and about thirty yards away. Jim and Loren joined me. Bill was down in the bottom of the gully with his hounds.

Jim pulled a handful of bolts from his quiver and stuck them in the soft ground beside him. Then he raised the crossbow and took careful aim. The bear had swung himself up on the limb. He was swaying back and forth, preparing to jump over the pack onto the bank.

The crossbow gave its stinging twang, and the bolt stuck in the bear's throat, pinning him to the tree. The bear jerked his head, making the shaft vibrate like a tuning fork, and tore himself free, pulling the bolt from the trunk. Jim recocked the bow and fired another bolt. The bolt went completely through the bear's body at the shoulder and came out on the other side. The bear grabbed the protruding head and bit it off with a snap of his great jaws. Then, grabbing the trunk, he slid down the tree like a fireman on a pole.

"Shoot!" yelled Bill. "If he hits the ground he'll run for a week. The dogs can't hold him now!"

Halfway down the tree, the bear's grip relaxed and he fell among the hounds, dead. There was a whirling mass of hounds over the great brown body. Then the tangle cleared as the hounds stretched the dead bear, three of them pulling at the head and three others straining at the rump.

We climbed slowly down the side of the gully. The hounds were still worrying the dead bear. Red's head and shoulders were streaked with blood from the mauling the bear had given him. The scarlet blood showed up vividly against the hound's ocher and white markings. Blue limped. He was still lame from the time when the three-hundred-pound bear had rolled on him earlier in the fight. Scout had a torn ear, and Chief carried claw marks on his shoulder. The other hounds were unhurt.

Jim's first bolt, fired while the bear was still on the ground, had gone through the chest and one of the lungs. The bolts fired through the neck had nicked the bear's windpipe. The third shaft, fired into the bear's shoulder, would have passed through the animal and kept on going if the bolt's feathers hadn't caught between two of the bear's ribs. Loren found the head of this bolt in the bear's stomach. After biting off the broadhead, the bear had swallowed it.

Since then I've seen many medieval tapestries and engravings of bear hunts with hounds and crossbows. Of all the millions of people who've looked at these works of art, I suppose I'm one of the very few who know what it was really like, can recall the screaming of the hysterical hounds, the deep, coughing roar of the bear, and dull twanging note of the bow as the bolt leaps away. As the tapestries often show, even a mortally wounded bear with a bolt in him can do a considerable amount of damage before he falls. In medieval times the hunters always carried spears equipped with a crossbar just above the head so the charging bear even when impaled couldn't force his way up the spear shaft and kill the man in his dying agonies. We could have used some of those spears that morning in New Hampshire.

Today, there's an even grimmer use for the once-forgotten crossbow. In Vietnam, both the Viet Cong and our men are using them, usually with poisoned bolts. Because the bows are silent, they are the perfect sniper's weapon. Lieutenant Colonel Floyd Lien, of the 1st Logistical Command in Vietnam, has been kind enough to send me detailed descriptions of the Montagnards' bows. He says:

"There are three distinct styles of Montagnard crossbows. The Rhade tribe use a long, slender bow with a long, slender straight stock. The Mêo use a wider and thinner bow with a curved stock. The Jaré use a Mêo-type bow with a stock patterned after a gunstock. All use a similar release mechanism. No metal is used in any of them. The triggers are made of horn, hoof, or hard wood. Bowstrings are made of hemp, root, bamboo, or other fiber material. The strings made of bamboo are quite interesting; they split the bamboo at either end into many fibers, plait the fibers into a rope, and then backsplice to make an eye. Arrows are of split bamboo with barbed points. The butt of the arrow is split; a folded palm-leaf vane is inserted and the end bound with thread. Many of the war bows pull 150 pounds; short pull with only about a six-inch brace. The string is slack until the bow is cocked."

The Viet Cong also use these bows. On one occasion, our forces captured forty Viet Cong crossbows in a raid near Ankhe. The Viet Cong have even devised a huge crossbow with eight-foot bolts, on the principle of an ancient catapult, for shooting down helicopters.

I talked to a young G.I. who was so impressed by the effectiveness of the Montagnard crossbows that he's got several bows from George Stevens of Arkansas for himself and his friends serving in Vietnam. Because he was uncertain of the legal status of using poisoned weapons, he asked not to have his name used.

"We follow a Viet Cong patrol going single file at night, and keep picking off the last man. If he's hit in the heart, he drops without a cry. With poisoned bolts, even a flesh wound is fatal. The trick is to get your man silhouetted against the sky. Often it takes them some time to realize what's happening. When they do, we open up on them with shotguns loaded with buckshot."

Anyone interested in using a crossbow in this country should first check with his local game commission. Because they are silent, the bows make perfect poachers' weapons, and are outlawed in several states.

CHAPTER 6

Ferrets—Underground Warfare

According to a beloved American tradition, every boy should have a dog. Judging from English literature of the last century, a dog was considered an unnecessary luxury for youngsters, but every boy had a ferret. He used the ferret to bolt rabbits into nets, and made his pocket money selling the rabbits to butchers, as many an Englishman fondly remembers. Gamekeepers, poachers, and ratcatchers also had ferrets. Although most descriptions of rural life in England contain references to ferrets, I know of no account of their use in America. Yet ferrets were employed in this country on a scale unheard of in Europe, and were even used against such formidable quarry as raccoons, mink, muskrats, and foxes.

From the beginning of time, hunters have longed for some device to bolt quarry from holes and burrows. The ferret was the answer. There are Egyptian frescos dating from the Eighteenth Dynasty showing nobles hunting with trained ichneumons, a weasel-like animal that was apparently used to retrieve injured ducks in dense cover. Later, a smaller Asian weasel, called *Mustela eversmanni,* was domesticated and probably crossed with the European polecat to give it more size and stamina. The domestic ferret (*Mustela furo*) is the result of this cross, and averages about a foot and a half long, including a five-inch tail, and stands some three inches high. The females (called "jills") are much smaller but are better ratters, as the big males (hobs) are often too large to go down the holes. Ferrets have become so completely domesticated that they cannot fend for themselves in the wild, and a lost ferret will starve to death. The wild black-footed ferret of our western plains is a completely different animal. Domestic ferrets are quite slow, and cannot catch quarry unless they happen to bottle up some unfortunate rats or rabbit in a dead-end hole. In hunting, their work is to drive out the quarry, not to kill it.

Ferrets have played a surprisingly important role in the history of man, mainly because before the widespread use of poisons they were the only effective means to control rats. Rats are more than a nuisance; they are a definite menace, as certain species of rat fleas carry the deadly bubonic plague—the terrible Black Death of the Middle Ages that once wiped out 60 percent of the population of Europe. Even today poison is ineffectual against plague-bearing rats, as the infected fleas leave the bodies of their hosts as soon as they grow cold, and contaminate other rats. But when ferrets are used, the rats are driven out of their holes, killed, and the bodies burned immediately. For centuries, the chief ratcatcher was an important official in European courts.

Ferrets were brought to this country in 1875, and soon proved so popular that the demand greatly exceeded the supply. During the early part of this century, an ambitious young man named Levi Farnsworth started breeding ferrets in New London, Ohio. Soon he was doing a $10,000-a-year business—which in those days was quite a sum. He required 190 acres of wheat and the meat of 50 horses a month to feed his stock, as commercial raisers of ferrets feed them mainly on a special mash made of ground wheat mixed with whole milk, plus some meat. Before long, Levi had plenty of imitators. By 1914, New London was shipping an average of 200,000 ferrets a year, and became known as "Ferretville." The breeders exported ferrets to Europe, India, and South America.

Ferrets were used not only on rats and rabbits (their only quarry in Europe) but on just about every animal that has to be bolted from burrows. They had other uses too. When telephone companies started to put their lines underground, the only way they could run the wires through the long pipes was to start a rat through the pipe with a ferret after him, the ferret wearing a harness to which was attached a light string that later was used to pull the wire through the duct. When plague was reported in Montana during the early part of this century, men with ferrets and dogs were sent out to kill the infected squirrels. One man with two dogs and a ferret killed sixty-two ground squirrels in two hours.

When state after state passed laws against the use of ferrets, the great ferret-breeding establishments at New London closed. But after the last war, there was a demand for ferrets for laboratory purposes. Biologists found that ferrets are useful for developing a serum against influenza, ferrets, like humans, being highly susceptible to this disease. Levi Farnsworth's son, Dick Farnsworth, renovated the old ferret barns his father had built fifty years earlier and went into partnership with another young man named Morry Smith. I traveled to New London to talk to them. The boys showed me around.

The ferret barns were long, low buildings resembling small plane hangars. Down the center of each barn ran a narrow aisle, and on either side of it were the pens, fronted with wire and open on the top. Around the tops were wooden overhangs, projecting downward to keep the ferrets from climbing out. When we entered the barn, scores of ferrets began scrambling over the wire like squirrels, giving their curious chittering calls.

Dick Farnsworth told me: "About two-thirds of 'em are bought by laboratories. The rest are sold to private individuals for ratcatching and hunting. People drive here with license plates on their cars from states four hundred miles away."

As the boys walked down the long aisle between the pens, they occasionally reached into the enclosures and brought out a squealing, kicking ferret. The furious animals tried to bite, but the boys held them in a special grip that rendered them helpless.

"We're getting ready for the spring breeding season, and that's always a tough time," Dick said. "It's hard to tell whether the jills are being mated or murdered. A jill has to be half killed before she can be bred. Apparently the hob has to prove to her that he's tougher than she is before she'll yield to him. The hob grabs her by the neck, bites clear through to her backbone, and then shakes her until she's groggy."

Ferrets have two litters a year, with six or seven young to a litter. "We've found that the best ratters are jills after they've had their first litter," Morry Smith told me. "They seem to develop a craving for blood then. I've dropped a rat in with a bunch of young hobs, and they don't pay much attention to him. Then I've put the rat in with a jill that's just had a litter, and she'll nail him before I can get my hand out of the pen."

There are two types of ferrets: the brown with black markings, called a "fitch," and the albino variety, called the "English ferret." The English ferret was developed so that ratting terriers could more readily distinguish the ferrets from the rats. The two types interbreed freely, and the young are either pure white or fitch, never piebald.

The ferrets got very little meat. "It seems strange that such a little killer as a ferret can be raised on wheat mash and milk, but apparently the milk takes the place of blood for them," Dick explained. "We tried giving them skimmed milk, but they have to have lots of cream. Rat-catchers who have only a few ferrets raise them on wholewheat bread with milk and a little raw hamburger."

Professional ratcatchers usually break in young ferrets by keeping them in a loft full of old drainpipes so the animals will get used to running through long passageways in complete darkness, although this isn't really necessary, as ferrets will go down a hole naturally. The ferrets must also get used to the ratting terriers, and sometimes even sleep with them. When the little fellows are six months old, the trainer gives them mice to kill. Later he puts in rats whose long incisors have been broken out; otherwise the young ferrets might get so badly bitten that they'd develop a dread of the rats.

The mere presence of a ferret in a hole drives rats mad with terror. A ferret follows rats by their scent, like a miniature bloodhound, and no matter where the rats hide he will eventually "ferret them out." A ferret that is a "killer"—that is, one that deliberately tries to corner rats to kill and eat them—is not considered a good ratter. He wastes too much time and it's too hard to get him out of the hole. Killing the rats is the dogs' job.

A local farmer was having trouble with rats in his chicken house, and the boys offered to show me a rat hunt. We drove over to the farm, the boys carrying a couple of pet ferrets in their coat pockets like kittens. When we arrived, the farmer's whole family turned out for the hunt. "If we'd announced a week ago that we were going to have a rat hunt, half the township would turn up," Dick said. "Every farmer who has a good ratting dog would be here, ready to bet on him. That's one reason why ratting with ferrets is so popular; it's as much a sport as a business."

Dick and Morry inspected the chicken house. It had a flooring of heavy mesh wire, raised about six inches off the ground. The space between this mesh and the ground had become honeycombed with rat passages. The rats lived on the scratch feed put out for the chickens, occasionally taking eggs or a newborn chick.

The baseboards on the outside of the chicken house were riddled with chewed half-moon holes. In some places the farmer had laid new boards, and the rats had simply burrowed under them. The boys stopped up most of the holes to keep the rats from bolting in all directions. The farmer stationed his dog at one of the remaining openings. Morry went around to the other side of the building and fed his slim jill into the hole.

The ferret sniffed at the tainted earth for several seconds and then started to tremble with excitement. Her tail fluffed up until it looked like a bottle brush. She began to dig frantically, and a shower of earth spurted up behind her. Gradually she disappeared into the tunnel. Dick took his ferret out of his pocket and put her in one of the chewed holes at the baseboard. The ferret turned and came back. "That means there aren't any rats in that particular hole," Dick said. He tried the ferret in another place. This time, after some frenzied sniffing, the ferret poured herself in.

"Now we'll see some fun," said Dick. Inside the chicken house we could stand on joists running beneath the wire-mesh flooring and watch the hunt underneath our feet. For a few seconds, nothing happened. Morry had just started to say that perhaps the rats had moved into the corncribs for the winter when a rat dashed across the floor under our feet like a flicker of brown light. While Dick was still yelling "There goes one!" another rat exploded out of a burrow.

He ran about in aimless terror, then dived down another hole. I saw a rat appear apparently out of nowhere and run desperately back and forth along the baseboards, seeking some way to escape. Another panic-stricken animal collided with him. The two rats squeaked, bit at each other, and vanished down holes. There was a miniature explosion in the ground directly below me, and a rat came bursting straight up through the loose earth. Then rats seemed to come boiling up through the ground in all directions. There were darting brown forms every place you looked. If it hadn't been for the wire flooring, we could have conducted a massacre with a couple of dogs.

I saw the first of the ferrets come up through a hole in the ground. She was moving slowly, stopping to sniff around, and obviously nervous in a strange place. A rat darted by her, actually touching her nose. The ferret hesitated, snuffed the ground where the rat had passed, and then started to follow him. She found another hole, and promptly vanished again. Instantly a rat tore out of the far end of the burrow. In his hurry, he bumped into the chicken-house wall, nearly knocking himself out. He rushed around crazily, nearly colliding with the first ferret. Almost quicker than the eye could follow, the ferret grabbed him by the throat. The rat squealed, kicking wildly. The ferret continued to hold the rat until his struggles became weaker, and finally stopped. Then she released her grip, sniffed at the body, and went on with her hunting. She made no attempt to eat her kill.

The chickens, lined up on their perches over our heads, clucked anxiously like old ladies at a prizefight. As ferrets cannot climb board walls, the hens were perfectly safe. Dick told me that ferrets used on rats become "wedded" to their prey, and won't bother adult poultry. But they will kill baby chicks, afterward dragging the bodies of their victims into a heap. They will also sometimes collect the corpses of rats and mice. Ferreters call this "piling up." Occasionally a ferret will bring a rat up out of a hole after he has killed it, almost like a dog retrieving. However, this is unusual.

I noticed that after a few minutes, the rats got over their first wild hysteria and began to keep out of the ferrets' way. Ferrets are very nearsighted, and hunt mainly by scent. As the rats know their own underground system of passages, and are much faster than ferrets, they can stay away from one or two ferrets indefinitely. The trick is to take advantage of the rats' original terror and stampede them out to the dogs as quickly as possible. The ferreter must use a number of ferrets working together so the rats find them wherever they turn. It is very important for the dogs not to scratch or bark at the holes, for if they do, then the rats know what's waiting for them, and double back, scattering to avoid the ferrets.

A good dog doesn't stop to worry the rats—he kills each one with a single bite, usually tossing the dead rat up into the air as he runs back and forth among the fleeing vermin. Often a fast dog will have a couple of rats in the air at the same time. Usually there are men with clubs to help the dogs, but the terriers do most of the actual killing. Rats turn so quickly a man has trouble hitting them.

Herded across the floor by the ferrets, the rats finally collected in one corner of the chicken house. There was a dead-end burrow there, and into this cul-de-sac the rats poured. Either by accident or design, the dozens of struggling rats kicked down earth around the entrance of the burrow and gradually blocked it up. As Morry said, "They crawled into that hole and then pulled it in after them."

The falling earth apparently cut off the scent, for the ferrets ran desperately back and forth over the closed entrance. Dick finally had to rip up the wire flooring and dig the rats out with a spade. For months the farmer's dog had been waiting for a chance to get at those rats. This was his big opportunity. There were a few seconds of leaping brown shapes, shrill squealing, and the frantic dog knocking us aside to get at the rats. Then the massacre was over, and the floor was polka-dotted with dead vermin.

I asked how you got a ferret out of a rathole if he decided to stay in. The boys said that a ferret nearly always follows a rat out of the hole unless he finds a litter of young. Then he usually gorges himself, afterward lying down to sleep off his orgy. However, he usually comes out the next morning looking for food.

Keeping "killer" ferrets from catching and killing rats instead of driving them out to the dogs has long been a problem with handlers. "Killers" are often the most experienced ferrets, but this vice makes them more trouble than they're worth. Some ferreters put a muzzle, called a "cope," on "killers," but if the ferret runs into a really tough old rat, he may be killed, as he has no way of defending himself. Other ferreters put a harness on their ferrets and keep a long line attached to them. The great trouble with this device is that the line usually gets entangled in the burrows, and the floorboards have to be ripped up to get the ferret free.

Using ferrets on wild game is illegal in most states, but as Dick Farnsworth remarked, "It's mighty funny how right before the hunting season we get a big rush of orders from all over the country."

Rabbits make the best quarry. Like rats, rabbits go stark mad with terror when they know a ferret is starting down a burrow toward them. The boys introduced me to an old-time farmer in New London who had ferreted rabbits for years. He described a typical rabbit hunt:

"We'd start out early in the morning right after a big snow. Sometimes we'd carry the ferret in a little hay-filled box with a handle—like the carrying cases they make for cats—but most times I'd just stick him in my pocket. If we had a rabbit hound, he'd jump the rabbit and run him down a hole. Then we'd leash up the dog and I'd get out my ferret. He'd sniff a little at the hole, then start down.

"Man, oh, man, you never saw a scared rabbit until you see one with a ferret after him! If the ground was frozen hard, you could hear that old rabbit pounding up so fast it sounded like a horse galloping. When he came out of the hole he was flying. He'd jump eight feet without touching the ground. Every time we took out a new man, I'd bet him a dollar he wouldn't hit the first rabbit. The guy would get all set, but when the

Bill Green's hounds
hold the mountain
lion at bay on the
cliff face

The mountain lion
treed — two arrows
have found their
target

The mountain lion shot by Edwin Drexel with bow and arrow

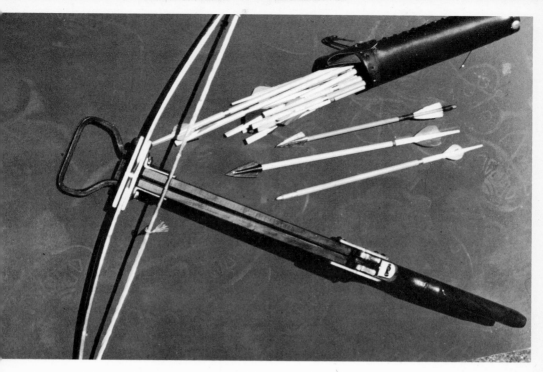

ABOVE: The crossbow used on the bear hunt in New Hampshire. BELOW: Shown uncocked (above) and cocked (below), this crossbow, made by Earl Powell, is mounted on a rifle stock and can be cocked without lever or winch by placing a foot in the stirrup

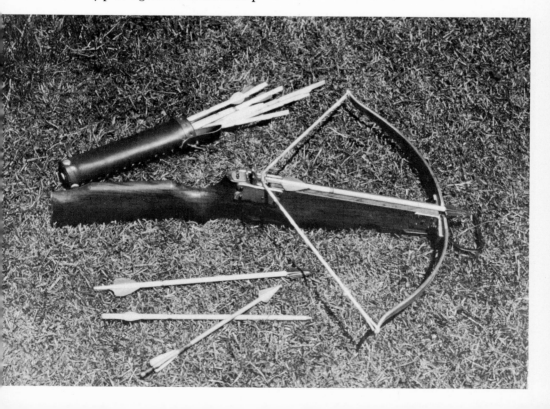

Dan Mannix's pair
of ferrets, Snoopy,
the white hob,
and Lady

Snoopy catches a
barn rat

rabbit came busting out of there it'd go so fast he'd never lead it enough. Once I saw a rabbit hit a man in the stomach and knock all the wind out of him. The rabbit kept right on going."

On muggy days, rabbits for some reason are more reluctant to bolt. Occasionally a rabbit would come out with the ferret hanging to him. As with rats, a jill is generally used because a hob can frequently seize the rabbit as it rushes past him, and kill it. Then the ferret will lie up to eat his kill. After the hunters get tired of pounding on the ground and trying to dig the ferret out, there's nothing to do but leave the ferret's carrying box beside the hole, preferably with a freshly drawn rabbit inside, and hope the ferret will eventually come out and curl up in his familiar nest. Hobs used on rabbits often are coped or carry harnesses.

Game commissions often use ferrets to catch rabbits alive for restocking. A bag or net is held at the mouth of the hole; nets are better, as a bag darkens the entrance and sometimes makes the rabbit turn back. Purse-type nets operating on the drawstring principle were once made for this purpose, and could be bought in any general store.

At first, ferrets in this country were used only for ratting and rabbiting, as in Europe, but soon Yankee hunters began training the big hob ferrets to attack and drive out almost any animal. For this work, you need an exceptionally powerful and aggressive hob. The hobs grow to be three times as big as the jills. For a ferret to make a straight-on attack on a coon or a fox would naturally be suicide. He makes darting attacks, chittering his war cry, and nipping. Eventually the quarry will get tired of the persistent attacks, much as a bear will run from a barking dog. If a man or his dog stays so close to the mouth of the burrow that the quarry is afraid to bolt, or if once the quarry is flushed, they allow it to duck back into the hole, the animal will almost certainly kill the ferret rather than come out a second time.

Old Billy, a famous ferret who chased out eighteen mink for a trapper in one season, performed the amazing feat of bolting a full-grown coon. The coon was in a hollow limb, and Billy's master put the hob in after him. The men could hear the coon hissing and Billy chittering. Suddenly the coon ran out on a limb. As soon as he saw the men, he tried to go back, but a shot knocked him down to the dogs. As the coon must have weighed at least thirty pounds, and Billy about two, this was quite a stunt.

Ferrets have been used on skunks, mostly just to show if the skunk is in the hole. If the hunter puts his ear to the ground, he can hear the skunk patting with his forefeet, a skunk's warning signal before he discharges his musk. Usually the ferret backs out hastily, especially if he has been sprayed once before. Then the man starts digging. But sometimes a ferret will fight and drive a skunk out.

Woodchucks generally refuse to bolt, and often kill the ferret. Foxes are surprisingly easy to bolt, as a fox in a burrow will rush out if anything touches him unexpectedly in the dark. Of course, this doesn't apply to a fox who knows that men and dogs are awaiting him above ground. Opossums usually play dead.

"In the old days, small game was plentiful and there weren't any game laws," a New London farmer told me. "We used to go out with our ferrets all the time. I had one old male named Dick, the best ferret I ever saw. He was tame, smart as a dog, and would tackle anything.

"Dick could follow your trail like a dog. When he was a yearling, he was great on rabbits. Then he got so smart that he started killing them before they could get out. I'd never put a cope on him 'cause you never knew what he might meet down a hole. I remember that once he killed a rabbit, and laid up. I left him in the hole and went on home. The next morning, Dick was back in his pen. He'd followed me back to the farm by my trail.

"They say ferrets are cruel animals. I guess they are. But when Dick was killed in a fight with a mink, I felt as bad as if a dog had been killed. Taking Dick for a day's hunting in the woods and then coming home in the evening and seeing that smart little white head poking out of my pocket—well, I couldn't ask for any better sport than that was."

Neither Farnsworth nor Smith are in the ferret business anymore; and years later, when I wanted to get some ferrets to clean out the rats in our barn, I had to go to another dealer. I don't like poisons; in spite of the claims made for them I've lost livestock through using poison, and several friends have lost valuable dogs. I got my pair from a state where keeping them is legal, and installed them in a large, roomy cage in the living room.

My ferrets weren't vicious, but making pets of them was like trying to domesticate a current of electricity. Both were convinced that no hole was so small that they couldn't go down it (they were usually right) and that there was something interesting hidden in every part of the room. I have never seen such curious creatures in all my life.

The first time I let the hob out he was convinced I had a couple of mice hidden in my shoe. He stuck his nose between my ankle and the vamp, gave a loud sniff, and then started burrowing in. I had to take the shoe off, and he promptly dived in. Meanwhile the jill had humped herself into the kitchen, at the strange inchworm gait all weasels have that doesn't look fast but covers an amazing lot of ground, and climbed on top of the stove to supervise Jule's cooking. Preparing a stew while a ferret is trying to snatch pieces out of the saucepan is not one of Jule's specialties, and the ferrets finally had to be locked up.

They did bite occasionally, but never maliciously. I doubt if they could see more than three feet, so they depended almost entirely on their noses. We soon discovered that in spite of everything I'd heard, milk was bad for them; it gave them violent diarrhea. I've had the same experience with all weasels, including Ottie, my otter, and pet skunks. Every expert on keeping weasels recommends warm milk as the major part of their diet, and in every case I've tried it the milk scours the animals badly. There was no doubt they loved it. Put a saucer of warm milk in the room, and both ferrets went mad. Questing about like hounds on a hot scent, they would often run over the saucer, sending the milk in all directions, and keep right on going. If you tried to pick them up at such times to show them the saucer, they'd turn on you. Once the milk was gone, they were friendly again.

I finally compromised by giving them pablum with a little warm milk, egg, and hamburger. I've also been told that giving weasels meat makes them mangy. This hasn't been my experience. They weren't especially fond of meat, but it never caused mange.

I named the hob Snoopy because of his desire to stick his nose into everything. You could usually tell where Snoopy had been from what was sticking to the end of his nose: jam, milk and, when we let him outside, bits of eggshell and occasionally feathers. He found eggs in the barn, and the feathers came from starlings who liked to mob him and would occasionally fly too low. Whenever he found anything new, he'd make a quick check to see if it was good to eat. If it wasn't he dropped it immediately and never bothered with it again.

The little jill was much gentler, and liked to climb on your shoulder and snuggle under your chin. This always made me a bit nervous, as she usually made a quick check of your ears, lips, and nose before settling down to make sure you hadn't anything edible on them. However, as she never bit once she had got used to us, we became used to this investigation. We named her Lady. Both were scrupulously clean, and spent hours working their fur like cats. As Lady was brown, dirt didn't show on her, but after Snoopy had come out from investigating the barn he was almost black, and required a complete dry cleaning. Sometimes Jule would help him with a damp cloth.

Both were playful, especially Lady. When we let them out of their cage, she would bounce around like an animated rubber ball, sometimes turning a complete somersault. Most of the time they slept so deeply that you could pick them up and turn them upside down and then put them back in the cage without waking them. When they did awake, they moved so fast it was almost impossible to keep track of them. Lady would dive under our living-room couch, and while her tail was still disappearing her head would pop out at the far end.

By the end of a month, my ferrets were so tame that they'd come when called, and even Snoopy had stopped biting. With the help of our terriers, I cleaned out the barn of rats—the rats that weren't killed vacating the premises. Then I decided to use them to get rid of a muskrat colony undermining the banks of our pond. Because muskrats naturally take to water as soon as they are bolted, I decided to use a .410 shotgun rather than the dogs.

There was no trouble finding muskrat holes around our pond; the whole bank looked like a Swiss cheese. Remembering that ferrets like to work down, I went to the top of the bank, walking lightly so as not to alarm the muskrats. Then I tried putting my hunters down the holes.

Indoors, the ferrets had always been only too eager to go down anything that looked like a hole, but here they didn't get the idea at all. As far as they were concerned, I'd taken them out for a game of tag. Lady kept trying to play with me, jumping sideways and making mimic attacks on my fingers. Snoopy ran around investigating every clump of grass, every stone, and every root—in fact, everything except the holes.

Luckily, I'd taken some hamburger with me, and I threw a little down a hole. Lady promptly dived after it, and Snoopy, seeing she was after something, rushed over and tried to pull her out by the tail. Lady chittered furiously but wouldn't come out until she'd eaten the hamburger. I tried them on some more holes, but as they always came out again after eating the hamburger, I'd about decided I was on the wrong track when Lady suddenly went into action.

She'd gone down the wrong hole looking for hamburger and started to back out when I saw her freeze. She remained motionless for a few seconds, and I could hear her sniffing loudly. Then she began to dig frantically. Slowly she disappeared.

Snoopy hurried over, but he was far too big to fit down the hole. He ran to one nearby and poured himself in. He vanished, all but his plumed tail, which began to lash furiously. Then, with an eager wiggle, he went underground.

I picked up the gun, went to the water, and waited. For a while nothing happened, and then a curious moaning came from the bank. I don't know if it was the ferrets or the muskrats; it didn't sound like either of them. I began to be afraid the ferrets were being killed.

Then a muskrat darted out of one of the holes just at water level. While he was running along the bank I knocked him over with the .410. Almost at the same time another muskrat appeared, and I was about to fire again when I saw Lady hanging to him. The muskrat dived into the pond, and as he disappeared I saw him lock his teeth in Lady's head. When they came up again a few feet away, Lady had let go and was gasping for breath, but the muskrat made a determined attempt to drown her. I waded in and after a few wild grabs got hold of her. She was bleeding badly and almost unconscious. I put her down on the bank and rubbed her with my shirt. She came around after a few minutes and started to clean her fur like a cat.

Another muskrat ran out, apparently in a hysterical frenzy, for instead of taking to the water he ran around in circles until I shot him. Two more bolted, and then I heard a sound as though a junior earthquake were getting ready to be born: hissing, snarling, and a chattering noise like a squirrel scolding.

I sprinted back to the barn, got a spade, and started digging. I had to be careful not to dig too fast, as I might drive the spade through the ferret. When I broke into the burrow, I found what had happened. Snoopy had a big muskrat trapped at the dead end of a burrow that had been hollowed out as a nesting place. They were fighting.

When I broke in, the animals separated. I dropped the spade and reached for the gun, but to my surprise the muskrat, instead of running, went for Snoopy again. He reared up on his hind legs, apparently to get Snoopy by the back of the neck, but Snoopy sidled up to him with the same sidelong gait both ferrets used when playing with me. Suddenly he flipped over on his back and grabbed the muskrat by the throat. He threw the muskrat down, but in doing so lost his hold. Snoopy was panting so heavily he kept his mouth open and didn't try for another grip, holding the muskrat down with his forefeet. The muskrat was equally exhausted and lay there gasping for breath.

They stayed there so long I put down the shotgun and reached for the spade to finish the muskrat off. As I raised it, the muskrat made a desperate effort to escape. He grabbed Snoopy by the shoulder and regained his feet. He'd put up such a fight I was willing to let him go, but Snoopy felt differently. He fell on his side, locking his teeth in the muskrat's neck and shaking him as a terrier would shake a rat. In a few seconds the muskrat kicked convulsively, stiffened, and died.

After a few days' rest, I tried Snoopy again. This time he went down the burrows at once, but no more muskrats came out. Checking the muddy bank, I couldn't find any fresh tracks. I think the whole colony probably moved out the night after my first hunt.

I never used the ferrets on muskrats again for fear they might be hurt. I did, however, use them on rats. A colored family who'd had a lot of trouble with rats asked me if I'd bring Snoopy and Lady over to do some exterminating, which I was only too glad to do. Unfortunately, the children must have talked. A few days later five game wardens arrived at six o'clock one morning with a warrant to seize my pets and fine me $50 for illegally possessing ferrets. Sportsmen have had a law passed against the use of ferrets, feeling that the little animals compete with them as predators. I could not save my pets.

The house has been a sadder place since their passing. They no longer jump out of their box to play with me and our Cairn terriers in the morning. The rats have returned to the barn, and in spite of the services of an expensive exterminator they continue to thrive. I am sorry that such brave, friendly little animals had to be sacrificed to preserve the majesty of the law.

CHAPTER 7

The Boomerang—
the Stick That Kills

A real hunting boomerang is a dangerous weapon and should be treated with respect. A boomerang can't, as has been reported, cut off a man's head; but listen to the account of an expedition to Alice Springs, Australia, that was attacked by aborigines armed with boomerangs: "Several horses were knocked down and some of our party received wounds over an inch and a half deep."

First of all, let's get one misconception straightened out. There are two kinds of boomerangs: a "war," or "hunting," boomerang that flies straight and does not return, and a "return" boomerang, which, as far as I can discover, is basically a toy, although under some highly special circumstances it may have a utilitarian use.

Most people say: "But I thought the whole purpose of a boomerang was to have it returned to the thrower if he missed, thus saving him the trouble of having to go after it. If a boomerang doesn't do that, what good is it?" This requires some explanation.

Suppose you see an animal you want to kill and you're still in such a primitive state of culture that you haven't invented the bow and arrow. So you throw a stone at the quarry. Even if you're Robin Roberts you can't throw the stone more than two hundred feet, and even then the stone has lost so much power it won't hurt the quarry. Also, you have to score a direct hit. A curved throwing stick, or boomerang, is far more effective.

A hunting boomerang is about a yard long and usually only slightly curved. One side of the boom is flat. The other side is carved to form an airfoil. In other words, the boom closely resembles the wing of a plane, except for the fact that the boom is curved. The boom speeds toward the target spinning sideways, and can go a surprising distance. It is said an Australian expert can throw a boom with deadly effect at seven hundred feet. I can't, but I can throw one 540 feet with force enough to crack an inch-thick tree limb.

A boomerang, then, only can not fly farther than any other hand-projected missile; it will also hit harder. Furthermore, you have a greater chance of hitting your target. A three-foot boomerang spinning sideways cuts a three-foot swath, so if you throw within a yard of your target it will still make some sort of contact. With a stone you haven't any margin of error at all.

A boomerang is especially effective when thrown into a flock of birds. It whirls through the flock like a buzzsaw and often knocks down two or three birds, so in this respect it's more effective than a shotgun. The main trouble is that if the birds are in full flight they can see it coming, and avoid it. Try using it on a flock of ducks just as they are rising from the water and unable to maneuver effectively because they're trying to gain altitude.

The boomerang—or "throwing stick," as many experts prefer to call it, since to most people a boomerang *has* to return—is by no means peculiar to Australia, although the Australian aborigines have carried it to a higher state of perfection than anyone else, mainly because they were never able to devise a more effective long-distance weapon. The Egyptians used throwing sticks for waterfowl in the Eighteenth Dynasty, and a wall painting on the prince's tomb at Beni-Hasan shows a group of desert Semites armed with S-shaped booms. An S-shaped boom operates on the same principle as the ordinary single curved boom. It's simply two C-shaped booms with the lower one reversed and fastened to the bottom of the other.

Throwing sticks are still used by some of the tribes in the Sudan, generally with one tip broad and flat like a paddle, apparently to increase its hitting power. In India, booms are made of ivory or steel with a knob on one tip to give the thrower a better grip. The steel booms are sharpened along the outside edge, and were used by the Maravar warrior caste in battle. The most curious are the "beaked" war boomerangs used by certain South Pacific tribes. These boomerangs are heavy, almost straight clubs with a short "beak" a couple of inches long projecting from one end. When a native throws a boomerang at an enemy, the man usually tries to ward it off by holding up his spear. A beaked boomerang hits the shaft, slides along it until the beak catches, and then spins around the spear, finally hitting the man holding it.

Throwing sticks have been used since time immemorial by the Hopi Indians of Arizona, and they still use the curved sticks for hunting jack rabbits. A few summers ago, I had a chance to go jack hunting with a group of Hopis from the Second Mesa, about seventy miles northeast of Flagstaff.

The Hopis use boomerangs because the sticks are cheaper to obtain than cartridges, and can be used over and over. Virtually the whole population of the mesa turned out for the event—the young men who were doing the actual hunting rode ahead on their ponies, and the women and children followed behind on donkeys to carry the kill and pick up the boomerangs, which were all nonreturning.

Suddenly there was a wild yell. A jack rabbit had bolted out from under a clump of sage and was streaking across the desert, a flicker of gray and white. Instantly half a dozen riders were after him, leaning forward on their horses' necks, spurring for all they were worth. One man straightened up, his hand shot back over his shoulder, and his boom flashed away, skimming low over the ground. Fast as the rabbit was, the boom was even faster. I saw it catch up to the rabbit, but he saw it too, and dodged. The boom hit the ground a foot in front of him, sending up a spray of sand. But the boom turned the jack, and he darted back toward the line of riders. Two more booms shot toward him, whirling like pinwheels as they went. One was too high. The rabbit dodged the other. The high boom spun off at an angle, and one of the riders had to pull his horse back on his haunches to avoid being hit. Then a boom hit the jack. He lay kicking in the sand with a broken back. One of the little boys slid off his donkey and, rushing in, grabbed the still-struggling animal by the hind legs and dispatched him with a single efficient blow behind the ears. Already another jack had been sighted and the riders were off again, leaving the boys and women to collect the fallen booms.

Two old Indians who had followed the hunt on foot were talking together contemptuously of the younger men's technique. Through an interpreter, I asked them how it should be done.

"In the old days, we used to hunt on foot," one of the old-timers explained. "That required real skill. These youngsters just ride up on the rabbit and they're so close that they can't miss. But if you're on foot you have to know what you're doing. The best throwing stick I ever owned used to shoot straight forward and then suddenly turn sharp right. You aimed behind the rabbit, and it would turn and overtake him."

"My best one used to go straight and then turn and go down," the other said. "You had to aim over the rabbit."

Talking to these old men, I realized that neither of them had the slightest idea of the principles on which a boomerang operated. In some prehistoric era an Indian had discovered that a curved stick flew better than an ordinary one, and the Hopis had been using curved sticks ever since. But they had never made any attempt to find out why one curved stick flies better than others.

These two old men had probably owned hundreds of throwing sticks. They had prized two of the sticks—not because they flew well but because the sticks happened to be of such design that they always flew in the same way. One of the men explained: "When you carve out a throwing stick, you never know how it will behave. Most sticks fly every which-way and never go the same way twice. But once you get a stick that will always fly consistently, you know what to expect. It's like a gun that always throws a certain amount to the left or right; you can allow for it when aiming."

Although the Hopis were short on theory, I learned a lot about practical boomerang techniques from them. The sticks they used were much heavier than the commercial comeback type, and closely resembled the Australian booms but weren't as well made. The Hopis had no interest in trying to make the booms rise in the air because they used them only for rabbits. They wanted a boom that would skim hard and fast and stick close to the ground, so the stick had almost no airfoil. I also noticed that every man used several booms. Often he would deliberately throw ahead of the rabbit to make the animal turn, then throw to one side or the other to bewilder the jack before trying for a knockout blow. Occasionally a rabbit would become so confused that he'd start running in a small circle, and a man could rush in and grab the animal with his hands.

When I returned home, I decided to make some booms of my own. Making a boom turned out to be a far more complicated job than I had realized. The boom must be perfectly balanced so that you know what it will do, and having only one boom is almost useless. In duckhunting, especially, you have to throw a series of booms—one after the other—into the flock so that while the birds are dodging one, they run into another.

This means all the booms must be exactly alike in shape and weight, for you can't alter your throwing style for each boom, especially when you're throwing them as fast as possible.

A hunting boom should be made of the heaviest and toughest wood available—hickory or oak being probably the best. Simply outlining the shape of the boom on a plank and then cutting it out is useless; the boom will break the first time it hits against the grain. A round of the proper wood has to be bent so the grain follows the bend. I was able to get this done by a maker of barrel staves in the Pennsylvania Dutch country. He has the apparatus for steaming wood to make it pliable. How else you could do it I have no idea. The aborigines simply keep looking until they find a crooked branch bent in the right shape. This can take months; but those boys have nothing but time.

I have read it is possible to join two curved pieces of wood with a half-lap and then glue them together. I could never make this work. No glue I used would hold, and even bolting the pieces together wasn't successful. A boom hits with astonishing force, and the bolts wouldn't hold. However, you may have better luck.

Most hunting booms, whether Australian or Hopi, are almost straight. I could never make these fly correctly; it was like trying to throw a club. Mine had an angle of about ninety degrees and a definite airfoil, so they were much easier to throw.

I found the best-sized boom for me was 24 inches from wingtip to wingtip, with the top of the curve 14 inches high. The widest part of the boom (at the apex of the curve) should be about $2\frac{1}{2}$ inches across, and the arms gradually taper down to about $1\frac{1}{2}$ inches. The length of an arm should be about six times the width of the boom at the center. The airfoil has to be whittled out with a knife and then worked down with sandpaper. It rises fairly abruptly from the outer edge of the boom to a ridge running the length of the boom (and naturally following its curve). The top of this ridge, the thickest part of the boom, should not be more than a $\frac{1}{2}$ inch. The airfoil then tapers more gradually down to the inside curve. There is no airfoil on the reverse side of the boom; it is perfectly flat.

Booms vary greatly in design, depending on how far and in what manner you want them to fly. All the commercially made booms I have seen are very different in size, weight, and degree of angle. If you're interested in boomerangs, I'd suggest you buy some of the factory-made ones and experiment with them before trying to make your own.

To throw the boom, stand with the wingtip resting in the palm of your right hand with the flat side away from you and the apex of the curve back over your shoulder. Bring your arm straight back and throw directly at the target. At the instant of release, give a snap with your wrist to start the boom spinning. This snap has been compared to the motion made when snapping a whip and the wrist snap made when skipping a stone over water. I should add that Bud Carlell, who is a professional boomerang thrower, never uses any snap. His advice is, "Just throw the thing away as though you never wanted to see it again." But most people do use the snap.

When the boom leaves the hand, it should be spinning so fast it looks like a discus or a miniature flying saucer except that it is moving vertical to the ground rather than flat. As the boom continues forward, it gradually loses its momentum and turns over on its side. Without the airfoil, the boom would now drop; but because of the airfoil, the boom is supported in the air and glides along on the principle of a spinning gyroscope. This whirling motion adds enormously to its velocity and causes it to go such amazing distances that the boom seems to be flying of its own volition. The boom actually gives the impression of being alive, and I have never seen anyone who wasn't astonished at the illusion of free flight as the boom soars away toward its target.

My booms were much heavier than the plywood commercial booms, and harder to throw, but they built up much more force. The first time I threw one it hooked to the right and hit the side of our barn. It knocked a chip out of the solid stone. My son and some of his friends got interested and started throwing with me, for boomerangs attract kids as a velvet collar attracts dandruff. We soon made two important discoveries:

1. Never throw in the direction of the sun. Occasionally with a bad throw the boom will shoot upward at an angle of 45 degrees, hesitate, and then come sliding back at you as though down an inclined plane, gathering momentum every second. If it's coming at you out of the sun's eye you can't see to dodge it, and being hit in the face with a hunting boomerang is no joke.

2. Never throw a boom while someone is out in the field looking for one he's just thrown. Until you get reasonably expert with them, you can never tell what a boom will do. You throw one in a direction entirely away from your friend, who's wandering around with his head down, and suddenly the boom turns in midair and heads for him. You shout, "Look out!" and he straightens up with no idea in what direction to look. Al-

ways remember that these things are not toys, but weapons designed to kill or cripple.

I tried duplicating an East Indian boom by studding the outer edge of one of mine with razor blades. This might have been effective against human beings, but I found it did not add to the boom's usefulness in hunting. The boom's power lies in its crushing force—it's like hitting the quarry with a club. If you can hit a flying bird with enough force to stun it, you don't need to worry about slashing it at the same time. However, wrapping some No. 14 copper wire around the tips of a boom did give it more striking power.

After practicing for a few weeks, I decided to go duck hunting. My biggest problem was to find a place where I could try out my booms undisturbed by gunners. I figured that hitting a flying duck with a boom would be enough of a job without having to dodge shotgun shells at the same time. Fortunately, I knew an experienced old duck hunter named Harry who, in the summer, ran a camp on the shores of a lake in the northeastern part of the United States. In winter there were always plenty of mallards, red-legged blacks, and teal either rafted up on the lake or feeding in the logins near the far end. Harry owned the property and didn't allow shooting there except for himself and a few friends. I decided this was the place.

I wrote Harry, explaining what I wanted to do, and a few days later I got a note from him saying to come ahead, although I could tell from the tone of the letter that he thought I was crazy. I put my collection of boomerangs in the back of my car and drove up. Harry's camp is twenty-five miles from the nearest paved road, and he and his family had moved into the kitchen of the lodge and seemed holed up for the winter. Harry looked the flying sticks over and listened while I explained that this was just an experiment to see how effective the most primitive of all weapons could be.

"I can think of a hell of a lot better ways of getting a duck than hitting it over the head with a club," was Harry's verdict. "But with those things, you want to be as close to the ducks as you can get. Suppose you and me go out real early tomorrow morning in a canoe. Maybe we can skull some up. Do like I tell you, and I'll put you within twenty-five feet of 'em."

Harry shook me awake at four the next morning. It was bitter cold, but after a couple of cups of scalding coffee I was semiconscious. With flashlights, we went out to the canoe rack in the boathouse and hoisted out one of the canoes. We carried it down to the wharf and slid it into the black water.

There was a full moon. The firs showed black and pointed along the rocky shoreline as we glided across the lake. Luckily for me the wind had died down—even the faintest breath of air affects the flight of a boomerang. A low mist hung over the water, splitting into smokelike wreaths as the bow of the canoe cut through it. It was a long paddle across the lake, and before we reached the far side the moon and stars had begun to wash out in the faint light of the dawn. The sky turned green-blue, and then the east was shot with pink. "You're in luck," said Harry, speaking for the first time. "Regular bluebird weather."

As the red sun rose, the mist still was hanging low over the water and I could hardly see ten feet ahead. Harry skirted a rocky promontory and turned the canoe toward the mouth of a stream that fed into a lake at the far end.

Then I saw my first ducks—a flight of four blacks. They were flying in high above the mist toward the stream. I saw them set their wings and drop their feet for a landing, and then they vanished into the mist. A moment later I heard their splash as they hit the water. They must have awakened a red squirrel, for I heard him scolding, and a grouse went up with an explosion that sounded as loud as a shotgun blast. Harry leaned forward and spoke in a low voice:

"Now, this stream's got enough bends to break a snake's back. We'll go up it real slow. Every time we go around a bend, you get ready with your sticks, 'cause maybe there'll be some ducks. When you see 'em, keep your eyes just about closed. If they see the gleam of your eyeballs, they'll fly. Don't go knocking those sticks against the side of the canoe, neither. And don't talk. I'll try to take you up as close as I can, but when you see 'em jump, you throw. Throw about six feet above 'em as they leave the water. But don't make no quick movement until you're ready to throw."

I nodded, and Harry sent the canoe up the stream, which was about twenty feet wide, the banks covered with shadbush and maple. The mist was thinning now, lying in long wisps from bank to bank. Without lifting the paddle from the water, Harry forced the canoe ahead by turning the handle with a continual corkscrew motion. It was absolutely noiseless, and there was no flash of white water.

Then through the thinning mist I could see some dark forms on the still-darker water. For a moment I couldn't be sure that they were ducks, and I had to blink my eyes. As I did so, the group began to move away. Harry followed them, the ducks swimming rapidly about five hundred feet ahead of the canoe. I gripped the boom, and waited.

The ducks—they were mallards—stopped and began milling about, obviously uncertain whether or not to fly. Harry gave a thrust with his paddle that drove the canoe toward them . . . forty feet . . . thirty-five . . . twenty-five. Then an old drake gave a sudden alarm and leaped into the air, and the rest followed. As they flapped up, I threw the boom.

It skimmed over the water, turned over on its side, and then suddenly rose to meet the flock. I hadn't led the drake quite enough, and the boom passed under him. It was headed straight for another duck, but at the last instant she saw it coming. She made a frantic wing-over, and I could hear the sound of the boom hitting her outstretched primary feathers. I quickly threw a second boom—a heavy Australian one. It went wild—shot over the stream and hit the bank fifty feet away.

I knew what had gone wrong with the second boom. Each of the two booms required a completely different type of throw, and in the excitement I'd forgotten to change my style. When you're throwing hard and fast at a flock of ducks, you don't have time to alter your manner of throwing to fit each boom. I remembered reading that the aborigines regard a perfectly matched pair of booms as a priceless possession, an heirloom to be handed on from father to son. Now I could see why. The Hopis use half a dozen different booms, but they trust to luck and numbers rather than to skill and accuracy in throwing.

"Well, you hit one. That's better than I expected," remarked Harry. He sculled me over so I could retrieve the booms, and we went on. This time I selected two of the booms I had made myself, which flew pretty much the same way.

For a long time we didn't see any more ducks, and finally Harry headed for the logins—the flooded area studded with shadbush and a few small trees. Although we'd occasionally come to a comparatively clear place, I was getting discouraged, for I was sure that even if we did find ducks I wouldn't stand the slightest chance of getting them. The smallest twig will deflect a boomerang.

Harry gave a low grunt. I saw a little bunch of mallards—perhaps the same bunch we'd seen before—swimming among the bushes. Harry turned the canoe toward them. The mallards kept the bushes between them and us, making no attempt to fly. They seemed to figure that they could outdodge us.

Several times we were so close I was tempted to use my heavy Australian boom and knock them over on the water, but I wanted to try a wingshot. Suddenly the ducks decided that they'd had enough of the game. While they were deep in the shadbush, the whole bunch leaped into the air. We could see them go up, but the bush was so thick I don't believe you could have got one with a shotgun.

I threw the boom straight up, flat side to me, airfoil side out, knowing that it would shoot up and then turn sharp right. As the ducks cleared the bushes, they hesitated a moment. In that moment, the boom came whirling in among them. I heard the slap of the wood striking against wing feathers. Then I heard a thud. A duck came slanting down, so mixed up with the boomerang it was hard to tell which was which. I jumped out of the canoe up to my armpits and waded in. The duck had taken a crippling blow, one wing was broken and the breastbone smashed. I don't think a soft-nosed bullet could have done much more damage.

I was now convinced of two things. First, it is almost impossible to hit an individual duck with a boom—all you can do is throw into a flock and trust to luck. Second, you have to time your throw so the boom passes through the bunch at the moment when the birds are practically stationary—either when they have just finished their jump from the water or when they are about to land and are backing with their wings.

Although ducks will avoid a boom if they see it coming, it doesn't frighten them even when it passes within a few inches of them. Apparently they don't recognize it as a lethal weapon or possibly they think it's some sort of screwy bird.

I spent three days with Harry and made about thirty throws with my booms. I got three ducks—not a very good average—but I was always trying for wingshots. On several occasions if I had thrown my heavy Australian boom right into the center of a flock, I would have probably knocked down several, but this was a little too much like pot hunting. The Australian boom flew close to the ground and had a short range. My booms would go up some fifty feet in the air and had a killing range of about thirty yards.

As far as I know, the return boomerang cannot be used for hunting. Trying to hit a moving object with a straight-flying hunting boomerang is tough enough without using a boom that flies in the form of a great circle. Also, a return boomerang has to be light enough to "soar" easily, and a light boom will not give a knock-down blow. The return boomerang is therefore only suitable for exhibition work. There may be a few exceptions to this rule. Edgar Waite of the South Australian Museum once saw natives using return boomerangs during a duck hunt, but not to hit the ducks. A returning boomerang seems to hover in the air, and the effect is very like that of a soaring hawk. As long as these strange objects were kept whirling over their heads, the ducks were afraid to fly and allowed the men to herd them under nets hidden among some thick reeds.

For exhibition purposes or for boomerang contests, the return boomerang is king. Boomerang clubs are quite popular in Australia, and there was even an attempt made to have boomerang throwing introduced into the 1956 Olympics as a recognized sport. The contestants can compete for accuracy (usually by standing in a four-foot circle, and the thrown boom must return and land within the circle), longest-flying boom, distance, throwing two booms at once, and stunts. Some of the stunts a really expert thrower can perform are incredible. It is possible to throw a boom so it will hit the ground, bounce up, and still return. A boom can be made to return, stop, go to the left, then to the right, and then drop at the thrower's feet. Booms can also be made to hover overhead, then drop until they almost touch the ground, finally returning to the thrower. An Australian expert was able to throw a boom so it made five complete circles and then took an apple off a boy's head. This last feat certainly must have taken some doing, but the others are fairly standard stunts regularly featured at contests.

To perform such feats, a special boomerang—or boomerangs—must be used. The return boomerang must have an angle not less than 70 degrees or more than 120. For best results, the tips of the wings should have a slight skew; the wood must be steamed to make it pliable, and then the tip of one wing is slightly twisted so the inner edge is raised and the outer lowered. The same is done for the tip of the other wing, but in the opposite direction. When the thrown boomerang turns over on its side and starts revolving, this skew pulls it around so it will go in a circle.

The skew can be approximated by shaving the inside of one wingtip and the outer tip of the other. The skew is not absolutely necessary to make a boom return. If the boom is correctly made and balanced, it will return without this feature, but the skew adds greatly to its effectiveness.

In general, there are two types of homing boomerangs. One travels in a circle. It is thrown slightly to the thrower's right, at an angle of about 30 degrees. It then swings around in a great arc and returns to him. The other type shoots upward and forward, stops, and then glides back to land at his feet. The first type is the more dramatic, but much harder to make and throw.

Most commercial boomerangs are made of plywood or plastic. They are perfectly suitable for youngsters, although even these can give you a nasty crack on the head if carelessly used. A good rule is: When a boomerang is in the air, everyone present should keep an eye on it.

Naturally enough, boomerangs fascinate aeronautical engineers and physicists Dr. Newton Gaines, chairman of Texas Christian University's Physics Department, used to use boomerangs to demonstrate physical principles to his classes. The doctor is the author of an interesting booklet "The Boomerang—a Neglected Device for Teaching Physics." Colonel John M. Gerrish, who makes commercial boomerangs, is an aeronautical engineer.

The great pleasure in boomerang throwing comes from watching the flying sticks wheel and soar in the air. One boomerang expert defined it as "playing with a trained eagle." Watching a boom that you've designed yourself compete with a bird on the wing is about as big a thrill as you'll find.

CHAPTER 8

The Plucky Little Terriers

Pound for pound, the terrier is the bravest of all dogs. Bred to be small enough to go down a hole, he is descended from the great British mastiffs that went into battle beside their masters and terrified the Roman legions. When Symmachus, a fourth-century Roman politician, imported some of these giant dogs for the gladiatorial games, the populace protested that they should have been confined by iron cages like any other dangerous wild animal. Throughout the Middle Ages a few wealthy families maintained these enormous animals as watchdogs, but keeping one must have been almost as difficult as keeping a pet lion, and cost as much to feed. They were also used to hold dangerous game such as bear, wild boar, and wolves. Today, large fighting dogs are not used with big game as they are too ungainly to avoid a charge and are so easily killed, but when a hunter had to face the attack of an infuriated animal with sword or spear, dogs large enough to slow the quarry down by sheer weight had to be used.

Later, these great fighting dogs were bred down for bull and bear baiting. The dogs used in bear baiting were comparatively small, quick animals that could run in under the bear's blow, get in their bite, and leap back before the bear could hook them. As the bear was kept chained, the men did not have to worry about stopping his charge. Bull baiting was invented by the butchers who needed some device to hold a steer steady while they killed him. So the butchers developed the bulldog, a squat animal with an undershot jaw that could grab a steer or bull by the nose and hold him until the butcher came in with a knife. The bulldogs were trained to get a hold and keep it no matter what punishment they took. They are the ancestors of the modern English bulldog.

Terriers were developed by crossing the quick-moving bear-baiting dog with the powerful bulldog. They were originally intended to bolt quarry that had gone underground, and their name comes from the Latin *terra,* meaning earth. They were probably developed by the peasantry as "vermin dogs" rather than by the nobles who hunted with hounds. Later, bigger types of terriers, such as the Airedale, were bred as watchdogs and to handle large game, but strictly speaking no dog too big to go down a hole is a terrier.

In the Middle Ages badgers were virtually the only wild animals ordinary people were allowed to hunt, as all other types were reserved for the nobility. Badger digging was the poor man's hunt and was developed to an exacting science. When I was in England, I asked a friend of mine, John Copely, if he could take me badger digging. John had taken me otter hunting, stag hunting, hawking, and beagling, but now he looked doubtful.

"I really don't know if I can arrange that," he told me. "It's a rough business, you know. I've seen a badger tear the lower jaw off a terrier; and on another dig, one dog came out of the earth with his left eye and ear gone. Badger digging is still widely practiced, but the people who go in for it don't like onlookers. Still, I'll see what I can do."

In the United States, badgers are found mainly in the western states, although they occasionally turn up as far east as Ohio. A big boar badger may weigh up to twenty-five pounds, and is a rough customer. The dogs used weigh only about half that, so the odds are all on the badger. The European badger lives in a maze of underground passages called a "sett." Often one of these setts covers over an acre of ground and may have three or four levels, each with its own network of passages. Working in the pitch dark, the terriers have to locate the badger (or badgers) and fight the animals until the men can dig down to them.

I was in luck. Two weeks later, John called my hotel to say that he had arranged to have me go on a badger dig. The dig was to take place on the estate of a Lord Canworth (I'm not using his real name, as he asked me not to) in Sussex. A badger was destroying a valuable growth of rhododendrons on the estate by constant burrowing, and Lord Canworth wanted the animal caught and liberated elsewhere where he wouldn't do damage.

"Arranging for a badger dig wasn't nearly as hard as I'd thought, for the old sport has suddenly become popular again," John told me as we drove down to Sussex from London in his car. "You see, some years ago a blasted French doctor had the brilliant idea of getting rid of the rabbits that were eating his garden by catching two of them, inoculating them with a highly infectious disease called myxomatosis, and then turning them loose. The scoundrel was so successful that he managed to wipe out all the rabbits in France. Somehow the disease jumped the Channel, and has virtually destroyed all our rabbits also. Now, a badger's principal food is rabbits . . . mainly young rabbits that he digs out of their burrows. With the rabbits gone, the badgers turned to killing domestic poultry. Naturally, all the farmers are up in arms against the poor badgers. Rather than kill them, sportsmen have taken up badger digging so the animals can be moved to other areas."

Lord Canworth's estate covered several hundred acres. Most of it had been plowed up for farming, but the grounds around the old Elizabethan manor house were still untouched and the trees and shrubbery were the finest I'd ever seen . . . as they should have been, for highly trained gardeners had been working on them for the last five hundred years. Lord Canworth met us at the door. He was a slender white-haired man in his late sixties, as thin as a swagger stick and just as straight. He was going on the dig with us.

"I must admit that I was somewhat taken aback when John suggested that you come along," he told me as we started out toward the rhododendron thicket. "You see, badger digging with terriers is regarded as cruel by many people but this animal must be removed and I simply won't allow gins [steel traps] set on my property. I once lost two of my best hounds because of gins."

Lord Canworth explained that when the badger is to be taken alive, long-handled tongs are used. The ends of the tongs are curved so as to fit around the badger's neck without injuring him. While the dogs are holding the badger at bay, a man can slip the tongs around the animal's neck and lift him out of the burrow. He is then put in a sack for later release.

Although terriers have been used to bolt all sorts of wild animals from holes, the test of a good terrier has always been whether or not he could stand up to a badger. "No other animal that takes to the ground can put up such a fight as old brock," said Lord Canworth, "brock" being an affectionate English term for a badger. "If your terrier flunks on badger, you can still use him for fox, otters, or stoats, but badger is the real test."

In an effort to develop dead-game dogs, terrier enthusiasts adopted the now almost forgotten business of badger baiting. A badger was put in a small barrel to represent his burrow, and a terrier was sent in to "draw" him; that is, to grab the badger by the head and pull him out of the barrel. It took a good dog to do the job, and the fights between the two animals were long and bloody. Some of the badgers themselves became famous, like "Old Hoary" who killed six terriers in two days in the London pit in 1763. For several hundred years, badger baiting might almost have been called the national sport of England, at least in country districts. Farmers would come for miles to pit their favorite terrier against some well-known badger.

"But the dogs developed for badger baiting couldn't be used for hunting wild badgers in setts," John told me. "The badger-baiting dogs had a strong bulldog cross to give them weight and bigger jaws, and not one of them could have got into a badger hole. Also, a badger-hunting terrier is not supposed to draw a badger out of a sett, except possibly under very exceptional conditions. A terrier's job is to hold the badger at bay until the men can dig down to him."

When we arrived at the rhododendron thicket, we found the gamekeeper chatting with three young farmers. Each of the farmers had two or three tough little terriers on leads. The dogs knew well what was up. They stood rigid and stiff-legged, their ears pricked up and their eyes following every motion. They were so tense that I had the feeling if you snapped one's tail, he'd give off a note like a twanged violin string. Three of the dogs were fox terriers (but shorter legged than the standard). A couple were rough-coated Norwich terriers. There was a terrier that looked like a light Sealyham, and the rest were what might be politely called Border terriers—a rough-coated, short-legged, tough little dog who was always ready for a fight, and didn't care who knew it.

"Which is the best breed for badger?" I asked.

This got a laugh. "There's a bit of a question about that, sir," said one of the younger farmers. "We breed our tykes for brains and 'eart [gameness]. Folks used to look at my father's dogs and tell him, 'Sam, those terriers are the wrong color.' He'd say, 'There ain't no *good* terrier that's the wrong color.' That's the way it is, sir. We're for performance, not for shows."

The owners gave me permission to examine their terriers. The dogs averaged fifteen pounds and stood about fourteen inches high. Most of them were rough-coated, with ears close to the body. The nice-looking "prick ears" of a show terrier are a disadvantage to a badger dog because a badger can grab them. All the dogs had powerful jaws—a straight bite —not undershot. John told me that these working terriers are often called "Jack Russells" after a famous sporting parson who lived in the middle of the last century. Parson Jack Russell is credited with having created the modern working terrier, breeding away from the highly specialized "badger-baiting" dog back to the hard, capable hunting terrier used for actual fieldwork.

As we started up through the rhododendrons, John said to me: "He's quite right. The dogs aren't mongrels by any means, although they aren't bench show dogs. Any one of these chaps can trace his dog's blood lines back for half a dozen generations . . . all hard-plucked, keen terriers."

"Quite so," remarked Lord Canworth. "Still, I'm sorry the Anti-Blood Sports Society and other groups have made it hard for the big terrier clubs to operate. There are about seven of them . . . the Working Terrier Association, the Parson Jack Russell Terrier Club, the Oxford Badger Club, and so on. The clubs try to breed for conformation as well as intelligence and pluck. Conformation is important, you know. Your dog should have powerful hindquarters but be small enough to get through a narrow pipe [burrow]. He should have a short muzzle, for a badger will bite off the nostrils of a snipe-nosed dog. He should have a thick coat with a good undercoat. That's important, for otherwise earth gets rubbed into the skin and causes eczema. Remember that often a dog will be underground for twenty-four hours. I've known a dog to be in a sett for two days."

I asked how the dogs were trained for badger digging. John explained that many enthusiasts build artificial setts equipped with trapdoors at intervals so a panicky terrier can be taken out. Food is put in the fake sett, and the puppies are encouraged to run about in it. Then a dead badger is pulled through with a string, and the puppies are allowed to catch and shake it. "Often the trainer bangs on the top of the sett with a shovel to imitate the sound of digging so the dogs will get us to it," he added. "Sometimes rabbits in wire cages are put in the sett, and if the dogs bark at them the trainer lifts the trapdoor and punishes the pups. There're often rabbits in real badger setts, and you don't want your dogs to riot on [chase] them."

When we reached the place where the badger had been digging, the men fastened their dogs to trees, making sure no two dogs were tied close enough together so they'd foul each other's leads when they got excited. "That often causes fights," John told me. Then the men laid out their tools. There were shovels, picks, and spades, and also several pieces of apparatus peculiar to the sport. I recognized the long-handled tongs, but the rest I didn't know. One was a long, hollow metal rod with a sharp point on one end and a crossbar on the other like the letter T. Two cups, like old-fashioned ear trumpets, were fitted over the ends of the crossbar.

John explained: "That's a listening rod. If you think the dogs have the badger bayed, you drive the sharp end of the rod into the ground and put your ear to one of the cups. In that way, you can locate the dogs' exact position. Sound actually travels better through ground and metal than it does through air, you know."

There was also a long stick with a loop of tarred string on the end. If the badger was in a spot where the tongs wouldn't reach him, this stick was run in the hole. Usually the badger grabbed the loop of string, and then the man could quickly twist the loop around his muzzle and pull him out. There were also a square-shaped spade for blocking runways, and a curious-looking device like half a bucket on the end of an iron pole. This was to scoop out earth in a burrow to let the dogs through a narrow passage.

"Most of these tools have probably been in the men's families for a hundred years or more," John told me.

The whole sett was carefully examined before the terriers were put in. As English badger setts go, this was a comparatively small one, measuring about a hundred square yards. There were eight entrances. "In a really big sett, there may be fifty or more entrances," Lord Canworth told me.

One of the men wanted to block all the entrances except two. "Happens old brock bolts out o' one we're not watching, and there he is among the tied tykes," he argued. "I lost a good dog that way onct, I did."

"Nay, man, how will the tykes breathe down there if ye block the earths?" protested another. "Brock'll nah bolt with my Nancy and Jim's Ripper. Have no fear."

At last they compromised by stopping two holes.

"Why don't they just turn the dogs loose?" I asked.

"The whole lot would be into the sett before you could say 'knife,' and then there'd be the devil of a row," said John. "The dogs would probably start fighting among themselves. They'd certainly get in each other's way."

The sett was on the slope of a hill, and it was decided to put three dogs in the highest holes and let them work down. "Better make it one dog and two bitches," suggested Lord Canworth.

"Aye, sir, we'll do that, but all our dogs has worked together before," said one of the men. "They know each other same as Christians."

The men went toward the tied dogs. The dogs went crazy with excitement, leaping to the ends of their leads, barking, whining, wriggling, and prancing on their hind legs to get at their masters. The men had all they could do to unfasten the selected terriers, for the straining dogs pulled their leads so tight it was hard to get enough slack to free the snaps. The collars were removed to make sure that they didn't catch on underground roots. Then the men, carrying their terriers, went up the hill and slipped them into the proper holes. Two of the dogs disappeared into the burrows so suddenly they seemed to vanish by magic. The third one only plunged her head in.

"Ai, your tyke's afraid of the dark, Jim. Give her a torch!" shouted one of the farmers.

"Nah, there's a bit o' root here. Pass up the spade," called Jim, who was lying on his belly, looking down the hole. But before the spade could arrive, the terrier had dug her way in and was gone.

Everyone lay down with one ear pressed against the ground. I did the same. The tied terriers were making such a constant whining that I couldn't hear until I put a finger in my other ear to shut out the noise. For a while, all I heard were faint noises. There was a sudden rumble like a miniature subway train rushing past underneath. It was gone in a second. One of the terriers suddenly popped out of a lower hole some twenty yards from the hole where he'd been put in. He shook himself and looked up at his master.

"Naught there, Jacky lad?" asked the farmer. The terrier wagged his stump of a tail and dived down the hole again.

"Dogs often have a hard job locating the badger," John explained to me. "This sett probably has three 'stories,' and the badger may be in any one of them. As soon as he hears the dogs, the badger starts shifting around to confuse them. In a few minutes the whole sett is full of fresh badger trails, and the dogs have trouble trailing him. Of course, it's black as the inside of an ink bottle down there, and the dogs have to rely entirely on their noses. A good nose is far more important to a terrier than most people realize. The badger knows the sett and the dogs don't, so after laying false trails he'll often den up in some out-of-the-way pipe, leaving the dogs to run around the sett until they're tired."

"They've found something!" shouted one of the men lying on the ground. "They're throwing their tongues now! That's my Nancy, hear her?"

I put my ear to the ground again. Then came the rush of the "subway train" a second time. I could hear the barking of the terriers as they chased it. The noise came dimly, as though very far away.

"About six feet down, wouldn't you say?" John asked a farmer.

"Closer to eight, I'd say, sir," said the man without lifting his head. I found out that an experienced badger digger can tell from the sound of a dog's barking exactly how far he is beneath the surface, although unexpected strata of especially hard or soft earth may occasionally fool him.

"He's shiftin' fast," said a farmer with his ear plastered to the ground. "Happens it's a rabbit, I do believe."

"Never fear, man. I heard my tyke growl. He'll nah growl on a rabbit," said another.

"But it might be a fox," said Lord Canworth, who was flat on his belly with the rest of us. "He is certainly running very fast. Hardly like a badger."

"There's badgers in there, I'm sure, sir," said the gamekeeper. "I sprinkled fresh sand before all the holes last evening. The tracks were going in, none out."

One of the farmers had taken a flashlight and climbed down the hill to the lowest hole of the sett. This hole went straight in like a tunnel. It was so big that the man was able to crawl in up to his waist. The underground rumble sounded again, this time going downhill. Suddenly the man in the hole shouted: "I seen 'em go past! It's a big old brock. My Nancy and Jim's Ripper is after him."

"Three dogs can't hold him," said one of the farmers, getting to his knees. "Let's put in Jock and Dandy, eh?"

Two more of the terriers were untied and fed into holes. One of the holes was as perpendicular as a well. The dog's master lowered him in by the hind legs until his front legs could find a hold, and then let him go.

A moment later, one of the men shouted, "They've fixed [bayed] him, I do believe! They're right under me."

"Naw, they're still running. They just went past me," called another, his ear to the ground.

"Now they're here!" shouted John.

A bellow from the man up the hole. "They're a-runnin' him! They went past again."

One of the frantic terriers burst out of a hole, ran around and plunged down another. The sight drove the tied dogs mad. One of them rolled on the ground, tearing at his leash.

"Watch that dog!" snapped Lord Canworth. "He'll bite through his lead in a moment."

Before anyone could move, the terrier had chewed loose and hurled himself down a hole.

"Oh, damn, he has his collar and a foot of lead hanging from it," said Lord Canworth irritably.

"Not your hard dog, is it, Harry?" called one of the men anxiously. He was in a different part of the sett and couldn't see the dogs for the rhododendron stems.

"Nah, my tyke's tied with a chain," Harry called back. A "hard" dog is a purely fighting dog, usually almost pure bull terrier, who is used only when it is necessary for a dog actually to fight the badger rather than simply chase or bay him . . . corresponding to the "catch-dogs" used with big-game hounds.

"Thank heaven for that," muttered Lord Canworth. "Those hard dogs are as apt to fight the other terriers as the badger. Nothing's worse than a dogfight in a pipe where you can't reach the dogs."

The man in the bottom hole crawled out. "Give us another terrier 'ere, Bill!" he shouted. "They're running past regular now. We'll 'ead 'im off!"

Another terrier was released, and the man crawled back in the hole, holding the dog by the hindquarters, ready to slip him when he heard the badger coming past again.

"Can't hear a thing now," said one of the men. "Could be they've lost him."

"More likely he's bayed in some far part of the sett and we can't hear the dogs barking," said Lord Canworth. "Let's spread out a bit."

We scattered among the rhododendrons. A few minutes later, the gamekeeper shouted: "They're here! Right under me. They've got him bayed. I can hear the terriers barking."

One of the farmers rushed to the spot and flung himself face down.

"Aye, they're holding him. That's my Ripper barking at him. Where's the bloody spades?"

I ran up and listened also. I could hear the steady, rhythmical barking of at least two terriers, a very different sound from the wild yip-yipping of the chase. The farmer stamped on the ground to let the dogs know we'd located them and were coming to their help. Instantly the barking increased in pitch and volume.

Two men came up with spades and began to dig. John brought the listening post and stuck the point in the ground. He listened at one of the cups on the crosspieces, moved it a few feet, tried again, and then called: "I'm right over the pipe. They're about six feet down, I'd say."

I listened at the other cup. The noise was much clearer. I could distinguish the sound of at least three of the terriers. Then came a low sound like gurgling water. It was instantly followed by screams of fury from the dogs. "They're fighting him!" shouted John. Promptly every man fell flat on his face to listen. The place looked like a battlefield with prone corpses scattered about. I heard one of the dogs suddenly scream, but whether with rage or pain I couldn't say.

"Nancy's bitten," said her owner, his ear pressed to the ground. "Brock's in the end of a pipe, and the dogs can't get behind him."

"Bad show," said Lord Canworth. If two terriers, working from both ends of a pipe, can trap the badger in the center between them, they have the quarry at a disadvantage. If he tries to attack one dog, the other nips at his rump and forces him to turn. This badger had taken his stand at the foot of a deadend passageway and had his back to the wall. He could charge forward and bite a dog without being afraid of a rear attack.

"Harry, get your hard dog!" shouted Nancy's owner.

"Now just a moment," said Lord Canworth authoritatively. "The hard dog can't get past the others to reach the badger, and he'll start fighting with them in his excitement. That will be far worse than any damage the badger can do."

The barking stopped. "The dogs know we're coming and they're probably lying down facing the badger," guessed John. But a moment later, Nancy popped out of a hole. She was badly bitten about the muzzle, and one ear was in shreds. A first-aid kit was produced, and her owner carefully doctored the injured terrier. Then Nancy was tied up. She made no objection, but lay down contentedly after drinking a little water. She evidently considered that she'd done her part.

One of the farmers put his ear to the ground. "Dig a bit and let's see if the tykes talk," he said. The two men with the spades set to work. After a few minutes the farmer stood up again, shaking his head. "No use. He's dug himself in, I do believe."

When a badger finds himself hard pressed he will, if he can shake off the dogs, dig in the roof of a pipe to make a barrier behind him. This trick has a double advantage: the dogs can't get through and the fresh earth cuts off the scent. The terriers should keep pressing the badger hard enough so he hasn't a chance to dig, but the little bitch Nancy had been so badly bitten that she had to turn back and had given the badger time to drop the ceiling before the rest could come up.

"I'm afraid we've lost him," said Lord Canworth, his ear to the listening rod. "Now that the dogs aren't holding him, he's probably tunneling off in some other direction, and he can dig faster than the men can. We'll never catch up with him."

"Ah, should 'a put down Harry's hard dog. He'd 'a held him," said Nancy's owner.

One of the farmers vanished into the rhododendrons and returned in a few minutes with a very small fox terrier. "Jock's got the best nose," he announced. "Not much o' a fightin' dog, but he's got a prime nose. Let's see what Jock says."

After considerable discussion, one of the holes was selected and Jock slipped into it. Again, everyone lay down to catch the sound of Jock's barking—if he did begin to bark. After a long time, John spoke up. "I can just hear him. He's over there to the left." He pointed.

The other men couldn't pick up the faint noise with their unaided ears, so the listening rod had to be moved. "Aye, that's Jock," said the owner when he put his ear to one of the cups. "But terrible deep down, seems like."

Now came the sound of the other terriers in the sett racing through the cat's-cradle of passageways to Jock's help. Occasionally one would obviously find himself in a deadend pipe, and we could hear his irritated whines as he tried to find a way into the spot where Jock was still barking faintly but steadily. Then another terrier joined with Jock, and we could hear the double barking. Then another.

"They've got him between them this time!" shouted the gamekeeper. "A good six feet down. Dig, lads!" and he grabbed a shovel himself and sank it into the ground.

Four men were digging, three with shovels or spades and the fourth using a pickax. As before, the sound of the digging encouraged the dogs, and we could hear the barking more plainly. The badger could also hear the digging, for another fight started. It raged back and forth under us. The men in the rapidly deepening pit reported that they could feel the vibrations of the struggling animals through the soles of their shoes. A Border terrier came up, badly bitten around the head and neck. His owner tried to grab him, but the terrier disappeared down another hole almost as quickly as he'd appeared.

"That's where brains come in," said John approvingly. "Two of the dogs have the badger boxed in a pipe between them, but the rest are making sure he doesn't get away down a side passage. When they can't reach the place where he's fixed by running through the sett, they come up and go down another entrance to make sure there's no way he can break out."

"I believe the badger's trying to dig in again," John reported. "But the dogs seem to be holding him."

There was the sound of another scuffle, and this time through the listening rod I could hear the hissing of the badger mixed with the snarls and growls of the terriers. Then there was a general mix-up, the dogs screaming with pain and fury and the badger grunting and hissing as he charged into them. The men with the tools were working desperately, but you don't dig through six feet of earth in a few minutes. The Border terrier reappeared with fresh cuts on his head, and this time his owner grabbed him. While the man was doctoring him, I had a chance to look at the injuries. They weren't clean bites. They looked as though someone had grabbed pieces of the terrier's hide with a pair of powerful pliers and torn off hunks of hide.

"Look 'ere!" said the Border's owner, rubbing the dog's fur. " 'E's in sandy soil, 'e is. The tykes can't 'old 'im in that. 'E'll dig 'isself clear for a fact, 'e will."

"I'm afraid you're right," said Lord Canworth. "If you think it safe, we'd better use the hard dog."

Two more of the terriers came up, both more or less chewed. That decided it. The hard dog was brought up . . . in this case not a bull terrier, but a powerful little Sealyham. "Rather long-legged to work in a pipe," said John doubtfully as the dog's owner took off the collar.

"I'm more concerned about the width of his chest," remarked Lord Canworth. "Legs can be tucked out of the way in a fight. A big chest can't."

The hard dog was poured into the biggest of the entrances. There was a long pause while the men continued to dig as though their lives depended on it. Then the most God-awful racket burst out. You didn't need to put your ear to the ground or use the listening rod to hear it. I expected to see the dogs and badger burst through the earth.

"He's running again!" yelled John at the listening rod.

" 'Ere they are!" shouted one of the farmers, halfway down one of the holes with only his legs sticking out. "They just went past me. I saw Jock. He's bleedin' terrible bad."

"Now they're under me!" called another man, ear to the ground. "They've stopped him, but he's trying to dig." Two men joined him, and put their ears to the ground. "That's my Dandy, a-fightin' of him," he shouted.

"We've hit stones," called one of the diggers. "Get the crowbar here, quick!"

"Get me another terrier 'ere!" yelled the man down the hole. "It's a fix."

"Naw, it's no fix. Old brock turned to fight. There, they're running again. You hear my Gyp runnin' him?"

"They're back under us," called one of the diggers. "It's a proper fix this time. Rock [the hard dog] has him! Listen to that row! Rock is trying to draw him [has the badger by the head and is trying to drag him out of the pipe]. Brock'll kill him. Dig, for Gawd's sake!"

The earth came vomiting out of the pit from the shovels. There was now only room for two men to dig at a time. When one man was too exhausted to keep up the pace, he vaulted out of the pit and another jumped in to take his place. The noise below us was continual. Rock had evidently taken his hold and was refusing to let go. There was no danger of the badger digging himself in now, but there was a danger of the dog being killed before the men could reach him.

A yell from the diggers: "We're through to the pipe!" The men had been sinking the hole behind the dog (with the help of the listening rod they knew exactly where the animal was) rather than straight down on top of the fighting animals. Otherwise there would have been a good chance of burying the dog under the loose earth or breaking his back with a chance blow from the pick. I looked into the pit, now as deep as a man's shoulders. Using the tool that looked like a half bucket on the end of a handle, the men were clearing out the earth that had fallen into the pipe. The pipe was about a foot in diameter, perfectly smooth and round. It was as though the men had dug down to a length of sewer pipe and broken through the top.

"Give us a torch here!" shouted one of the diggers. He crouched down and stuck his head into the hole in the top of the pipe. "Aye, I see 'em. He's a rare big un. Rock is holding him. Let's have the tongs." The tongs were hurriedly passed down, and the man, lying on his side at the bottom of the pit, reached into the pipe with the curved ends.

Suddenly hell broke loose. The badger burst out of the broken pipe with Rock still hanging to him, and grabbed the man by the forearm. The man roared with pain. Two more terriers exploded out of the pipe and fastened on the badger, screaming like banshees with the DT's. "Block the bloody pipe!" someone yelled. "Get 'im off 'arry!" shouted another. Harry was trying to tear the badger loose. He finally succeeded and then pulled himself out of the pit, leaving the other digger leaping around like a ballet dancer trying to avoid the dogs and badger, who were rolling around together, barking and hissing. "Use the tongs, man!" cried the gamekeeper. The digger managed to grab the tongs, and at the same moment Rock got the badger by the head and the other terriers grabbed him by the hindquarters. The dogs stretched the badger out between them, straining in opposite directions. The man locked the tongs around the badger's neck and lifted him up, the dogs still hanging on.

"Get your tykes loose!" roared the digger. The dogs' owners fell into the pit and managed to wring the terriers off the badger. Then the badger was lifted out of the pit. A sack was got ready, but first Lord Canworth examined the badger for injuries.

"No marks on him," he reported. Badger hide is remarkably thick and tough, and although the dogs had pulled some hair out of him, the badger was otherwise unhurt. Still using the tongs, the man lowered the badger into the sack and then tied the mouth of it. The bitten dogs received first aid.

On the way back, Lord Canworth remarked: "Terriers bred for badger digging have been used in Europe to hunt wild boar, in Africa for jackal and warthog, and in Scotland for wildcat. All very fine, I'm sure, but it's rather a pity to waste their talents in that fashion. After all, for a real exhibition of pluck and brains, nothing can equal a good badger dig."

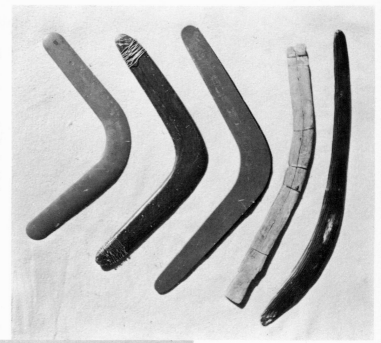

LEFT TO RIGHT: Plastic return boomerang, used for practice; commercially made wooden return boom, its tips wrapped with copper wire to increase hitting power; another commercial return type; Hopi Indian nonreturn hunting boomerang or "throwing stick"; hunting boom used by Australian aborigines

The Hopi Indians of Arizona have hunted jack rabbits with boomerangs since time immemorial

Stop-action photos show the author's boomerang hitting and bringing down a duck

Dan Mannix duck hunting with a pair of boomerangs

A terrier digs its
way into a badger's
sett, or network
of tunnels

The terrier's job is
to hold the badger
at bay underground
until the men can
dig down to it

CHAPTER 9

The Bola—
the Flying Snare

I first discovered the existence of the bola as a small boy when I saw the late Douglas Fairbanks use one in *The Gaucho*. Fairbanks made that bola of his do everything but talk. The bola is a deceptively simple looking device—three balls each with a three-foot length of rawhide tied to it and the rawhide thongs fastened together at the ends. Gauchos use it instead of a lasso. You swing the contraption around your head until you've built up enough momentum, and then let go. As the bola flies through the air, the thongs open until the bola resembles a flying spider. When it hits a running animal, it wraps itself around the quarry's legs and brings him down. After watching Doug tie up hordes of villains, rescue beautiful girls, and scale balconies by means of his bola, I was determined to have one.

A good many years passed before I was able to achieve my ambition, for bolas, as far as I have been able to discover, are not available in the United States. When I went to Argentina on assignment for a magazine, I kept a sharp lookout for bolas but didn't see any until I reached the Duke Jones *estancia* near Bariloche. There I discovered that bolas really exist and are still used.

The Jones estancia, or ranch, is a simple little place not much bigger than the state of New Jersey, but to the Joneses it's home. The country is either absolutely flat (pampas) or perpendicular (the Andes). The

Joneses were originally a Texas family who arrived in Bariloche some fifty years ago by way of Chile over the Andes. Their home is a Victorian mansion of the early Charles Addams period, complete with gingerbread curlicues, every stick of which had to be brought in by pack horses over the mountains. It looks incredibly out of place in the middle of some of the world's most magnificent scenery, and the furnishings, which consist largely of boars' heads, stag horns, spurs, whips, and lassos, do nothing to dispel the illusion of a mild case of the DT's. But if the nooks and crannies of such a home collect dust, they also collect memories as no modern house can do. Everything in the house has a story behind it— including the Joneses. Here were the *facones* (long knives) with which the Jones boys kill wild boar, riding the animals down, jumping off their horses, and stabbing them. Here were the silver-handled *rebenques,* a sort of heavy quirt, they used for breaking wild horses. Here were the heavy wool ponchos they used as coats, blankets, and sleeping bags. Here also were the bolas, some bound in silver, others with strands of twisted cougar hide, still others light enough to entangle a duck on the wing. There was a whole armory of them.

Mrs. Jones showed me around. There are several "Mrs. Joneses" in the clan, including one grand old lady in her eighties who can remember Indian raids across the Chilean border. My hostess was a slender lady in her forties who was able to ride any horse on the estancia, shoot a gun, or throw a bola. She told me something about the strange instruments.

"We call them 'boleadoras,' " Mrs. Jones explained, taking one down and twirling it expertly around her head. "There are still wild horses on the estancia, and the men hunt them when they begin to run off our domestic stock. You aim for the horse's front legs and generally catch him by the rear ones. A horse who has been boleadoraed before and managed to escape gets very cunning. Instead of kicking and fighting, he stops dead, and sometimes the boleadora will fall off his legs. We also use them on the wild cattle in the mountains."

The cords used for the boleadoras were spiraled from the neck of a guanaco, a llama-like animal. The balls were small round stones in leather bags made of guanaco hocks or the neck pouches of rheas, the South American ostrich. Some of the balls were old billiard balls and others were simply sacks filled with buckshot.

"Frankly, we don't encourage the gauchos to use boleadoras too much," Mrs. Jones explained. "They like to play a game with them. One man rides at full gallop while a friend boleadoras his horse by the front legs.

The horse turns a complete somersault and the rider has to land on his feet. You use up too many horses doing it—gauchos too."

As is usually the case with supposedly simple weapons, a boleadora is more complicated than it seems. It's really composed of two lengths of rawhide, not three. One length has two balls of equal size tied at the ends. The third cord is half as long and is tied to the exact center of this strip. The ball at the end is smaller than the other two and somewhat egg-shaped. This cord is called the *mañeque*.

For the first time I learned how to use a boleadora. The operator holds the small egg-shaped stone (I'd been holding it where the three cords join in the middle) and swings the boleadora first vertically and then horizontally around his head to get his aim. When the two large balls are behind him, he throws the small mañeque ball directly at the target as if he were throwing a baseball. The boleadora revolves slowly and does not open completely until it hits the target.

"The great advantage of a boleadora over a lasso is range," Duke Jones told me. "You can throw even a comparatively light boleadora forty yards, while the maximum range with a lasso is about thirty feet. Also, you don't have to get your horse into position for a throw with a boleadora as you do with a lasso. The disadvantages? Well, there's too much chance of hurting the animal to use it on prime stock. Either the animal is hopelessly cut up fighting the cords or a ball hits him on the leg and breaks it. If you're after wild horses and don't mind killing a few, or if you're trying to get a half-wild range steer for butchering, they're all right."

The traditional quarry for boleadoring is the rhea. These miniature South American ostriches stand about as high as a man and weigh about seventy pounds. A good horse with a sudden burst of speed can get a man within boleadora distance of a rhea for a few seconds. In those seconds, he has to throw the boleadora, aiming for the bird's neck.

When I was in Patagonia, in the extreme southern part of Argentina, I had a chance to talk to gauchos about rhea hunting and even go on a hunt. These men live on the open pampas where the wind blows steadily 365 days a year and they've got so used to leaning against it that if the wind ever stopped they'd fall flat on their mustaches.

Gauchos are usually described as Argentine cowboys, which is like describing a werewolf as a Transylvanian lap dog. These fellows spend most of their time on top of their scrawny little horses, sitting on saddles composed of half a dozen sheep skins cinched together, living mainly on *mate,* a seminarcotic green tea that they brew in small gourds about the size of a baseball.

Their principal recreation, aside from carving each other up with facones, is boleadoraing passing rheas. This sport combines business with pleasure. It's a real test of a gaucho's skill to get his horse within throwing distance of the racing birds without ending up in the hospital—which, as there aren't any hospitals, is an important consideration. Also, every part of the rhea is useful. The gauchos eat them, make tobacco pouches of the neck pouches, sell the feathers for dusters, use the skin for wallets and belts, and take the pepsin out of the stomach for medicine.

"Then, too, the rheas kill our dogs," one gaucho told me, indicating half a dozen wolfish-looking monsters that seemed capable of licking their weight in Bengal tigers. "Only last week I lost one that way. Some rheas were grazing with the sheep, and one of my dogs ran in to drive them away. A cock rhea struck at him with his spiked toes and disemboweled the dog before I could come up."

A rhea has three-clawed toes on each foot (an ostrich has only two), and a cutting downward blow from the foot of an infuriated rhea is no joke. One man said a rhea had even attacked him while he was on horseback. "I was coming over a little rise, and the horse nearly stepped on a cock bird sitting on his nest," he told me. "The cock jumped off the eggs and went for me. My horse reared so badly I was left sitting on the eggs."

There was a reserve near a lake where a small flock of rheas were allowed to run wild and unmolested. A gaucho promised to round up the birds and let me see how the boleadora was used. Not being able to stay up with him on horseback, I was posted at a strategic point and told to lie down and watch.

Rounding up rheas is quite a job, and it was a long time before the first birds appeared. There were three of them, a cock and two hens. They came skimming across the ground with their wings out like ships under full sail. They had the wind behind them, and although they cannot fly, their open wings helped to carry them along.

As the birds came closer to me, the rider suddenly bent forward and, putting spurs to his horse, burst into a gallop. Until then, the birds had been trotting along, going only fast enough to keep an appreciable distance between them and the horse. Now they closed their wings and went into full stride, their legs moving so fast that they blurred like the blades of an electric fan. But it took a few seconds for the rheas to build up to their maximum speed, and in those seconds the rider was able to get within throwing distance. As he began to swing his boleadora, the cock broke away from the hens and shot off at an angle. The gaucho kneed his mount, and the trained horse swung to cut off the bird like a cow pony following a steer. Suddenly the rhea opened one wing, dropped the other so the primaries nearly touched the ground, and spun around, "turning on a dime," to double back. As he swung, the gaucho flung his boleadora. It was at least double the distance at which he could have used a lasso.

The triple cords flashed through the air like an octopus and caught the bird around his outstretched wing and one leg. The rhea seemed to explode. He must have been keeping his feathers close to his body while running, and the sudden shock of the striking boleadora caused him to shoot out every feather at what seemed to be right angles to his skin. For an instant he looked five times as big as he had before. Then he went down with the boleadora wrapped around him.

The gaucho slid his horse to a Number 11 stop, hitting the ground before the animal had stopped moving. The sight of the man galvanized the struggling rhea to a supreme effort. Struggling to his feet, he managed to take off again in spite of the boleadora. The gaucho swung back into the saddle and took after the now crippled bird, uncoiling his lariat, but before he could catch up with him the bird had reached the lake. Without pausing, the rhea plunged into the water. Using his long legs and paddling with his free wing, he seemed fair to escape, but before he could go far the long rope had shot out and the noose dropped around his body. The gaucho hauled him in, hand over hand.

I helped to get the boleadora free. It was a surprisingly tough job. The rhea fought with his powerful legs and dagger-sharp claws while the guanaco-hide cords of the boleadora twisted themselves into such a hard knot it looked for a while as though they would have to be cut. Finally, by tying the cock's legs together with the lasso and having me hold the head to keep the rhea's potent beak out of action, the gaucho was able to get the tangled cords free. The bird was uninjured, and departed at a thirty-mile clip after his harem.

Later, I talked to the gauchos about their peculiar weapon, which is found nowhere else in the world. The origin of the boleadora is the *bolas pérdida,* often called the "most primitive weapon in the world." It was developed by the early South American Indians many centuries ago, and consisted of a round stone tied to a single rawhide thong. To keep the thong from slipping off, the Indians would carve a groove around the stone and then tie the wet rawhide in place. When the rawhide dried, it contracted so tightly nothing could get it loose. Some of these old bola stones with their grooves still occasionally turn up like arrowheads.

"When an Indian went into battle, he'd carry a number of these bolas with him," I was told. "He'd whirl a bola around his head by the thong and then let it go toward the enemy. When the Spaniards came, the Indians would sometimes tie burning grass to the bolas and use them to set fire to houses or wagon trains. Because you lost a bola when you threw it, like throwing a stone, they were called *bolas pérdida,* or lost bolas."

The modern boleadoras can also be used as weapons. I was shown a set with very heavy stones called "Las Tres Marías." "The cords on this one are made of cougar hide, which stretches and ties into such tight knots that it cripples whatever it hits," they told me. "Boleadoras like this were used in war, usually to trip the enemy's horses. About the only way to escape was to hold your poncho by one end and swing it back and forth behind your horse. Then the boleadora caught the poncho instead of the horse. General Paz, who led an uprising against the dictator Manual Posas, in the 1850's, was thrown from his horse by a boleadora like this, and captured."

"Sometimes in the old days two gauchos would fight with their boleadoras," another man added. "Did you ever read 'Martin Fierro'? That's a famous poem about the gauchos, and gives a description of a boleadora fight."

Later, I looked up the poem. Martin Fierro was a gaucho who came across an Indian tying the wrists of a white woman with the entrails of her baby preparatory to raping her. Martin had a facon and the Indian a boleadora, which he used as a flail before throwing it. Here's the account:

"One of the balls grazed my arm; a hair more and it would have broken the bone. The balls whizzed like bullets. The Indian would feint with the right-hand ball and then strike with the left. Suddenly he threw it. I went down, but the woman grabbed the boleadora before it could completely twine around me. I managed to cut one of the cords with my facon and free myself. Then the Indian was helpless, and I went in with the knife."

In 1870, the Paraguayan dictator Solano López marched against Argentina with his Irish mistress, Margarita Lynch, riding by his side. The Paraguayans would have won had not the Argentine gauchos pulled López from his horse with their bolas and cut his throat. Margarita was also captured with bolas, and after the gauchos had finished with her she was shipped back to Ireland.

The last great bola fight was in 1882. The Manzanos and Vuriloches Indians made their last stand on Mount Villegas against the Spaniards, defending themselves with bolas. They did considerable execution with them, but the firearms of the white men eventually triumphed.

When I left Patagonia, I took with me a collection of boleadoras, including some of the small bolas called *avestruceras* that are used on small game. As there are not many rheas in Pennsylvania, for a while it seemed as though my hard-won experience with boleadoras would go to waste. Then one afternoon, while strolling through the quiet halls of the University Museum in Philadelphia, I paused thunderstruck before a case of Eskimo weapons, one of which was the damndest-looking bola I'd ever imagined. It was composed of eight ivory balls, each no bigger than a large marble, all fastened by individual rawhide cords, about thirty inches long, to a central core surmounted by a cluster of feathers like the bird used in badminton. The cords were looped together in an elaborate series of slipknots, for some reason I couldn't imagine.

I asked to speak to the curator of Eskimo artifacts, and a very pleasant lady opened the case and got the device for me. "These are used by the Point Barrow Eskimos for wildfowling," she explained. "During the spring migration, you never see an Eskimo without several of these hung around his neck. Even the women and children use them. The balls are made of walrus ivory and, as you can see, are slightly egg-shaped. Each has a hole drilled through the small end to hold the cord. There's one length of sinew for each pair of balls; that is, a ball is tied at each end of one cord which is then doubled. The doubled ends are fastened together with several lashings of sinew and the feathers attached to make them fly straight. The bola is held at the base of the feathers, swung around the head, and then thrown. Up to a distance of forty yards, it's quite effective."

"Why are they looped up with those slipknots?" I asked.

"That's so a man can carry several bolas at one time without having them take up too much room. The knots are very ingeniously tied so a man has merely to jerk both ends of the bola simultaneously to have all the knots open together."

From my brief acquaintance with our feathered friends, trying to lasso one with eight balls struck me as impractical. It was, therefore, by sheer chance that I happened to broach the subject to a friend who was once a professional duck hunter and lives near Havre de Grace on the Susquehanna. Thirty years ago, my friend, whom I'll call Jake Homer, could average a kill of one thousand ducks a season, but nowadays, if you even saw that many ducks on the Susquehanna, you'd lay off the stuff. Jake is retired, and devotes his time to carving decoys out of white cedar. They sell for $30 each, and he's two years behind in orders.

One evening Jake and I were discussing unusual hunting techniques, and Jake mentioned a method he was willing to bet a bottle of Jack Daniels I didn't know. "I read about it in an old Dan Beard book when I was a kid," he explained, thus reluctantly admitting that during a misspent youth he'd wasted valuable time reading that could have been devoted to shooting. "By golly, I think the thing's still around here somewhere." Searching in the recesses of his workshop, he produced a true Eskimo-type bola. The balls were made of one-inch ball bearings encased in leather bags.

"You can actually catch a duck with this article," he explained, whirling it around his head. "I practiced on a neighbor's muscoveys. It worked fine but it didn't do the muscoveys any good, so Pa told me to quit."

"Did you ever try it on a wild duck?" I asked.

"No, but all you'd need to do was to find a duck that was blind, deaf, dumb, and flying backward."

I told Jake that the Eskimos did it regularly, and he expressed doubt.

"I'm not saying that you couldn't do it with green wildfowl that haven't been burned out." He meant birds that had never been shot at. "But where are you going to find birds like that around here?"

I had seen plenty of them in Tierra del Fuego. The Emperor geese there will let a man get within five yards of them before flying, but our native wildfowl have become too smart.

Still, the idea appealed to Jake. "It's illegal as hell, but we might try bushwhacking a pair of Canada geese nesting around here just to see if it could be done. Only the gander, of course. The female would be on the eggs anyhow. As this isn't gunning season, he wouldn't be on the alert and we could scull up close to him. But I wouldn't want to hurt the old character."

The light *avestruceras* I'd brought back from Argentina couldn't possibly hurt a goose. They were true boleadoras—three-ball jobs. I decided to tie two of them together and experiment on a wild goose.

A few days later, Jake and I set out at dawn in his bushwhacking boat. It had a high bow to hide the men and a strong flair amidships where we sat, or rather lay. Jake was in the stern, working the sculling oar and lying on his left hip. I lay in front of him with my head against his right knee, the bola in my hand. The sculler must keep the bow of the boat toward the quarry until the last instant and must take care not to scull faster than driftwood would normally float to avoid alarming the game. These boats are the only way of reaching ducks rafted up on a seaway, although today they are seldom used.

A low mist hung over the river, sucking away to the sides as the high bow of the boat knifed through it. The marsh where the geese were nesting was on the other side of the river, and by the time we reached it the mist had begun to lift. Lying on my back, I saw a flight of mallards pass overhead, already beginning to set their wings for the pitch, but they saw us and flared off, quacking loudly. I twisted around to look at Jake, but he shook his head.

"You'd never get those things," he whispered. "Even if you caught 'em on the water. All you have to do is move a finger and they're off."

I sank back again. The boat was entering the mouth of a narrow creek with high mudbanks on either side. Jake sent the boat ahead by a steady twisting motion of the oar that was absolutely noiseless. The creek had begun to widen now, and the water was shallower. Masses of arrowhead began to appear, and tall reeds. The sun was sucking up the mist like a vacuum cleaner.

Jake nudged me slightly with his knee. I turned my head slowly. This was a flooded area, with bushes growing half submerged in the water. On our left was a small island where some stunted pines grew. From what Jake had told me, I knew this was where the goose had her nest.

Something was gliding slowly among the bushes. I saw a flash of the typical white cheek marking and knew it was the gander. At the same time, Jake gently swung the bow of the boat toward the bird. Still lying prone on the bottom, he forced the boat forward.

I could no longer see the gander; I could see nothing but the sky. From the motion of Jake's hands, I knew we must still be going forward. Jake kept inclining the bow toward the left. Then he nudged me again.

As slowly as possible, I lifted my head. The gander was only a few yards away, swimming toward us. He was suspicious of the boat and had come over to investigate.

Jake stopped sculling and allowed the boat to drift. The gander was only about ten yards away now. He seemed half angry, half fearful of the boat. Then he decided that he'd had enough. He began to turn away. As he turned, I straightened up and swung the bola.

Instantly the gander gave an angry hiss and, kicking with his webbed feet and beating with his wings, tried to take off. Still in a kneeling position, I gave the bola a last whirl and let fly. Even as I threw it, I knew that I'd miscalculated the distance.

But I hadn't counted on the extraordinary properties of the strange weapon. As the bola flew through the air, it opened like a charge of shot, the spinning balls covering an area six feet in diameter. Even so, it was about to miss the gander, passing just behind him. But the bird panicked as the strange object rushed at him. He flared to one side, striking at it with one wing. The long flight feathers grazed one of the balls. The effect was magical. Instantly the whole apparatus seemed to change course and swing toward the gander as though it were magnetically attracted to him. The balls spun around his wing, tail, and body. The terrified bird came crashing into the water.

"You got him!" yelled Jake, and standing up, put his full force on the sculling oar. I scrambled to the bow, leaning over to pick the struggling bird out of the water. But the gander was still able to swim. As I reached out, he dived, came up again a few feet away, and tried to fly. Even crippled as he was, he could go faster than the boat.

If I'd had another bola with me, I could have caught him easily enough, but I hadn't thought to bring a spare. It was nearly an hour later that we got him cornered among the bushes and, jumping overboard up to my waist in mud and water, I was able to grab him. The bird was unhurt, but we had to cut the bola to get it loose.

Since then, I've made up a couple of light Eskimo-type bolas for use around the farm, using three-quarter-inch wooden balls, as anything else is too heavy and apt to damage the quarry. Although I doubt if the bola will ever take the place of the shotgun as a hunting device, it comes in very handy for catching ducks, chickens, and guinea hens, either in the spring, when a female has a clutch of young and you want to put her in a coop, or in the autumn when you want to catch certain individual birds for butchering. It's the most practical way I know of catching a semitame bird alive at twenty yards or so. The only trouble is that sometimes the bola only wraps about the bird's neck or body and she flies off with it. You'd be surprised how tough it is to get within throwing distance of a bird a second time. Those things learn fast.

CHAPTER 10

Aquatic Hunting—Fishing With Trained Anhingas, Cormorants, and Otters

Most of the unusual types of hunting I've tried were fairly strenuous, so it was with relief I discovered one exotic sport that was definitely restful. While in England, I ran across an old print showing Charles II reclining on a barge, surrounded by a bevy of luscious girls while a troupe of trained cormorants worked their tail feathers off catching fish for the party. This struck me as a sport that had possibilities. No worrying about whether the fish were biting or getting your line tangled in bushes. You just sat around while the birds did all the work. I decided to get a few cormorants and revolutionize the great American sport of fishing.

Cormorant fishing originated in the uplands of China because the narrow streams and fast currents make the use of nets impractical. There are records of it going back to 1000 B.C., and it was probably old then. As cormorants, like hawks, will not retrieve, the Chinese thought of the clever device of putting collars around the birds' thin necks so they could not swallow the fish. They also kept a string tied to the cormorant's leg so he could be pulled back after making a catch. In China, fishing with cormorants was considered a commercial venture, and only professional fishermen practiced it.

Cormorant fishing was introduced to Europe as a sport apparently at some time in the seventeenth century. Europeans manned the birds as they did hawks; the birds were trained to fly to the fist for food, were hooded (a completely unnecessary precaution), and worked free. They still had to wear their collars, but after a bird had caught a fish the cormoranter "made in" to him, calling to the bird and holding out a small minnow. When he was able to put his hands on the bird, he ran his closed hand up the bird's neck, forcing him to regurgitate the fish, and then rewarded him with the minnow, which was small enough to slip past the collar. The bird would then resume his fishing.

Cormorant fishing became popular, as it could be practiced during the summer months when hawks are molting and can't be flown. Louis XIII had a number of trained cormorants at Fontainebleau, and built a series of fishponds where the birds could fish while the king and his court watched from the bank. The birds were under charge of the Royal Keeper of Cormorants, who was still on the payroll in the eighteenth century. In England, James I had ponds built at Westminster for his cormorants and trained otters. During the last century, there was a revival of the sport both in England and in France, the French sportsmen even going so far as to dress up like Chinese mandarins for the occasion. It then disappeared again. Cormorant fishing is still practiced in Japan, although more as a tourist attraction than as a commercial enterprise.

I first tried this novel type of underwater falconry in Acapulco, Mexico, using anhingas, or (as they're sometimes called) snakebirds. Anhingas are considerably smaller than cormorants, and can't catch as big a fish; the big Oriental cormorants can catch fish weighing up to nine pounds. They can also swim faster than anhingas, but as I couldn't keep up with the anhingas I was just as glad not to start out with the bigger birds. Also, anhingas are far commoner and easier to obtain than cormorants.

Anhingas are about the size of a mallard duck, but with very long necks and thin, rapier-like beaks. Although web-footed, they have claws on the ends of their toes and can scratch like cats. A newly caught anhinga will strike for your eyes with his beak, and they are marvelously accurate. One of them got me in the left eye, and for a while I thought I'd lost the sight of that eye. Anyone working with them should wear a fencing mask until the birds are manned.

I named my pair of anhingas Mr. and Mrs. Izaak (after Izaak Walton). The female was brown, with a triangular white frontispiece, and the male was black. Later, I got another female, although the original pair preferred to work together, often helping each other land a large fish.

I put jesses, swivels, and leashes on the birds, and trained them like hawks. They manned very quickly and seemed to enjoy being handled and stroked. They were both haggards, fully adult when caught, and at first would eat only live fish that they caught themselves from a basin. Unlike hawks, they seldom "bated"; that is, they did not keep jumping off my fish to thrash desperately with open wings. After a few attempts, they accepted the situation philosophically.

Their training began in a friend's swimming pool where I liberated a number of small bait fish. The birds didn't seem to see their quarry until they dived. If I watched the fish, they seemed to be going like flashes of lightning; but when I watched the birds, the fish by comparison seemed to be poking along with weights tied to their fins. The birds swam with their long necks outstretched, their knitting-needle beaks following every twist of the quarry. They carried their big webbed feet back under their bodies and kept them moving all the time like outboard motors. They climbed out on the edge to eat their catch and always tossed the fish into the air several times before swallowing it—to make sure of getting the prey headfirst.

Getting the fish away from them was a tough proposition. The inside of an anhinga's beak is covered with fine hairlike spines, all pointing inward to help them hold a captured fish. Cormorants don't have this device. It seemed as though the birds could control the spines, erecting or flattening them at will, but possibly I am speaking only from bitterness.

The collars were equipped with tiny buckles so they could be taken off in a moment. This turned out to be very important, as some fish have a thornlike dorsal fin and the birds can't regurgitate them without tearing their throats. When either of the anhingas caught one of these stickle-backs, we simply took off the collar and the fish was swallowed.

We took the Izaaks down to the beach every afternoon, being careful to choose a bay where the water was calm and clear. Fishing with the anhingas was like falconry in fairyland. My wife and I wore diving masks and went down with the birds. We swam past towers of pink coral with purple and green seaweeds waving slowly in the crevices. Blood-red crabs scampered over the pink rocks. Schools of big turquoise angelfish swam above the coral, which was covered with vivid green algae. Occasionally we'd see a little octopus pouring itself over the rocks.

Looking up, we could see the webbed feet of the anhingas and the ripples their bodies made on the surface. Every now and then one of the birds would stick his neck underwater for a quick survey. The birds' eyes have a transparent eyelid, called the nictitating membrane, that they can lower at will and seems to serve the same purpose as diving goggles; it enables them to see underwater. Whenever they saw a school of fish they would come shooting down through the water, leaving a cloud of bubbles as the air in the feathers was forced out. Because the bird's feathers do not shed water like a duck's, the Izaaks quickly became waterlogged and would have to sit on the side of our outrigger canoe to dry out before resuming operations.

Catching fish wasn't easy for the Izaaks. All the local finny residents were smart enough to live near the coral rocks, and each fish had his own individual hole—just like a rabbit. When my wife and I were swimming around, the fish would sometimes nibble at our toes, and one little fellow who was defending his nest actually bit me on the nose. But as soon as the birds appeared, every small fish would vanish in a breath. The angelfish hung around, but they were too big for the anhingas to handle. Our birds liked something under a pound. They would occasionally grab a big fish by the tail, but it always wriggled free.

Jule and I would try to chase fish toward the birds. I had a spear that I used as a shepherd's crook to herd the fish along. Whenever we'd get one well away from the rocks, one of the Izaaks would come plunging down, leaving a trail of bubbles. The startled fish, which had just been playing with me, would streak away with the snaky-necked bird shooting after it. Sometimes Izaak would hit his victim so hard he'd harpoon it with his beak, and often he stuck his lower mandible clear through it.

Often the fish would dodge and double back. Then Mrs. Izaak came to help her husband. The birds would turn with a terrific swirl of water that often threw the fish off balance, and then one or the other of the birds would grab him. Sometimes the fish would wriggle under a stone, and Izaak would pull it out by the tail or a fin. Usually it would struggle free and escape, for Izaak wouldn't get up top speed after his initial dive.

Several times we saw the anhingas follow a fish right to the surface, where it would leap clear of the water. Occasionally it landed on the rocks in trying to avoid the birds, and flapped about while they swam around looking for it. Once, when Izaak was playing submarine, his wife was sitting on a rock, and a fish Izaak was chasing popped up beside her. Mrs. Izaak promptly swallowed it. Izaak saw his meal go and, climbing out of the water, began to bite at his wife's throat pouch and neck, following the fish on its way down to the collar. Mrs. Izaak resented this, and a fight followed, with much hissing and blowing out of throat pouches—like tiny balloons—and long beaks dabbing around with the speed of infuriated stilettos.

The best catch we ever made with the birds was in a little bay that was no more than knee-deep. A line of rocks fringed the place and, unlike the coral reefs, had no holes where fish could hide. There were many little channels, but they all came to dead ends. Schools of triangular fish would swim in long ribbons toward the beach and then shimmer out again. These small fry were just right for the anhingas. I would wade around with Izaak on my fist until I saw one of the silvery ribbons. Sometimes Izaak would see it first and jump off, making a splash that scared everything within fifty feet. The little fish were strangers in the bay, for they invariably dashed up the blind rock channels and Izaak would nail them at the end. It wasn't nearly as much fun as the deep-water fishing, but it was nice to see the poor anhingas occasionally get a fish—which seldom happened among the reefs.

We liberated the anhingas when we left Acapulco, and I thought our fishing days were over; but many years later, while in Florida with John Hamlet, we got on the subject of cormorant fishing. John had a permit to get some young cormorants from the nest, and generously allowed me to go along. I took two of the fledglings with me to Pennsylvania.

I believe my birds were a male and female; at least one was considerably bigger than the other, which with hawks would mean a difference in sex. The smaller bird was nervous and unpredictable. One moment he'd be very tame, and climb into my lap, hooking himself up with his beak like a parrot. Then without any warning he'd give me a nasty nip with his hooked beak. As his beak was always covered with fish, the wounds usually became infected. The female was shyer, and avoided me, but when she did come around she never made any attempt to bite.

I named the smaller bird Ichi, from a Japanese word meaning "the boss." When working a number of cormorants, one bird quickly establishes himself as the dominant one and keeps the others in order, and the fisherman calls him the "Ichi." The bigger bird I called Mrs. Ichi. They weighed about seven pounds, and ate enormously. Keeping their mews clean was a steady job.

When the birds would fly to my fist for food, I got some live bait and put it in our fishpond. Now I had just the reverse of the trouble with the "haggard" anhingas. These nestlings wouldn't pay any attention to live fish. They would swim right through the fish to get a piece of chum I tossed into the water. Only by alternatingly throwing in live fish with chum could I get them interested.

Like the anhingas, the cormorants could see underwater, but they didn't trust entirely to sight. When they were swimming around underwater, they could hear the sound of chum being thrown in and would swim toward the noise. If I wanted to call them, I just spanked the water with my hand.

When the birds were used to live fish, I took them down to a stream where there were plenty of small brook trout. In a wild state, cormorants don't live solely on fish. They'll take frogs, small snakes, crayfish, or anything easy to catch. My pair behaved like a couple of setter pups turned loose in a field who'd rather chase rabbits than find a covey of pheasants. All the fish automatically disappeared the instant the birds landed on the water, but the Ichis didn't care. There were plenty of frogs about, and the cormorants were willing to settle for them. But I wasn't.

I knew of a pool where a big trout hung out under the shelter of some willow roots. Though I'd never been able to make the old fellow rise to a fly, I hoped that now I had a surprise for him. I carried the birds over and put them on the bank and then moved around until I got the reflection of light on the water just right. The trout was lying under the roots, holding himself steady by little movements of his pectoral fins. I tossed a bit of bait toward him, and both birds dived after it, making the water swirl around them.

Ichi grabbed the bait and spun around underwater, heading back for me. Mrs. Ichi was about to follow him when she stopped and peered under the roots. Suddenly I saw her long neck dart in among the tangle, and there was an underwater explosion. Mrs. Ichi backed water desperately, beating with her wings and trying to brace her webbed feet against the roots for a better purchase, but she had the trout by the tail, and not even the bird's hooked beak could hold the slippery scales. The trout darted out, nearly colliding with Ichi, who'd swum back to see what was going on. Both bird and fish went downstream with the full force of the current behind them.

Mrs. Ichi took off and began to circle in the air, honking like a wild goose for her mate. I started running. The stream ran through a wood, and I made a shortcut around it. By the time I reached the other side, there was no sign of either bird. I was still whistling for them when Mrs. Ichi shot past my head in a long dive, missing me by inches. She paid no attention to me; she was looking ahead. I heard a splash as she hit the water and disappeared. From her great height above the trees, she must have seen Ichi far downstream.

I started running again, but before I could reach the place where Mrs. Ichi had landed I saw both birds swimming back upstream, their long necks stretched out and their powerful webbed feet kicking like outboard motors. Suddenly Ichi struck out. There was a white flash an inch in front of his beak as the trout did a barrel roll to avoid the blow. He must have doubled back, for both birds swerved, their torpedo-like bodies making the water churn as they spun around. Then they went downstream again.

I followed them, falling into deep holes and going up to my knees in mud. I finally saw Mrs. Ichi ahead of me, swimming around in a small pool. Every few seconds she'd stick her head underwater for a look, like a periscope in reverse. When I reached the pool, I found it was full of underwater growth, and Ichi was working back and forth through the tangle like a bird dog in thick cover. The trout must have dived into the weeds like a rabbit into a brier patch.

As I came up, the trout darted out. Ichi was deep among the plants and didn't see him, but Mrs. Ichi did. She went down in a straight plunge, using her wings underwater to shoot herself along at top speed. Ichi saw her and whirled around, meeting the trout as he doubled away from the female. Before the fish could turn again, Ichi had grabbed him, latching onto the slippery quarry with the hook on the end of his beak.

Although the trout weighed only a little more than a pound, it was all the bird could do to hold him. The fish broke away once, but the cormorant grabbed him again instantly and surfaced with the kicking fish in his mouth. Juggling him around, Ichi swallowed his catch head-first, as far as the collar would allow, and then swam ashore, Mrs. Ichi following. I retrieved the fish, and gave the birds the head and tail, first removing the collars so they could swallow.

By the end of the first week, I'd forgotten all about my dreams of sitting on a barge while the birds did the work. The cormorants could both swim and fly, and they covered a heck of a lot of ground in a short time. I had to keep them in sight, for too many unexpected accidents could happen. Once I found Mrs. Ichi almost dead after swallowing a large stickleback that she couldn't get past her collar. The spine on the fish's back had gone through her throat, and she was lying flapping on the bank, barely able to breathe. I had to race back to the car and get a pair of small pliers so I could reach down the bird's throat and snap off the spine. A few days later, I arrived just in time to keep a farmer from potting both birds with a shotgun. The cormorants had followed a trout downstream into a pool where the farmer kept some ducks and were diving among the ducks, trying to locate the fish. The ducks had never seen anything like cormorants before and were yelling their heads off. The farmer told me afterward, "I thought those things were some sort of underwater hawks."

Learning how to handle the birds turned out to be quite an art. Often I'd see a fish lying in the warm shallow water close to the bank, but I couldn't make the cormorants see it. By the time I finally got them over to the spot, the fish would be gone. But after a few days the birds began to realize that when I shouted and made a throwing motion, I wasn't doing it just for exercise, so they'd go over to investigate, keeping their heads underwater as they swam to see if anything darted back from the shallows into the deep water. I also found that although Ichi was the quicker of the two birds, his judgment wasn't to be trusted. When the cormorants came to a pool, Ichi would dart about, prodding with his beak in the likely places, and then give up if he didn't find a fish. Mrs. Ichi would take fifteen minutes to check the place. Then she'd flap her wings, wash herself, and climb out on the bank. When she did that, you could be sure there were no fish in the pool.

My birds, being nestlings, were easy to tame. They'd followed me around like pet ducks, making a gobbling noise somewhat like a turkey when they thought they weren't getting enough attention. Several times, when I had them on their perches, they managed to break the leather straps around their legs (being in water so much rotted the leather, although I kept it constantly coated with daubing), but they never tried to escape. They'd waddle to the back door and stand there gobbling for me to take them fishing. If I wasn't home, they'd go fishing on their own, flying back at sunset.

I never saw the birds dive into the water from a height after a fish, as do pelicans. Even wild cormorants seldom dive from more than ten feet or so above the water, and mine never learned the trick at all. Of course, I was using them mostly in shallow streams where high diving wasn't possible. Once underwater, however, they could swim any fish down in a straightaway race. The birds propelled themselves along with their wings to get going and then "coasted," relying on their momentum to cover the quarry. Because a cormorant's feathers are as tough and wiry as whalebone, they don't bend in the water as would those of an ordinary bird.

In a stream the advantage was with the birds, but in a deep pond the fish had the edge. The most elaborate hunt the birds made was in an old quarry after large-mouth bass. In wet weather, a little inlet full of water lilies ran from the quarry into a swamp, but the end of the inlet was closed off during a dry spell. The cormorants soon found out about the inlet and, working like a team of dogs herding sheep, would drive sunfish into the dead end and then clean up on them. The bass living in the lake would occasionally be caught in these drives, but they had enough sense to double back before reaching the inlet, and the birds were so intent on the sunnies that they let the bigger fish go. But one afternoon they got a bass cornered. He was forced into the inlet with both birds blocking the entrance.

Bass for supper, I thought, but the fish, once he realized that he was trapped, turned and went right for the birds. The cormorants were wing to wing, waiting for him, and he didn't have the chance of a cat locked in a telephone booth with two bull terriers. The fish swerved, as though to dodge, and then suddenly jumped clear of the water over the backs of the startled birds. They tried to turn, their beaks snapping like rattraps as they struck at him in midair, but they got in each other's way and the fish reached the open water. He made a crash dive and headed for the water-lily stalks at full speed, with the cormorants plunging down after him.

The fish swerved back and forth among the thin stems like a skier going between poles, but the birds followed just as expertly until the bass reached deep water. Neither fish nor birds seemed able to swim straight downward; both descended in a series of circles. If only one cormorant had been after him, the fish would have gotten away, but the birds separated, so when the bass was avoiding one in his series of descending rings, he encountered the other. Ichi finally managed to grab the fish with the hooked end of his beak and bring him to the surface.

The birds were so tame that I allowed them to swim free on our pond with our ducks and geese. They would come up to the house every evening to be fed, and my only concern was what to do when the pond froze over in winter. But one morning Mrs. Ichi took off from the pond, and flying in a series of great circles, rose gradually out of sight and never came back. A few weeks later, Ichi did the same. I expected them to return, but they never did. I think and hope they are now back in Florida with their friends and relations.

The most entertaining of all fishermen is an otter. Ernest Thompson Seton says: "On watching a gamboling fox cub, a fawn or an ocelot, one is apt to be carried away and declare each in turn the most beautiful and graceful creature ever seen, but it is the otter that stands out as the most beautiful and engaging of all elegant pets. There seems no end to its fun, its energy, its drollery, its good-nature and its postures of new and surprising beauty." I might mention they've also got big teeth, and a tendency to use them.

Otters are aquatic weasels. They are remarkably active. Although always found near water, they often go ten miles in a single night. They can stay two minutes underwater, and Izaak Walton thought they were a species of fish. They are monogamous, the pairs staying together and fish-ing as a team, one driving fish to the other. The dog (male) otter may reach thirty pounds, and is a terrible fighter. A single otter can lick two seventy-five pound otter hounds. In Wales, an otter killed a famous otter hound named Beauty by fastening onto her nose and dragging her underwater. The Welsh still put flowers on the hound's grave. Curiously, an otter is not a powerful swimmer. Although he can go very fast down-stream, he can't swim upstream any faster than a hound. Young otters can't swim naturally; the mother has to teach them, and it often takes them three weeks to learn the trick.

Like cormorant fishing, otter training was first developed in China. Friar Odoric reported it in 1513, saying: "They fish by means of another fish called a diver. They keep it by a cord attached to a fine collar. It has a muzzle and neck like a fox, forepaws like a dog, hind feet like a duck and the body of a fish. It dives into the water and I swear in less than two hours it had filled two big baskets, always depositing the fish in the baskets."

A Chinese observer named Chang Tsu wrote that a fisherman would no more be without an otter than a hunter without a dog. Swinhoe saw a trained otter in China driving fish into nets for fishermen. When the net was lifted, the otter rode up on the top and then sat in the bow of the boat until his services were again needed.

At some time in the sixteenth century otter training was introduced into Europe. In Sweden, whole families were supported by a trained otter, fishermen selling their nets and tackle as unnecessary. Oliver Goldsmith says he saw an otter so perfectly trained that it would corner a school of fish in a pool and pick out any one that his master indicated. As late as 1880, otters were so frequently used by poachers to catch salmon that it became illegal to tame them, and so the sport died.

One year, while in Florida, I ran into a fisherman living on the edge of a cypress swamp who owned a pet baby otter. No sooner had I laid eyes on that otter than I was a gone gosling. Seton hadn't told the half of it. This otter was tamer than any dog. You couldn't sit down but what he'd climb into your lap, turn over on his back, and lie there sucking the end of his tail like a baby sucking his thumb, looking up with eyes full of limpid devotion. He went in swimming with the fisherman's children, frolicking like a porpoise, and went gallumphing after them when they ran back to the house, his long body humping up and down like a delirious inchworm as he strove to keep up. He ate his meals with the family, had his own plate, and slept curled up with the baby.

To my surprise the fisherman was quite willing to sell him for $100. Somewhat doubtfully I asked if the children wouldn't miss him. "Sure will," piped up one of the kids. "Pa said as soon as he was full growed we could skin him out and the pelt 'ud be worth $30 easy." When you're as poor as that family was, there isn't much room for sentiment. I bought Ottie, decoying him into the car with some hamburger. By the time I got back to the tourist court where my wife and I were staying, the back of the car looked as though it had been hit by a hurricane carrying a switchblade knife. Bits of the hamburger had got down behind the seats, and Ottie had dug them out, whistling and snorting as he ripped open the genuine leather covers and exploring the interior stuffings.

For the trip north, we constructed a special heavy-duty cage for Ottie, got him in with some food, and started for Pennsylvania. As we drove, Ottie cried so pitifully that Jule finally let him out of the cage. Ottie hung out the window, happily drinking in the wind, while Jule kept a firm hold on his tail, for he showed a tendency to jump out whenever the scenery looked interesting. After an hour or so, Ottie got bored with this recreation and began examining the car. The driving became a nightmare. Ottie was convinced that the buttons on the dashboard were eatable, and no amount of experimentation could disillusion him. He worked out an uproarious game that consisted of taking a flying leap from the rear seat and landing on top of my head. He crawled under the seats, managed to get himself caught, and then cried like a baby until we stopped and extricated him. Although his hind feet were webbed, he could use his front feet like a monkey, and took everything apart he could find. Finally we managed to get him back in his cage, where he moaned and wailed until a lady in a passing car screamed at us that if we didn't stop beating that child she'd call the police.

Ottie was hardly the perfect house pet. He went through the house like an unguided missile, took baths in the toilets, and then dried himself on the pillows. He climbed all over us, the table, and the food during meals. If you tried to sit down with a drink, he'd reach into the glass after the ice cubes, which he loved to eat. Jule tried to housebreak him with a small box of sand. Ottie would rush up to the box, put his forefeet on the edge, and then let go on the outside. Afterward he would run to us for approval, evidently thinking he had done everything expected of him. He loved playing with Tilly, our Cairn terrier, and the two of them would go rocketing through the house, leaving destruction in their wake. Finally we had to exile him to an outdoor pen. As otters can dig, climb, and bite through ordinary chicken wire, construction of a pen that would hold him was a major project.

I set about trying to train him. Ottie quickly learned to retrieve, although he was erratic about it. He would retrieve sticks and a celluloid boat we threw in our pond, but he always regarded the whole business as a game, and sometimes he just didn't want to play.

Getting him to retrieve a fish or dead bird was something else again. Ottie much preferred to eat the quarry, although after he was full he would usually retrieve it for fun. A Victorian otter trainer named Captain Salvin suggests, "If an otter persists in eating the fish he catches, give him a red hot one," although how you're going to do this the captain doesn't explain. The captain also says that a trained otter should always be kept on a collar and lead when he isn't actually fishing. I tried just once to get a collar on Ottie. I didn't repeat the experiment.

Like the cormorants, it was difficult to get Ottie to concentrate on fish. He preferred a mixed bag of frogs, crayfish, tadpoles, and even mud turtles, although he could make no impression on their shells. He caught his first fish by accident.

We were going along the banks of a stream and ran into mudbanks that took me over my knees at every step. Ottie, however, had no difficulty. When he came to a particularly bad place, he just lay on his stomach and slid along. He made better time sliding than he did walking. He used his tail for propulsion, and shot over the mud like a toboggan over soft snow.

Suddenly there was frantic splashing ahead. An eight-inch trout had been basking in the warm shallow water and was now trying desperately to reach the pond. Ottie took one look, gave a mighty push with his tail, and went flying over the mud. He shot into the water, and vanished.

I could follow his progress by a string of bubbles that rose to the surface, two by two in a perfectly placed series. Then the chain stopped, as though Ottie had paused to locate his quarry. The trout was also in deep water now, but Ottie was between him and the pool.

The water swirled as Ottie made his rush. Then the whole surface boiled as though two submarines were chasing each other. Ottie surfaced, the current surging around his chest as he treaded water. He'd got a mouthful of eelgrass, which he indignantly spat out. Then he dived again. Another commotion, and the trout flickered past me with the torpedo-like body of the otter on his tail.

If the trout had kept straight on into the pond, he would have escaped, but he tried to hide under the shelving bank. Ottie spotted him. The otter was in shallow water and lay stretched full out. So slowly that he hardly seemed to move, he began to move toward the fish, pushing himself along with his tail and an occasional motion of his forepaws. It was almost like watching a cat stalking a bird.

Suddenly Ottie arched his back and snapped himself forward. The motion was so swift and unexpected that he was under the bank before I realized that he'd left the mud flat. There was an explosion, and then I saw Ottie holding the trout with his forepaws, not with his teeth, as I'd expected. But a second later Ottie had killed the fish with a quick bite in the head and was towing him ashore.

According to Captain Salvin, the owner must now "approach the otter quietly, and taking hold of its long, strong tail, hold him with one hand while extracting the fish with the other, a move that calls for considerable dexterity."

Captain Salvin wasn't just whistling "Rule Britannia" when he said getting a fish away from an otter requires dexterity. Ottie hissed, snarled, grunted, and hung onto that fish with both forepaws and his jaws. At last I decided to let him keep that fish. It was his first catch, and he obviously wanted it more than I did.

In winter, I tried Ottie as a retriever. I knew he was interested in ducks. He'd managed to catch a couple of teal that had landed on our pond by stalking them and then making a quick rush. Curiously, he never bothered our domestic mallards and Moscovies, seeming to know they were members of the family. I thought Ottie would be the perfect retriever. He could run over thin ice, crawl through places impossible for a dog, and no winged duck could escape him by diving. Some diving ducks, when injured, will swim to the bottom of a pond and hold onto weeds. They're safe from a dog, but Ottie could follow them down.

A friend of mine was to do the shooting, as I suspected that keeping track of Ottie would take all my time. The blind was built on the edge of an old quarry where passing blacks and mallards often pitched as they traded back and forth between the river and the Chesapeake swamps. We were in the blind before dawn, with Ottie in a cage, because I knew that left to himself he'd play about in the quarry and no ducks would come in.

The moon was still out as we settled ourselves in the blind, and the distant edges of the quarry were swathed in light mist like the dry-ice fog used in murder-mystery movies. There was no wind, and the black water lay unrippled below us. My friend went out to set the decoys, the fine scum of ice along the edge crackling as he waded out in his hip boots.

We saw ducks passing high above us on their way to the swamps, but none dropped. Ottie was beginning to wake up now, and whine to be let out, but I didn't dare to open the cage as yet. The sun was high enough now to turn the glass eyes of the decoys red, and in a few minutes the birds should be coming in.

Over the blind came the quick whistle of wings. Hardly daring to move, I managed to glance out a small opening in the back of the blind. I caught a quick flash of passing red-legged blacks. They swung in low over the quarry, but at the last moment rose and circled again. Another whisper of wings and they came in again, this time bracing with their wings, their feet forward. As they drifted down, my friend stood up and fired quickly, left and right.

One duck folded in midair and crashed down on the thin ice. As the rest veered away, I saw another bird volplane down toward the open water. He landed with a heavy splash, dived, and then vanished among the dark shadows along the bank.

The dead duck lay like a black bundle on the ice. "A bad job for a dog," said my friend, reloading. "Let's see what your otter will do."

I let Ottie out and tossed a stone toward the quarry. Ottie rushed after it, rolled the stone over, and then went down toward the water. He saw the dead duck immediately and, after studying the situation, started across the ice. He broke through, pulled himself out, circled the quarry until he found stronger ice and then cautiously slid out over it. By spreading himself flat as a rug and shoving with his tail, he managed to reach the duck. After smelling it suspiciously, he started back shoving the duck ahead of him. Up the bank he came, looking like a miniature black Labrador, lifting the dead bird high above the frozen grass.

Getting the duck away from him wasn't as hard as I'd expected. Ottie seemed more curious than hungry. I sent him back for the winged bird.

Ottie swam around for a while before he decided to investigate the far bank of the quarry. He disappeared in the shadows, and then came a wild quacking mingled with splashes and the flapping of wings. The duck swam out with Ottie after him. Ottie paused and then dived. The duck continued swimming around, and suddenly vanished with a loud squawk. There was no sign of either of them for several seconds, and then Ottie appeared by the bank with the dead bird in his mouth.

Ottie retrieved several ducks that morning, always bringing them back underwater. Apparently he found it easier that way. He soon learned that when a gun went off, there was a dead duck somewhere about, and he'd dash down to the quarry after it. Unfortunately, my friend sometimes missed, and then it was impossible to convince Ottie that a mistake had been made. He'd scour every foot of the quarry looking for the duck, and my whistles and calls made no impression on him.

At one time, there were probably over 600,000 otters in North America. Today, there are probably less than 100,000. They have been killed not only for their fur but also because fishermen believe that they kill large numbers of game fish. If Ottie is any criterion, no otter is going to strain himself chasing game fish if he can find frogs and crayfish. As otters breed only once a year, and seldom have more than two young, they don't increase rapidly in numbers and can't stand much trapping. They certainly are among the most intelligent of wild animals and possibly the only wild animal that continues to be frolicsome and playful after they are full grown. Perhaps E. T. Seton wasn't so far wrong in his tribute to the otter after all.

CHAPTER 11

Steel in the Surf

Harpooning is more sportsmanlike than line fishing because the fish has as much chance to catch you as you have to catch the fish. For even fish that are not generally considered "gamy" may drown the fisherman or at least bite off a leg. Most big-game fishermen think that a marlin gives more sport on the end of a line than an octopus, but these gentlemen have never tried letting an octopus get a tentacle around their necks while they are underwater. Many of our aquatic friends have capabilities little suspected by people who have never tried sticking spears into them.

There are almost as many different types of harpooning as there are of line fishing. For fish weighing several tons, there is the thrown harpoon with a detachable head secured to a heavy line. For shallow water, a light, stabbing spear is often preferred. Skin divers usually like a steel spear discharged from a gun. Octopus hunters use a hook on the end of a long pole, and night fishermen stick to the ancient trident. Harpooning is more like hunting than ordinary fishing, and requires more action. Often when you are trying to sneak up on a fish with a spear, there is a bigger fish trying to sneak up on you. This adds an element of uncertainty that keeps things interesting.

The first principle of harpooning is not to spear anything bigger than you are—unless you can get out of the way afterward. I discovered this rule while trying to harpoon sharks near Acapulco on the Pacific coast of southern Mexico.

About fifty miles north of the town, the native fishermen wade out into the creamy surf and harpoon sharks as they rush in on the waves. The undercurrents are so strong that often a harpooner will be fouled by his own line flung back on him by the surf. Before the man can cut himself loose, the backwash has tied him and the shark together and carried them both out to sea. Then his friends grab the line and start to haul it in. Sometimes they bring up the fisherman and sometimes the shark. It's a wonderful sport.

Shark harpooning is seasonal. A few miles north of Acapulco begins a great fresh-water lagoon that runs for miles and is separated from the ocean only by a bar of white sand. Once a year after the rainy season this lagoon breaks through the bar and flows into the sea. Thousands of bass, cabezudo (mullet) and trout are swept into the salt water. Sharks collect like wolves around a broken sheepfold. This is the moment for the harpooner.

Along this section of the coast, breakers fifteen and twenty feet high come rolling in. Standing on the beach, the harpooner can see fish swimming in these perpendicular sections of ocean as though he were looking into an aquarium. When the black dorsal of a shark cuts the edge of the breaker like a knife sticking through melon, the harpooner wades out to meet the wave.

To be struck by the full force of one of those breakers would mean death. The system is to time your rush so that you can throw your harpoon and get back again before a wave breaks. If you miscalculate, you'll certainly lose your harpoon and possibly your life. A friend of mine who tried to hang onto his harpoon after he was caught in a breaker couldn't use his right arm again for ten days.

You spot a shark's triangular fin in an oncoming wave, and you run down the beach until you're opposite the point where the shark will be after the wave breaks. When the overhanging green wall has burst into a mass of soapsuds twenty feet broad, you wade out into the seething boil with your harpoon ready.

Suddenly the black fin rises above the white swirl. It may be a hundred yards away or it may be beside you. Not infrequently men have felt the sandpaper skin of the shark brush their legs while they were waiting for the fin to appear. When the fin shows, you force your way toward it through a swirl of water up to your chest. As the water is as opaque as milk, there is always a chance you may step on another shark.

Suddenly the foam rushes shoreward. The water abruptly clears. Below the black fin you can see the white shine of the shark. It is snapping at the terrified bass that are swirling around in the ocean currents. You hurl the harpoon. At the same moment, you start running for the beach, letting the loops of line hanging over your left arm pay off as the wounded fish thrashes toward the open sea. If the next wave breaks before you can reach the shore, the force of the water will probably carry the injured shark out to sea so rapidly that you cannot hold him. I have seen a harpooned shark that must have been at least fifteen feet long vanish in a torrent of foam and reappear almost instantly a hundred yards down the beach with the harpoon still sticking in him. The harpooner had to drop the line to keep himself from being carried down the shore with his catch. The undercurrents following a breaking wave are so swift and uncertain that a man may start to run for shore after throwing his harpoon and trip over the injured shark, which has been sucked between him and the beach.

Any time that I'm standing up to my waist in water harpooning a shark, I want to know where the shark is, but because of the terrific surf I might be standing in two feet of water one moment and the next second I'd be swimming for my life. I waded out to photograph one big shark that had taken the harpoon in his head. I took a shot at a nice safe distance and then started back just as a wave broke. The next instant the shark and I were thrashing about in ten feet of water, his tail beating against my camera and both of us tied together with the harpoon line. His big jaws opened and closed beside me and I could count his banks of teeth. Every time I tried to get away, I jerked him closer. My friend on the beach shouted hopefully, "Don't worry! He isn't a man-eater." He was probably right. He knew a lot about sharks, which is why he didn't go in wading with them. But I didn't want to have an arm or leg snapped off, even if the shark realized his mistake and spat it out afterward. Finally an Indian fisherman waded out and said he'd cut me and the shark apart if I'd pay for the harpoon head. I said I would. Harpoon heads cost $2.85, but I considered that one cheap at double the price.

Unless you take harpooning really seriously and start looking for whales, the biggest sea animal you are likely to spear is a manta ray. These gigantic creatures look somewhat like a barn door and weigh about half a ton. The manta has two stubby tentacles he uses to sweep food into his big mouth. When a ray grabs anything in these tentacles, he gets panicky and won't let go. There have been cases of rays grabbing the anchor chains of small boats and dragging them miles out to sea before the crew could cut through the chain. Harpooning a manta from a thirty-foot launch is no more exciting than shooting a cow from a truck, but try spearing one from a light native dugout.

I started out early one morning with two young Indian fishermen to look for "batfish," as the huge rays are called. In order for one to see the shadow of a ray swimming close to the surface, the sun must just be rising. We paddled along about a quarter of a mile offshore, watching the rounded tops of the swells for a ray's wing to break surface. The harpoon was laid across the bow with the line carefully coiled in a bucket to keep it from fouling anyone. Occasionally, men have carelessly put one foot in the center of the coiled line just as the ray started to run with it. They never repeated the experience.

Usually rays float near the surface, basking in the warm top water, occasionally lifting one of their vast wings in a lazy stretch. We had drifted uncomfortably close to the breaker line when the boatman shouted. A dozen yards ahead, on the side of a swell, we could see what seemed to be the reflection of a big cloud. We lost sight of the ray as the next swell rose to meet us. There are no landmarks on water, so as we slid down the other side of the swell we could not definitely locate the spot where we'd seen the ray. The harpooner stood up in the bow with his iron in his hand. The boatman moved the dugout slowly forward. We were all watching the water.

The tip of the ray's wing broke water about ten feet from the side of the dugout. The boatman started to swing the bow around when the ray's right wing appeared on our other side. "We're over him!" shouted the harpooner, and drove his iron straight downward. If he'd asked me, I could have told him right then this would be a mistake.

Suddenly the whole ocean exploded. The handle of the harpoon flew over our heads. The dugout was jerked over on her side and started to ship water. Spray poured over us. The harpoon line leaped overboard so fast that the coils didn't have time to straighten out. Both Indians were yelling, "Where's the manta?" and it was a good question, as a ray occasionally leaps clear out of the water and comes down on top of a boat.

The harpooner managed to take a turn with the harpoon line around a crude stanchion in the bow while the boatman swung the dugout around to head toward the ray. I pulled out an oarlock and tried to force the taut harpoon line into a groove cut in the bow that acted as a fairlead, but the ray had the line pulled so tight against the gunwale that I couldn't budge it. Then the big fish stopped and began to thrash around, bringing his wings down on the water with reports like a shotgun fired off in a tunnel.

The harpooner said, "Do you want to see me jump on his back?"

I said, "Are you kidding?"

"He'll never die with only one harpoon in him. I'll stab him in the head." He pulled off his shirt and pants, picked up a bait knife, and dived expertly overboard. Putting the knife between his teeth, he swam behind the big fish and trod water until the ray stopped trying to throw the harpoon head. Then the man gave a quick kick and, grabbing the ray by the head, pulled himself up on the broad back. He stabbed three times before the ray sounded. In a moment the fish surfaced again and seemed to be trying to scrape the man off with its wings. Suddenly the Indian gave a yell of agony.

I thought the ray had broken the man's back with its blows, and so did the boatman, for he brought the dugout in as close as he dared. The harpooner slipped off the ray's back and swam toward us painfully. When we pulled him into the dugout, his chest, belly, and legs were covered with bood. The ray's file-like skin had torn him every time the fish moved. The ray struggled feebly a few times and then began to sink. We paddled over to him and found that the fish measured eighteen feet across.

For several weeks I had been trying to find an Indian who would take me out torch fishing for *agujón,* or "daggerfish." The fishermen never let me go with them because they claimed it gave Acapulco a bad name to have Americans get killed there. Daggerfish are greenish eel-like creatures with long alligator jaws. You can always tell a daggerfish harpooner because he is covered with ugly, pucker-mouthed scars. Agujón fishing is done at night with the aid of a torch, so it's a spooky business.

At least two men were killed by daggerfish that summer. One man was stabbed through the throat by the agujón's beak as the fish leaped at his light. The other had a daggerfish impale him through the eye. The fish's beak was so deeply imbedded in his skull that he had trouble working the jaws loose. He bled to death before he could reach shore.

Finally one fisherman agreed to take me out if I would promise to spend the whole trip lying flat in the bottom of the canoe. "Sometimes there are five or six jumping at the light at the same time," he explained. "While you're watching one, two others stab you in the back. It doesn't hurt so much at the time, but when the doctors start cutting the beaks out of you afterward, that's really painful."

He selected a moonless night so that the fish would not be distracted by any light except the glare of his torch. The water had the smooth sheen of ink as we paddled out into the silent bay, and the paddles made little whirlpools of ghostly phosphorescence. Ahead, I could hear the suck of surf on a pile of coral rocks.

We began to pass blobs of hardened foam as big as powderpuffs. The fisherman stood up to light his fatwood torch. "This is where the agujón live," he told me. He picked up his three-pointed spear and stood with the blazing torch in his left hand while his son paddled the canoe. Sparks from the torch spluttered in the ebony water and popped over our hair and clothes.

Suddenly there was a splash near the canoe, and something like a fat arrow sailed over us. I saw the daggerfish hit the water twenty feet away and go skipping off over the surface like a skimmed stone. Right alongside the canoe I saw floating a long, thin shape. The fisherman struck with his trident. There was a moment of wild thrashing, and then he lifted up a writhing, open-mouthed monster four feet long. He dropped it into the boat. The tooth-studded jaws were almost as long as the fish's body. The boatman dropped his paddle and brained the fish with a club as the jaws bit madly at the seats and frames.

As I bent over to examine the weird beast, the fisherman grabbed my shoulder and jerked me into the bottom of the canoe. A fish flashed over us, and a drop of water from the flickering tail hit my neck. I sat up, and the fisherman promptly pulled me flat again. Another daggerfish ten feet ahead of the canoe came shooting at us. He passed over our heads and landed near the stern. A puddle of phosphorus flashed up in the water where he struck, and remained glowing like a beacon light.

As we came around, I could see the agujón tremble slightly and turn to face the light. "He's going to jump for you," said the son dispassionately. The fisherman drew back his trident as the daggerfish bounded up like a released spring. The harpooner knocked him back with the trident and then stabbed him through the body. The agujón bent like a snake and bit the spear handle, his teeth grating on the tough wood. A blow from the club finished him.

We got four more daggerfish in an hour. I asked the fisherman if he'd ever been stabbed by them. "Only three times," he told me. "Twice through my left arm that holds the torch and once through the chest."

He showed me the scars. He did not believe that the fish jumped directly at the light. He thought that they flung themselves wildly in any direction to escape.

The greatest of all harpooning is skin diving with a face mask. Without the mask the underwater scenery is a blur of colors and flashing shapes, but with the mask everything springs into focus. Fish more beautiful than hummingbirds and with stranger shapes than a drunk's dream hurry past. Once while I was stalking a two-foot red snapper, more brilliant than a goldfish, I felt a curious nibbling at my toes. A tiny iridescent fish scarcely two inches long had a nest of minute eggs on a rock, and my clumsy foot was scraping past them. The little mother was bravely defending her home and doing her best to drive me away.

The weirdest creature in this aquatic world is the octopus. I've been told that octopuses aren't very intelligent; if so, they go a long way on instinct. Watching an octopus stalk a crab is about as grisly a sight as I ever want to see. First, the octopus turns the same color as the bottom, which in itself is quite a stunt. Usually the unsuspecting crab is feeding in a foot or so of water. The octopus creeps toward him, allowing his spongy body to be washed back and forth by the tide as though he were a jellyfish. Finally he gets within range. Gathering himself together, he suddenly bounds forward, his arms shooting out like a fan. If he lands on top of the crab, he envelops his victim as though trying to smother him. Actually, he is working the struggling crab into position so his parrotlike beak can go to work on it. If the crab manages to break away, the tentacles go whipping out, trip the crab up, and the octopus makes another bound. I never saw the crab win.

The Acapulco octopuses grow to be about a yard across, not big enough to be very impressive but strong enough to hold a man underwater until he stops blowing bubbles. The tool for octopus hunting is a big fishhook firmly wired onto the end of a light iron rod about two feet long. You swim along the rockiest part of the shoreline until you see a little pile of crab claws or clamshells near a hole in the boulders. Then you swim down and look inside. You will probably see either a tangle of tentacles that look like a mass of seaweed or a dead eye regarding you out of a slick black mass. That's the octopus.

A few individuals have tried reaching in and pulling the octopus out by brute force. This is a very poor system, as the octopus can pull harder than you can and he has a habit of grabbing your arm and hanging on.

Terriers for hunting
wild badger are
bred for brains and
gameness

The bola is a
deceptively simple-
looking device

A gaucho in the Argentine shows how to swing a bola (Panagra Photo)

ABOVE: Jule Mannix fishing with the two anhingas, Mr. and Mrs. Izaak, at Acapulco, Mexico

LEFT: One of the cormorants trained by Dan Mannix for fishing

Handling cormorants is an art

Ottie, the Mannixes' trained
hunting otter, was keenly
interested in ducks

Because you can't breathe, he has only to hold on for a couple of minutes to get the decision.

The correct method is to reach in with your hook and give one quick jerk. If he won't come that first pull, he probably won't come at all. Sometimes an octopus will let go of the rocks to grab the hook and try to smother it as though it were a crab, and then you can bring him to the surface, clinging to the iron like a limpet. But so long as he keeps his tentacles fastened to a rock, even a small octopus can outpull a gorilla. The power in the tentacles is amazing. An Indian boy offered to pose for me with a little two-foot octopus on his shoulder. The creature suddenly clamped down on him, and he had a sore back for a fortnight.

Someday I hope to spend a few weeks traveling by canoe through the great system of lagoons and fresh-water inlets that surround Acapulco. These waterways contain everything from twenty-foot crocodiles to giant manatees. An Indian told me he had once seen a huge creature that looked like a sea horse but was as big as a Percheron swimming in one of the bays. I had just finished telling him that there is a giant squid thirty feet long hanging in the American Museum of Natural History in New York, and I thought he was trying to go me one better. Later, I found that the skeleton of a gigantic, sea-horse-like creature is actually preserved in Mexico City. The bones were found near Acapulco. I'll never again doubt stories Acapulco fishermen tell me about the ones that got away.

In the last few years, a new sort of fishing has developed that combines sports with a certain amount of profit—if you're lucky and skillful. Perhaps 20,000 people in America are experimenting with salt-water aquariums. Keeping salt-water fish is just about the most complicated hobby going, but the satisfaction of having a segment of coral reef in your living room with a pair of brilliant sapphire-and-turquoise Beau Gregory, a school of tiny sea horses, and perhaps a cheerful little porcupine fish that will feed from your fingers, seems to make up for all the cost and trouble. Until the knack of breeding these temperamental imports from the ocean is found, fanciers have to catch their own fish or rely on professional fish collectors. Nearly all the varieties suitable for home aquariums must be caught by skin diving with hand nets. Seines can't be used among the coral heads; hooks would injure the fish; and most of the more valuable types won't enter the baited traps, designed somewhat like a wire rattrap, that are occasionally effective.

Catching the tiny, iridescent salt-water tropicals can be dangerous. Russ Renand, a lean, wiry man in his forties who makes his living catching fish for fanciers, was swimming face downward over a Bahama reef when he saw a tiny flicker of color eighteen feet below him. That bright flicker might be a queen angel (worth $20) or a jewel fish ($25) or even a royal gramma for which any hobbyist would gladly pay $40. Russ was wearing a face mask and had rubber swim fins on his feet. He shot the air out of his lungs and dived. It was nearly his last dive.

The fish turned out to be a little blue angel, worth about $12 but still a good catch. In one hand Russ held a white net that he would use to drive the fish into the black net he carried in the other hand, but as he sped toward the fish the angel darted into a hole in the reef. Russ did not dare to put his net in the hole. The unyielding wire frame might push the valuable little angel against the sharp coral points and injure him. Instead, Russ put in his hand. Instantly he felt something grab him by the wrist.

"I knew at once it was a moray eel," Russ told me while we were discussing fish collecting in his Miami home. "Morays have fine, needle-sharp teeth and live in holes in the reefs. They get to be about six feet long and are as thick around as a man's thigh. I had enough air in my lungs for only a few more seconds, and the surface of the water seemed a mile away. I managed to brace myself against the coral, and pulled the eel's head out of the hole. Then I hit him as hard as I could with the wire frame of my net. The second or third crack he let go and I went for the surface. I still carry the scars."

Experiences like this keep the price of salt-water tropicals high; but as Russ Renand told me: "I took a man out with me who'd been complaining about my prices so he could catch his own fish. The first time he went down, a barracuda made a pass at him. He went flying out of the water and into the boat and refused to go down again. Later he told me, 'Russ, you could charge me $100 apiece for those fish and I'd say you earned it.'"

In spite of this, Russ Renand, like all the fish collectors with whom I spoke, gives a disgusted laugh at the idea of the job being particularly hazardous. Time after time I was told, "You don't worry about yourself —you worry about getting those fish back alive." A cake of ice in a blast furnace is a stable commodity compared to a cargo of live fish. The tanks in which the fish are kept must be constantly aerated and fresh sea water pumped in; if the pumps' batteries go dead, the whole catch is lost. An extremely hot spell, a storm that keeps the boat at sea for a few extra days, even anchoring in a choppy sea where the constant swishing of the water in the tanks makes fish used to the comparative quiet of the depths "seasick," can mean a 100 percent loss.

The collector must also know his fish. If he makes the mistake of putting a sargassum in with a load of demoiselles and cardinals, he will find himself with nothing but one very fat sargassum, even though the sargassum is only half the size of the others. A sargassum is equipped with a huge mouth plus a distensible stomach, and can engulf a fish two or three times his own size. Then there's the spotted-trunk fish that exudes poison when alarmed which can kill all the other fish in the tank. Sometimes the fragile little butterfly fish faint from terror, lose control of their gills, and drown. They must be kept in the dark to quiet their delicate nerves.

Not even the most experienced collectors are immune from disaster. Captain William B. Gray, a collector for the gigantic Seaquarium in Miami who does a $10,000-a-year business catching fish for private collectors, has collected fish in the Bahamas, Galápagos, and the South Pacific. Captain Gray told me, "Once I'd been collecting hard all day along the reefs and when night came, I went inshore and anchored for a few hours' sleep. I checked the pumps that keep fresh water from the sea circulating in the tanks, and went to bed. When I got up the next morning, all my fish were dead. I'd anchored near the mouth of a stream running into the ocean. It changed the salinity and pH (hydrogen ion content) of the water enough to kill my catch."

Competition between the fish collectors has led to "fish wars." Captain Gray uses fish traps to catch some of the hardier types of fish, and several times he has found his buoys cut and the traps missing. Even in the wholesale market there has been keen competition. One dealer decided to corner the market on lionfish, possibly the most spectacular of all the salt-water fish. The lionfish has reddish-brown markings fringed with white against a light-pink background and is covered with flowing fins somewhat like those of a veiltail goldfish. The dealer offered $150 each for these fish, bought in all on the market, and then upped the price to $200. The lionfish is hard to obtain, particularly as the fish has a row of long spines that secrete a poison as deadly as the venom of a rattlesnake, so the dealer felt that his monopoly would be hard to break. But for $200 a fish, collectors will take considerable risks, and within a few months the market was so flooded with lionfish that the price dropped to $25. It has now been stabilized at about double that figure.

The risks collectors will take to obtain a rare fish are incredible to anyone who hasn't been bitten by the fish bug. The Portuguese man-o'-war fish is a tiny blue-and-white fellow that makes his home among the trailing twenty-foot tentacles of the man-o'-war jellyfish. These jellyfish float on the surface of the water like multicolored globules blown from bubble gum, and their tentacles possess a venom so virulent that, as one collector described it, "It knots up your muscles as though you'd gotten an electric shock." To capture the minute fish, a collector has to insert a small hand net among the writhing mass of deadly tentacles and catch the little fish as they dodge about. Pulling the jellyfish out of water does no good, as then the fish simply scatter in all directions.

Octopus are fairly easy to catch but hard to keep alive. When excited, they squirt ink into the water, and then the whole tank has to be emptied and cleaned. The instant you put the octopus in again, he's likely to do the same thing. Another great problem with octopus is keeping them confined in an aquarium. Even an octopus no bigger than a man's fist has enormous lifting powers. Bob Straughan, owner of the Coral Reef Exhibit in Miami, had a baby octopus that lifted a heavy piece of plate-glass covering his aquarium with a twenty-pound hunk of coral on it. "Then when he got out and found where he was, he died of fright," Bob said bitterly.

An octopus can stay out of water for some time, and if the cover of his aquarium isn't clamped down he will go wandering about the house, generally causing considerable excitement. Being virtually boneless, an octopus two feet in diameter can slither through a half-inch crack under a door, so you never know where he'll appear. A California salt-water fish enthusiast had to give up keeping his octopus when the animal strolled across the living-room floor while his wife was giving a bridge party.

Perhaps the biggest collector of salt-water fish in America is Emil Hanson, who often spends several weeks by himself cruising off the Bahamas and Florida keys after his quarry. Emil has a twenty-eight-foot boat with a large tank holding several hundred gallons and two small skiffs. He values his outfit at about $15,000—"plus my own experience," he adds.

After stocking up with gas, food, fuel for the stove, extra batteries for the pumps, and ice, Emil starts off. When he reaches the reefs, he uses a glass-bottom box to study the underwater terrain. Different types of reefs mean different fish. Rocky coral growths, especially staghorn, mean angel and butterfly fish. Jewel fish are found only on the outer reefs at twenty-foot depths or more, while the curious little highhats prefer shallow, constantly moving water. For his diving, Emil usually uses a Desco with a seventy-five-foot length of hose. "Don't forget, it often takes half to three-quarters of an hour to get one fish," he reminded me. "With an Aqua-lung, just about the time you're ready to get the fish, you're likely to run out of air." Emil considers old wrecks good hunting spots, but dangerous. "Once the wind shifted while I was in a wreck using the Desco, and my tube got flooded. I nearly passed out before I could surface."

A collector has to be able to outguess the fish. Angels usually swim upcurrent to escape. Blueheads make big circles. Others will head for silty water or dart for their holes. While chasing them, the collector must remember not to touch fire coral, which burns like acid, and avoid the deadly red sponges. "If you brush one of them, you can hear your flesh hiss even underwater." Then there are sea urchins with quills like porcu-pines and the innocent-looking scorpion fish with his poisonous spines. Like most collectors, Emil doesn't bother about sharks. "I've had sharks charge and come so close I could feel the water push against me, but they always turned aside at the last moment."

Keeping salt-water fish has become so popular that conservationists are concerned that the demand will put too heavy a strain on some of the rare varieties. On the West Coast, certain rare fish are even protected by law. Perhaps the best-known West Coast collector is Donald Simpson, who captures rare fish both as a hobby and a business. Don is a lean, wiry man who has collected everything from cutthroat trout to sharks. Mrs. Simpson, his pretty, lively wife, generally accompanies her husband on his trips, which may take them anywhere from Oregon to southern Mexico. The Simpsons travel in a light truck equipped with an air pump to aerate the huge, seventy-five-gallon tanks that fill the back. While Don drives, Mrs. Simpson sits in the back, giving her husband minute-to-minute bulletins on the health of their catch.

Before starting out on a collecting trip, the Simpsons consult a govern-ment tide chart that shows the exact moment when low tide occurs at different points along the coast. Low tide is important, because the reced-ing water leaves tide pools where fish are trapped, and also uncovers the offshore reefs. Like all collectors, the Simpsons don't regard their work as dangerous, but occasionally they have close calls. Much of their fishing is done by running along the tops of the reefs, balancing with their long-handled nets like tightrope walkers carrying poles. When they see a wave coming, they stop on a serrated section of rock, bracing themselves with their nets. The water churns around their knees and then sucks back, occasionally taking one of the Simpsons with it. Don was once pulled off a reef, dragged underwater, and then flung back against the rock by the next wave. When he finally crawled back on the reef, he was slashed from neck to waist by the barnacles that studded the rock like broken glass on top of a wall.

Mrs. Simpson had an even worse experience with a stingray. She explained: "The rays lie flat on the bottom, almost completely buried in the sand, and if you step on one you can sometimes feel him wriggle and jump clear before he can strike you with the poisonous barb at the end of his tail. Unfortunately, I had the bad luck to step right beside one. He got me in the ankle, just above my sneaker. I don't believe there is any worse pain. I nearly lost consciousness. Don dragged me ashore, the ray still hanging from my leg. I left a trail of blood up the beach. Don tore the creature off, but my whole nervous system seemed to be knotted up with agony. The pain was so intense I couldn't scream, and worse yet, I couldn't faint. Don rushed me to a doctor, who cauterized the wound as though it were a snakebite. I couldn't walk for a week."

Although the Simpsons are enthusiastic propagandists for salt-water aquariums, they are somewhat alarmed at the rapid spread of interest. "I gave a talk on salt-water aquariums in San Francisco, and the next day the Bureau of Fisheries received six hundred requests for collecting permits," Don said apprehensively, "People don't realize the cost involved in collecting even as a hobby."

In addition to the usual apparatus used by skin divers, a fish collector needs nets (usually handmade for his special requirements), a seaworthy boat, a score or more of all-glass tanks (sea-water corrodes ordinary aquariums), air compressors, Neaprin suits (for cold-water diving) and a truck fitted up to handle fish tanks, plus aerators and filters.

Probably a collector's greatest thrill is to find a new species, completely unknown to science. Because no one knows what may come out of the ocean, every time a collector dives he is prepared for anything. Russ Renand told me of a man and his small son who stopped in to see his fish and stood staring at the seahorses. Later, the man came up to Renand and said seriously: "I told my boy that there wasn't any such thing as a fish with a horse's head. I see now I was wrong. Tell me, have you any mermaids?"

"I told him not as yet," Russ explained to me. "But I might catch one any day. I couldn't say what might be in the ocean. I've seen too many strange-looking fish down there among the reefs."

CHAPTER 12

Dangerous Game: Hunting American Big Game With Hounds

"Bee" Adkins was one of the last of the old-time dog men. When I was looking for someone to take me coyote hunting with Rani, my cheetah, I was told by professional hunters, "Bee is the only man who knows enough about coyotes to set things up for you—and he's the only man crazy enough to try." Bee went back to a fast-vanishing American tradition. When homesteaders began to cut up the open range, they found their livestock menaced by predatory animals ranging in size from wildcats to grizzly bears. There was only one way to keep powerful killers in check—the expert tracker and his pack of hounds. These men developed great strains of hunting dogs that will never see the inside of a dog show—the long-legged Walkers, the tenacious Triggs, and the fighting Plott hounds. A dog man not only depends on his pack for a living but must occasionally entrust his life to their courage and intelligence. Bee Adkins had devoted his life to knowing dogs, and was, when I knew him, employed by the Fish and Wildlife Service (now the Biological Survey) as a predator-control man. His job was to answer complaints and hunt down predators that had turned to stock killing.

The first day I spent with Bee, he had a call for his hounds. A young couple in southern California had put all their savings into a turkey farm. They ran out one night to find ten prize gobbers thrashing around on the ground, their legs neatly amputated at the body. A pair of coyotes had raided the enclosure and amused themselves by mutilating as many fowls as possible before the cries of the tortured birds woke the humans. The coyotes returned the next night and killed eighteen more turkeys. After a third raid, the couple called the mammal-control supervisor in Wilmington, California. He, in turn, sent a message to Bee Adkins.

Bee took me with him as well as six rangy hounds. He also had a tough bull terrier that rode in the front seat of the pickup between us. The turkey farm was about two hundred miles from Bee's home, and we got there shortly after dawn. The coyotes had been there the night before and had carried off two of their victims. "This probably means they have a litter of pups near here," Bee told me. Ordinarily, Bee did not use hounds on coyotes. The rangy prairie wolves can outdistance even the fast Walkers, for the hounds must trail as well as run, so Bee had intended to use traps. But to protect their pups, coyotes will stand and fight, so Bee put his hounds on the scent.

The hounds picked up the trail readily enough and followed it into a range of hills riddled with small caves. By now the sun was up and the hot rocks killed the scent. "They probably have a den in one of these pockets," said Bee, looking for tracks. The job seemed hopeless, as there were so many possible caves and the scent was going fast, but Bee put his old half-bred bloodhound Copper on the fading line. Then suddenly the dog coyote leaped up in front of the hounds. The pack broke into full cry, and the coyote deliberately waited until the leading hounds were only a few yards away. Then he whirled and began to lead the hounds away from his home and down the foothills where he could lose them in a tortuous system of arroyos.

This trick was his undoing. The coyote was looking over his shoulder to make sure the hounds were following him, and he nearly ran into Bee. Bee shouted, and the coyote stopped in astonishment. That instant's pause gave the Walkers time to reach him. Before the coyote could shake them off, the savage little bull terrier that had been following the hounds had dashed up. In a few seconds it was all over and the turkeys were avenged. Then, with the patient Copper who would spend all day puzzling out a scent, Bee located the den and collected the pups. The female coyote left the district and moved into the desert, where she could perform her natural function of destroying such pests as gophers and prairie dogs.

Bee lived with his wife, two children, and some forty dogs in a cabin halfway up a steep draw near Perris, California. On three sides the cabin was completely surrounded by high cliffs, but from the front door you could see down the draw to where the great yellow prairie stretched out as wide and flat as the ocean. Everywhere you turned there were dogs of all colors and sizes. A soapbox full of solemn hound pups lay beside the stove; three white bull terriers played with a ball under the eucalyptus trees; a Travis and bluetick hound would trot off side by side to look for wildcats in the hills; and dozens of black-and-tans, Plotts, and Walker hounds started barking at you from their kennels on the hillside. In a box by the back door were always a pile of coyotes' "scalps" that Bee had to send to the Fish and Wildlife Service as proof of his services, and in a locker hidden deep in a cool cave was a supply of bear meat from Bee's last hunt in the high Sierra. A couple of cougar skins, stretched out like rugs, were hanging from Mrs. Adkins's clothesline, and close beside them was a grizzly hide, pegged out on the ground and waiting to be scraped.

Bee spoke of the predatory animals that he had to kill with the quiet respect of an old-time professional soldier discussing an honorable and resourceful foe. One day I mentioned hearing of a female dog that had been bred by a male wolf. "The wolf must have been a very young animal, because an adult wolf would never be unfaithful to his mate," Bee told me seriously. Yet Bee was no sentimentalist. A few minutes later he was describing how a pair of wolves will train their young to kill by hamstringing a horse and letting the cubs drag him down. The parents will often mutilate twenty horses a day in this manner and then leave the tortured creatures to die of hunger on the desert. "When wolves start doing something like that, they have to die," Bee remarked matter-of-factly.

Bee got his start as a professional hunter more than forty years ago in southern Arizona. As a sixteen-year-old boy he began to trap wolves for the bounty. "I made over a dollar a day at it, which was more than a good ranch hand could get in those days," Bee explained. Because the wolves frequently managed to tear themselves free, most hunters were using a very heavy trap securely tied down. Bee experimented with light ones fastened to a drag. Instead of fighting these traps, the wolves simply ran off with them, but the drags slowed them down. Then Bee used hounds to track the animals. As Bee began to get a reputation as a hunter, ranchers hired him to kill cattle-killing bears, coyotes, mountain lions, and jaguars. After spending some twenty-odd years hunting predators in the Southwest, Bee heard that the Fish and Wildlife Service needed a man who could trap and who knew how to handle dogs. He signed up with the service and moved to California.

Bee uses two types of dogs in the pack—the "trail hounds" that follow the scent, and the "catch dogs" that bring the quarry to bay. Each dog has his own job to do. Among the trail hounds Bee always has some experienced old hound, usually a bloodhound, that will systematically work out a cold trail with the care of an expert accountant going over tangled books. But the painstaking bloodhound is apt to be slow, and when the scent becomes hot Bee lets the faster Trigg or Hudspeth hounds take over the trailing. Sometimes hounds that are excellent trailers have poor voices, so to keep track of his hounds Bee has a clear-voiced Brooke in the pack. Trail hounds are often very poor "treeing" dogs; they soon lose interest when the quarry climbs a tree or dives into a cave. The hunter needs a dog that will force the quarry to climb and then bark for hours to guide him. So Bee includes a Plott or bluetick hound with the others. All these hounds must learn to work together, each respecting the other dog's abilities and yet coming to his companion's aid if necessary.

The fighting "catch-dogs" are often Airedales or bull terriers. When the hounds overtake the quarry, the catch-dogs must hold the predator until the man can come up. Sometimes the catch-dogs are big animals with a strain of staghound or mastiff, and can pull down the quarry by main strength, but more often they are tough little terriers that rush in, grab a mouthful of fur, and then duck out again before the raging predator can turn on them. Occasionally the hounds will help the catch-dogs bay the game, and sometimes the catchdogs will find a scent that the trail-dogs have missed, but generally each type of dog keeps to his own specialty.

Because every species of wild animal has his own methods of outwitting dogs, Bee must vary his technique and his pack for different types of quarry. When an epidemic broke out among cattle in southern Texas, biologists at Tulane University suspected that the disease might be carried by peccaries—the wild pig of Mexico that occasionally crosses the border on foraging expeditions. Arrangements were made with the Mexican government to permit Bee to hunt peccaries in northern Sonora and bring back the stomach contents of a hundred pigs.

The temperature on the desert often hits 120 degrees, baking the scent out of the ground and the brains out of man or dog. The hounds were able to work only in the early morning or evening. During the heat of the day they lay in the shadow of the giant saguaro cactus, and panted. The desert floor was thickly sprinkled with pincushion buds from the cholla, called the "jumping cactus" because the buds seem to leap at a passerby. The hounds soon got their feet so covered with these spines that they looked as though they had been walking over porcupines. When they tried to bite out the needle-covered buds they got the spines in their lips and lay foaming and helpless until Bee could reach them. But they still kept after the pigs.

When the hounds finally ran down the peccaries, the pigs formed into a solid bunch with the old boars on the outside protecting the females and young. The hounds stood back while the catch-dogs rushed in, but even these warriors couldn't break the peccaries' iron formation. Bee fired over the herd and in an instant there were pigs and dogs scattered over the entire district. The catch-dogs worked in couples, one dog grabbing a pig by the ear while his companion seized the porker by a hind leg. As soon as the pig went down he began screaming for help, and the nearest boars rushed to his assistance. A sixty-pound peccary with three-inch tusks is a very formidable antagonist, and the catch-dogs, trying to hold down their prisoner, were at a disadvantage. So Bee decided to eliminate his pack altogether and hunt with only one dog.

He selected a big rangy dog named Sandy, half staghound and half redbone. Sandy's redbone ancestry bequeathed to him a reasonably good nose, and his staghound blood gave him long legs and determination. After Bee had scattered the herd by a shot, Sandy learned to cut out a pig like a sheepdog taking out a sheep.

In spite of his skill and intelligence, however, Sandy had several narrow escapes. Once, while Bee was hunting in the mountains, Sandy took after a pig that promptly bolted for a cave. Sandy knew if he took hold of the peccary the animal's cries would bring down the whole herd on him, but rather than see his quarry escape, the dog took a chance and grabbed the pig by a hind foot. Instantly the peccary screamed for help, and several of the other pigs charged in. A big boar drove his tusk through Sandy's chest and tossed him into the air while the dog's captive dived into the cave. When Bee came up, the hound seemed to be dying. His hindquarters wobbled so badly that he could scarcely stand and he was losing blood rapidly. Bee climbed into the hills, got a hatful of snow, and packed the dog's wounds. After a rest, Sandy struggled to his feet, limped into the cave, and drove the pig out.

"After that, whenever Sandy caught up with a herd of pigs, he'd climb on a rock and watch the back trail to make sure I was coming," Bee explained. "I'm convinced that Sandy could count. Often he'd bay several pigs in a cave, and after I thought that I'd gotten them all, Sandy would keep on barking. I always found another pig that I'd missed. The cave was so full of pig scent that Sandy's nose couldn't do him any good, and I believe he counted the pigs as they went in and then checked to see how many I brought out. By sending the rest of my dogs back and just using Sandy by himself, I got the hundred pigs in a month."

Like Sandy, many of Bee's best dogs are crossbreds. Purebred dogs are specialists. They were created to do a certain job and they usually can do it well. But the purebred can seldom adapt himself to changing conditions. One winter Bee got a request from some Mexican ranchers to hunt cattle-killing jaguars that had been destroying their herds. During his vacation from the Fish and Wildlife Service, Bee went to Mexico with his pack to catch jaguars. The experience cost him the lives of most of his purebred catch-dogs.

"My dogs were used to hunting wolves and coyotes," Bee told me. "With those animals, the catch-dogs have to barrel right in and take hold. If a dog tries to spar with a wolf, he'll get cut to pieces because that's the way a wolf likes to fight. But no dog can charge in on a jaguar and come out alive."

The first jaguar that the hounds started simply loped along until he had outdistanced Bee and then sat down to wait for the dogs. When the catch-dogs rushed in, the cat threw out a long paw tipped with curved talons, hooked the nearest dog by the shoulder, and pulled him in. Then the jaguar bit his prisoner through the head and sat on the body while waiting for the next dog. Before Bee could shoot him, the cat had killed four dogs, piling up the corpses neatly beside him like kindling wood.

"After that I got some crossbred dogs that weren't so dead-game but were smarter," said Bee. "The crossbreds would dance around the cat just out of reach, baying their heads off, until the jaguar got tired of the noise and climbed a tree. The crossbreds were fine for jaguar, but they wouldn't have been any good for getting a coyote out of a hole or pulling a wildcat off a rock."

The narrowest escape Bee ever had while hunting predators came from a jaguar. Because his pack had been used to running so many different kinds of game, the hounds had a tendency to "change." Often, when dogs are following a difficult spore, they will happen to strike a new hot scent

and change to the fresher trail. Many predators, when they find themselves hard pressed by hounds, deliberately hunt up another animal so
the hounds will take after the fresh quarry and give the predator a
chance to rest. Hunters call this "running trash"—"trash" being any
animal the hunter doesn't want his hounds to follow.

The usual method of keeping a dog from running "trash" is to obtain
scent glands from the trash animal, let the glands decompose, and then
smear them on the dog. After a while the dog develops such a dislike for
the odor that he refuses to follow it. Bee's hounds showed an under-
standable reluctance to run jaguar, and "changed" to some less dangerous game, such as peccary, whenever they got the chance. One evening
after a long run after jaguar the hounds barked "treed" at the entrance
of a small cave no bigger in circumference than a barrel. There were
plenty of pig tracks around, so Bee decided that the dogs were up to their
old trick of running pigs and had chased a hog into the hole. As he
needed fresh meat, Bee twisted some dry reeds into a crude torch and
crawled into the tunnel on his hands and knees.

Bee saw no eyes shining in the darkness and heard no noise. But
suddenly he felt a strong wind in his face, and something rushed toward
him. Though Bee doesn't remember pulling the trigger of his carbine, he
remembers hearing the gun go off. Then he fainted. When he recovered
consciousness he was lying several feet from the entrance of the tunnel,
and the dogs were mauling a dead jaguar.

Bee's present pack has never been known to "change" and is as
completely "trash-broke" as hounds can be. A great deal of the credit
goes to an old hound named Copper, the leader of the pack. "I'm not
saying Copper is the best dog in the world," Bee mildly explains, "but I'd
like to see one that's better." Copper's father was a champion bloodhound named Inspector. The dog became so vicious that his owner was
unable to enter him in dog shows and sold the hound to Bee for a
nominal sum. Bee bred Inspector to a bitch, half Walker and half bull
terrier. Copper is the offspring of this remarkable mixture of strains. He
is a big black-and-tan hound with the rare ability to interpret scent
intelligently and courage enough to act as a catch-dog in a pinch. He acts
as a top sergeant to the other dogs and has been known to give young
dogs that leave the pack to run "trash" such a mauling that the pups are
permanently cured.

Copper is technically known as a "strike-dog." When Bee casts the
pack, Copper is usually the first to strike the scent. While I was staying

with Bee a farmer called in to say a wildcat had been robbing his hen roost. I went along with Bee and the dogs. The hounds ranged out around the hen roost, heads down, snuffing loudly, their tails going like high-speed metronomes. Suddenly a young Trigg gave eager tongue and then waited anxiously while Copper hurried over to check the spoor with his educated nose. When the old hound turned away in disgust, the younger dog slunk away with his tail between his legs. A few moments later Copper's great bell-like cry boomed out. Instantly all the other hounds dropped whatever trails they were working on and rushed to the old dog. The whole pack started off in full cry and were soon so far out of sight that Bee had to track them to find out where they'd gone. An hour later, spent mostly running up the side of a mountain, we found where the dogs had checked by the banks of a stream. The cat had taken to water, but Copper was still slowly tracing the quarry by standing up on his hind legs in the stream and catching fragments of the cat's scent that had been caught by the overhanging bushes. The cat treed twice, but each time jumped over the dogs' heads when he saw us coming. Finally he turned at bay on the side of a cliff. The hounds collected around him, yelling "treed" but refusing to close with the fierce little fighter. A white bull terrier that had been puffing almost as much as I was in his efforts to keep up with the other dogs now charged in, knocking the hounds out of the way. He grabbed the cat and they slid down the side of the cliff together. The hounds followed, screaming with excitement, their toenails skating over the hard rock. When we reached the bottom of the thirty-foot incline, one of the terrier's ears was hanging in ribbons and his head was more red than white, but he was holding the dead cat. After sniffing the quarry, Copper turned away and walked slowly over to Bee for the casual pat on the head that meant he had done a good job. The bull terrier wanted no reward but the opportunity for a fight.

Although Bee speaks of Copper as being a virtually ideal dog, he actually means that the old hound's style of working blends in perfectly with his own methods. Bee and the twelve-year-old hound have hunted together for so long that the man can interpret the dog's slightest move, and Copper understands what Bee wants apparently by mental telepathy.

Another hunter who handled hounds differently might consider Copper simply a better-than-average dog. Last winter Bee loaned Copper to Howard Bilton, another professional hunter who lives near Glennville, California. Bilton hunts nothing but mountain lion. These big tawny cats have a fatal fondness for horsemeat, and as a result several states have put a $100 bounty on them. Last winter Bilton averaged nearly a lion a week, and to keep up this astonishing record he seldom spends more than a day running down a single animal.

"Copper is a grand old dog, but I couldn't use him for my style of hunting," Bilton explained to me. "He'll take a pack off on a three-day-old scent as readily as on a fresh track, and I can't waste time following a lion with that long a start. Now, one of the handiest dogs I ever got from Bee Atkins is a little cocker bitch named Birdie. Bee found Birdie when she was a puppy lying in a ditch. Her mother was a registered cocker that got bred by a street dog, and the owner threw the pups away. Bee kept her as a pet for his kids. One day for a joke he took her out after lion with his dogs. Birdie trailed the cat along with the hounds, and when the lion 'treed' on a rock, Birdie climbed up to pull him down, although she weighs only about twenty pounds. The lion grabbed her and had the dog's head in his mouth when Bee shot him. Birdie wouldn't run another lion for two weeks, but she's all right now."

Bilton's method of lion hunting is to put his dogs in a trailer and drive at thirty miles an hour over mountain roads. He is so expert at picking up lion tracks that even at this speed he can identify a cougar's pad marks. Little Birdie rides on his lap, and if the signs look good Bilton opens the door and lets Birdie jump out to investigate. If Birdie approves of the tracks, Bilton opens the trailer and lets out the hounds. "Birdie has only an average nose, so if she gives tongue I know the scent is hot and the regular trail hounds will run him down in a few hours," Bilton explains.

Bilton's strike-dog is a powerful animal named Red. Red is a fast, aggressive redtick hound that keeps going from "jump" to "catch." Once Red sighted a lion ahead of him on a long ridge. Instead of giving tongue as most hounds do at the sight of game, Red ran mute until he had got ahead of the cat. Then he turned and began baying. Caught between the dog and Bilton, the cat treed almost at once, and Red's strategy saved his master a three- or four-hour run.

"Red not only works as a trail hound, but he's a darn good catch-dog," Bilton told me. "Once the pack had treed a lion on a narrow ledge with a three-hundred-foot drop beside him. I could have shot the cat, but I was afraid he'd fall over the cliff and the dogs would follow him. My wife, who was below me on another ledge, suddenly called out, 'There's a bear after me!' I looked down, and sure enough there was a big black bear standing beside her and champing his jaws so hard the spittle hung down two feet. My wife had accidentally cornered him on a shelf of rock while climbing up to help me. I couldn't get a shot at him so I hollered to Red. He left the other dogs and climbed down after the bear. He and that bear had a real tough time of it. In the bushes Red could dodge around the bear and pull hair out of his rump, but in the open the bear nearly killed him. Finally I managed to shoot the lion so he'd fall on the shelf, and then I went down to help Red. By that time the bear had lit out for parts unknown. Red was pretty well cut up, but he was running again in a week."

Of all game that can be hunted with dogs, bear is the noblest and the most difficult quarry. A bear, on hearing the music of hounds on his trail, will often trot back to do battle with them, and not even a jaguar can put up such a savage and determined fight. On the other hand, a bear may run for miles—charging through bushes that a man would find impenetrable and climbing up cliffs that would impress a cougar. Although a black bear will usually tree, he often prefers to fight it out on the ground, getting his massive rump against a rock or fallen limb and swinging at the dogs like a boxer equipped with tenpenny nails in his gloves. Given a fair chance, he frequently attacks the hunter. When a bear charges, the man seldom has time for more than one shot. If he misses, only the dogs stand between him and a mauling.

Last winter Bee and his brother, Graves Atkins, agreed to take a sportsman out after a bear that had been destroying apple orchards by breaking off limbs to get at the ripe fruit. The bear was "spoiled"; that is, he had been run by packs of half-trained dogs until he knew more about hounds than most dog-men. The bear had burrowed out a series of tunnels through some thick blackberry patches, and when chased by dogs he would plunge into one of these tunnels, and wait. The dogs could come at him only one at a time. The bear would hold down a dog with his big paws, break the dog's neck with a quick bite, throw the corpse aside, and grab the next victim. Some hunters, reasoning that they were going to lose their dogs anyhow, would go to the city pound, buy up half a dozen dogs, and turn them loose on the bear's track. "Those men weren't hunting the bear—they were just feeding him," Bee said bitterly.

Knowing the bear's habits, Graves Atkins waited with the sportsman beside a narrow pass leading to the blackberry thickets. Bee took the hounds to the orchard and put Copper on the scent. As soon as the bear heard the dogs, he headed for the pass, with Copper and the catch-dogs hard on his black flank. True to their training, Bee's dogs tried desperately to bay the predator. Little Birdie would duck under the bear's body, nip him in the belly, and dash out again before the furious animal could find her. Copper ran parallel to the bear while one of the catch-dogs kept on the predator's other side. While the catch-dog distracted the bear by snapping and barking, Copper would leap in, grab a mouthful of hair, and spring back as the bear turned on him. Before the bear could reach Copper, the catch-dog would rush in and bite him in the rear. The dogs worked with such perfect coordination that one dog was always spitting out hair while the other was getting in his bite.

But this particular bear was dog-wise and, in spite of the punishment he was taking, kept running for his tunnels in the blackberry bushes. Graves and the sportsman were waiting on opposite sides of the pass, and as the bear passed between them the sportsman shot the animal through the flank. Instantly the bear whirled and charged. The sportsman tried to retreat, stumbled, and fell down. The charging bear grabbed the man's foot and in spite of his heavy hunting boot crushed the bones like cardboard tubing. Copper and three catch-dogs grabbed the bear by the flanks and almost literally dragged the three-hundred-pound monster off the man. One of the catch-dogs grabbed the bear by the nose and managed to hold him until Graves could put the muzzle of his .45 revolver into the bear's ear and blow his brains out. "It was a bad moment. . . . I nearly lost some good dogs there," said Bee, describing the incident later.

Hunting with dogs is a hard, dangerous, and not very remunerative job. If a man falls from a cliff or gets mauled by a predator, he is usually miles from his car, and no search party will be sent to look for him because a hunter is expected to be absent for weeks at a time. Often he has to spend the night on the trail with no covering but his dogs. Feeding a pack of hounds is so expensive that a hunter is lucky to break even at the end of a year.

One evening while Bee and I were returning from a particularly exhausting pig hunt in Sonora, I asked him why he had ever become a professional hunter.

"Because I like listening to the cry of hounds when they're on a trail," Bee answered, without hesitation. "Many's the time I've been so beat I didn't care if the game got away or not. Then those hounds would break into music, and it was four hours later before I'd stopped running. I've followed hounds up a cliff without giving it a thought as long as the dogs were talking on a scent. Then I'd look back over the place I'd just climbed and get so scared I'd have to sit down. When I get too old to follow a trail, I'll turn my dogs loose in the evening, sit on my back steps, and listen to them run foxes through the night. What with these new traps, poisons, and all such stuff, there'll soon be better ways of killing predators than using hounds. But as long as dogs will talk on a hot scent there'll be men who want to follow the sound of hounds in full cry."

CHAPTER *13*

Formal Hunting
With Hounds: Otter,
Stag, and Hare

Scent won't lie on running water, as every sportsman knows
. . . everyone, that is, except the English otter hunters who have been
hunting otters in rivers for nearly a thousand years. As an otter can swim
down a fish and is more at home in water than on land, I could never
figure out how hounds could trail these animals in fast-flowing water and
run them down. So when I went to England, I decided to solve the
mystery.

I was lucky enough to get the address of Mr. Richard Henniker, who
for many years has been secretary of two of the best known otter packs in
England. Over the phone, Mr. Henniker said that he'd be delighted to
take me otter hunting, and suggested that I come over that night for
supper. The Hennikers live in a "mews," a sort of courtyard at the far
end of one of the twisting old London streets. The mews was once part of
a stable where some forgotten nobleman in the Middle Ages kept his
horses, hounds, and hunting hawks. I went up a long flight of stairs in
the old building that has now been cut up into apartments and met the
Hennikers. Mr. Henniker was an energetic, enthusiastic man with a close-
clipped military mustache who works as an architect when not otter
hunting, and his wife was a tall, attractive woman who spends most of
her weekends wading around streams with her husband after hounds and

otters. The walls of their apartment were decorated with otter masks (heads) and rudders (tails), mounted on plaques with the date and location of the hunt.

"We're surprised and pleased that anyone in America should be interested in otter hunting," said Mr. Henniker after making me a whisky and water. "I believe in the States you trap or shoot them. Here we consider it more sporting to use hounds. It's our oldest field sport, you know. Started shortly after the Norman Conquest in 1066."

According to Mr. Henniker, otter hunting was originally simply a way to get rid of the otters, although it is now practiced as a sport. In medieval times fish were considered a valuable "crop," and many people depended on their hooks and lines to see them through hard times. The original otter hound was developed from a cross between the griffon (a type of French hunting dog) and the bloodhound, but today foxhounds are generally used.

"I can't understand how any hound can follow the scent in running water," I said.

This started a long, technical discussion on scent in which both the Hennikers joined. Although I've been writing about hounds for several years now, this otter hunting was by far the most complicated deal I've met. Yet as the question of scenting is the crucial one in this type of hunting, I'll have to explain it in some detail.

Because otters operate on both land and water, the otter hunters have two sets of terms to describe the scent, depending on where it occurs. If the otter runs overland, the scent is called the "drag" (because it comes mainly from the long, dragging tail). If the otter is swimming in the stream, he will occasionally touch a stone or push off from the bank going around a sharp bend. This is called a "touch."

In the water, the term "scent" is used only when the otter is free swimming and the stream carries the scent to the hounds swimming after him. Scent floats on the water, and the stream carries it to the hounds exactly as the wind carries scent to a hound on land. However, particles of this water-borne scent may be caught among reeds or rushes, and is then called the "wash."

"We'll pick you up at your hotel tomorrow morning at six," said Henniker. "Wear old clothes and don't forget you'll get wet. The hunt is meeting at an inn near Salisbury, about a hundred miles south of London. We'll draw the river there and you'll see some lovely country."

Mr. Henniker didn't mention that I'd also run about twenty miles and see plenty of mud, nettles, barbed wire, and brambles. Otter hunting is a strenuous sport. I innocently thanked him.

The drive down to Salisbury next morning was through some of the loveliest country I've ever seen, and the little villages looked so picturesque I expected them to be Hollywood props of old English towns. The inn was called the Red Lion and stood under a grove of huge trees. Most of the field, as the hunt followers are called, had already gathered in everything from bicycles to sport cars. They were of all ages, from toddlers who seemed barely able to walk to an old couple who crawled out of their tiny English car and tottered over to speak to Dick Henniker. I might add that later that afternoon, while the hounds were in full cry on a fresh drag and I was figuring how to get over a thorn hedge, something whizzed past me and took the hedge like deer. It was the old couple going all out.

Everyone except me carried an otter pole, a long, strong stick about six feet long. Many of the poles had notches and crosses. Dick explained that when a hunter was in at the death of an otter, he was entitled to cut a notch on his pole. If two otters were killed in one day, he cut a cross. Some of the poles had over a thousand marks. "You need a pole to vault over ditches, balance yourself in fast-flowing water, probe for deep places, help you through bogs," he explained. The officials of the hunt, including the Hennikers, who often helped with the hounds, wore a costume consisting of a green cap, a green coat with brass buttons, white serge breeches, and a red tie. I was introduced to the master of the hunt, Mr. A. M. Wadsworth, a thickset, pleasant man who was most cordial, although he obviously had a dozen things on his mind.

The professional huntsman was named Leigh Douse, a slender, quiet fellow whose father and grandfather had also been professional huntsmen. He had done nothing but handle hounds for various hunt clubs all his life, except for a six-year stint with the army during the war.

The hounds had arrived in a special van from the kennels, with a small box under it for the two hunt terriers who are used to bolt an otter from a hole. Douse and his helper, a young boy who was an apprentice huntsman, opened the door of the van and the pack poured out. I'd been used to the thin, rangy hounds used to track big game in our West, and was greatly impressed by these magnificent-looking animals. They averaged about seventy-five pounds and stood twenty-six inches at the shoulder. Whether or not they could have stood the long hard grind of tracking over the Mojave Desert or through the Sierra Madres like our Plotts or

Walkers, I wouldn't know. Dick said frankly that he doubted it. "We keep them heavy so they can stand the cold water better," he explained. "They aren't meant for long, fast runs." The hounds were English and Welsh foxhounds, with a few of the otter-hound cross.

Douse put his horn to his lips and blew a single blast. Instantly, the hounds gathered about him and Douse led the way toward the river. His helper followed behind the pack, occasionally snapping a long whip and calling, "Champion! Drop it! Get along, Willow!" as the different hounds showed a tendency to stray. The two hunt terriers trotted behind the hounds, and the field followed.

The river turned out to be what we would call a stream, some twenty feet across. It twisted across the fields like a snake with colic, making great S curves every few yards. "An otter going upstream will cut overland across those curves to save time," Dick told me. "Going downstream, he'll float with the current, making only an occasional touch. Douse will probably draw upstream, so the river will carry any wash there may be down to the hounds, but the best chance is to find a fresh drag across one of the bends."

When we reached the river, the hounds spread out and began eagerly searching up and down the banks. Douse slowly worked the hounds upstream, talking to them constantly, "Yoo-hope, lads. Loo to 'em, there, Despot. Hike to 'em [start giving tongue]. Lee over, lads, loo over [try the far bank]. Nothing, Furrier? Try back. Ah, what's that, then? Have a care, it's naught but a water rat. What's that, then, Beauty? [One of the bitches was snuffing feverishly, her tail going madly.] A slot [deer hoof-print]. Drop it, girl, drop it, I say." Douse touched the bitch with his pole, and the boy ran up, snapping his whip. Beauty turned away.

Two whips (experienced members of the hunt carrying whips) kept ahead of the hounds, making sure they didn't go too fast. Wadsworth and Douse kept with the pack, and the young helper brought up the rear. The field stayed well behind. Occasionally some overeager member would crowd the hounds, and then Douse would say plaintively, " 'Ware hounds, sir. *Please* 'ware hounds." Following the stream, we trudged through one farm after another and past great estate after great estate. Apparently no one bothered about trespassing on these properties, as nearly everyone in the English countryside is a sportsman and would never object to a hunt passing through.

"Hike to it, lads, hike to it," Leigh Douse called continually. Dick joined Wadsworth, who was checking the muddy banks for signs. They found some seal (otter tracks), but the hounds, when Wadsworth called them over, gave one sniff and hurried on. The seal was too old. Next, Dick came on some sprints (droppings), but Furrier, when his expert nose was called into play, turned away at once.

"At least three days old," said Wadsworth, turning over the sprints with his pole and watching the hound.

Suddenly one of the hounds gave an eager cry. Instantly the rest of the pack left whatever they were doing and rushed to him. They gathered around the spot, the younger ones whimpering with excitement. Douse stood leaning on his pole, watching them. "If old Councilor speaks on it, we'll have a hunt," said Dick beside me. Then two or three hounds gave tongue together, and Councilor's deeper voice joined them.

"Hark to Councilor! Hark to Beauty! Loo to him, lads!" cried Douse. The hounds rushed away in full cry, and everyone started running.

The pack vanished into a swamp full of high grass, and all I could see was a procession of waving sterns above the cover. The first step took me over my knees in mud, but the rest of the field, helped by their long poles, plunged on. Dick Henniker had forgotten all about me when the hounds gave tongue, and was thrashing through the swamp, brandishing his pole and yelling encouragement to the pack. I came on a man with a little boy; the kid couldn't have been more than six. He was stuck in a bog hole. As I passed, I heard him wail, "But really, Father, I can't go on!"

His father paused long enough to give him a hearty kick in the backside and say, "Get on with it, you little slacker," before plunging on after the frantic pack.

The hounds broke out of the swamp and streamed away across a meadow, yelling their heads off. By the stream, two people were waving their hats on the end of their poles, and pointing. They must have seen the otter when he broke out of the swamp and made for the river. I managed to get through the bog, and ran across the meadow after the pack. When I arrived on the bank, the whole pack was in the water, spread out like a fan, swimming upstream and still giving tongue. The field was running alongside.

"Please, gentlemen; please, Mr. Wadsworth!" It was Leigh Douse, his white breeches covered with mud, "There's a bridge two hundred yards upstream. Will someone run ahead and see if they can gaze him [see the otter]?"

"I will, Leigh," said Dick Henniker. He started off across country at a lope. I followed the hounds. Ahead, I heard someone shout and raise his pole as a signal that he'd seen the otter. The hounds turned in midstream and started to swim toward him.

"No, sir, no!" shouted Douse. "That was a marsh hen diving, sir."

Wadsworth cried, "Please let the hounds go on!" The whips ran along the bank, shouting to turn the pack back. "Bloody fool!" said Wadsworth, under his breath.

The pack began to mill around in the water. Then they turned and went downstream, gradually giving tongue again. Wadsworth looked at Douse. "What do you think?" he asked.

"I believe they're following the wash downstream. The otter's probably come to land and cut off the scent," said Douse. Then he added bitterly, "A pity that gentleman stopped them, sir."

The bridge was only a short distance ahead now, and Wadsworth ran toward it. I followed him and saw Dick Henniker leaning on the span, watching the water below him. "Did you see anything?" called Wadsworth.

Dick shook his head. "Water's so clear here I can see the trout. He couldn't possibly have come past."

The hounds were silent now. We went a mile, the hounds investigating every inlet and hole. "I still think he may have gone upstream, sir," said Douse to Wadsworth. "Perhaps he passed under the bridge before Mr. Henniker got there." Wadsworth shook his head. After another mile, Douse stopped the pack. "I think we might try back, sir," he said to Wadsworth.

"Try it, but I'm afraid we've lost him," said the master.

After a couple of hours of searching the banks, I was willing to give up and try for another otter, but Wadsworth wouldn't consider it. "We often keep this up for six or seven hours," he assured me.

An elderly gentleman walking beside us remarked: "Young man, don't be impatient. This is like a game of chess. Study the hounds, study the hounds. You learn more about scent in one day with the otter hounds than you will in a year fox hunting."

Champion, one of the old hounds, stopped and stood with his head up, sniffing. He was obviously scenting the breeze, and Douse stopped to watch him. Some of the younger hounds jumped a fox from a thicket and the whips had to turn them, but Douse remained leaning on his pole, watching Champion. Finally the old hound trotted across the pasture, still keeping his head high, to a drainage ditch that flowed into the stream. Champion vanished into the ditch. A few seconds later, we heard him yelling with excitement.

"Hark to Champion!" shouted Douse, putting his horn to his lips and blowing a quick, sharp blast. The hounds came bursting out of cover to run to him, those on the opposite side of the stream swimming across. "Loo into him, boys!" He started running toward the ditch, Wadsworth and I following.

"I hope Champion isn't rioting on a rabbit," panted Wadsworth.

"Never fear," said Douse confidently. "Not old Champion."

The rest of the pack quickly confirmed Champion's opinion. The field came hurrying up from their positions along the stream where they'd been watching for a sight of the otter. The hounds had checked, and were trying to puzzle out the scent in the dirty water of the ditch. "Muddy water kills scent," Wadsworth told me. "Once the hounds get it stirred up, they have to depend on bits of wash in the puddles."

Douse spared a moment from watching the pack to speak to Wadsworth. "Look there," he said, pointing with his pole. "This ditch runs straight into the river. The otter came to the mouth of it, and swam up without touching. The hounds followed the wash on downstream. That was the way of it, sir. Yoo-hope, lads. In to him, there!"

The entire meadow, which measured some twenty-five acres, was a checkerboard of drainage ditches. The otter ran up one and down another. From time to time some member of the field would see him and give a shout. Often when the animal was running across the field in plain sight and everyone was yelling, the hounds would be silent because they had lost the scent. A few minutes later, the pack would be tearing along, yelling with excitement on a hot drag while the human stood by in silence. I managed to ask Wadsworth how Champion had known the otter was in the ditch.

"The breeze was to us, and Champion air-scented him lying up there," said Wadsworth. "The hounds missed him the first trip because he was still wet, and a wet otter doesn't give off much scent. On the way back, he'd had a chance to dry out."

The last few hours had been leisurely, but now everything was crazy excitement. The hounds were pouring up one ditch and down another, in almost constant full cry. Occasionally you'd meet them unexpectedly going around a corner and had to jump fast, for the hounds thought nothing of knocking you down, and the weight of fifteen couples of seventy-five-pound hounds is no joke. I could see the rest of the field following as best they could, using their poles to vault the ditches. In their excitement, the hounds were constantly overrunning the scent; Douse's horn calling them back and the pistol-like reports of the whips sounded continually.

Then I saw the otter. He was running across the pasture by the river, his long, weasel body undulating like a snake as he loped along. Douse's horn screamed for the hounds. They burst out of a ditch, and the whips put them on the scent. They screamed with eagerness and rushed away, the foxhounds leading. Then I heard the pitch of their cries change. They had seen their quarry ahead. I saw the otter leave the ditch and plunge into the river in a long, smooth dive like a jet of oil, with the hounds after him. In the stream, there was a fierce fight, the hounds biting desperately around them in the water and all being carried downstream by the rushing current. "The first shallows are half a mile down," moaned Wadsworth, who had just come up. The hounds were swimming in circles now, trying to locate the otter; and once I saw him, a sleek, brown shape in the brown water, turning and twisting through the pack. Then he was off downstream like a torpedo, leaving the pack to struggle ashore.

Douse cast his hounds downstream. As we followed, it began to rain. Everyone was so wet by this time that the rain made little difference, and the Britishers, who are practically amphibious anyhow, merely remarked that a light rain improves scenting conditions. "If it begins to thunder, though, we're finished," Wadsworth remarked to me. "In thunder the scent goes down like a light dimming."

The rain grew worse, and even the most enthusiastic members of the field plodded along through the wet without showing much interest in the sport, when suddenly the pack exploded into full cry. Lord, what a sound that is! Instantly everyone forgot all about the rain, nettle stings, sore feet, and insect bites. The whole field started running, plunging through the river up to their waists, getting tangled up in thorn hedges, and falling in bog holes.

Most of us ran full tilt into the pack, which had made a *U* turn and were coming upstream again. Half of the hounds were in the water, the rest racing along the banks. The scent was obviously red hot, for the swimming hounds didn't bother to lower their heads to pick it up but were paddling along, heads held high, screaming with excitement. The field followed them, wading up the river when holding (bushes) along the banks were too thick or taking short cuts over pastures to hit another bend in the stream. I thought the otter must be right ahead of the pack, but within a hundred yards the hounds' cry died away and they checked. Here we go again, I thought.

Douse and Wadsworth stopped the pack for a few minutes to organize them and then put them on again. Still no trace of drag, touch, wash, or scent. Then several members of the field called attention to an old bitch who was sniffing hopefully at the roots of a tree. "An excellent marking hound, that," said a lady near me approvingly. It turned out that the otter had made directly for the roots of an old tree that grew partly in the water, gone up among the roots, and laid there while the too eager pack had kept on downstream, following the wash that was still carried on the surface of the river.

Douse blew three short blasts on his horn as a signal to bring up the terriers. There were two of them, a white fox terrier and a rough-coated border terrier. "We prefer to use white terriers," one of the whips told me, "because the hounds occasionally mistake a brown terrier for the otter, with unhappy consequences. However, the master generally holds the pack off until the otter is put down (bolted from the hole). It's considered sporting to give him several minutes' grace."

The terriers began to scratch and bark among the roots, and finally the white one forced his way in. A man watching the stream suddenly shouted and pointed with his pole. The water was smooth there, and I could see a succession of bubbles coming up . . . a pair of bubbles about two inches apart . . . a pause . . . then another pair about a yard farther on downstream. I recognized it as a "chain"—bubbles from the otter's nostrils as he swam underwater.

The hounds were put on at once. When they hit the place where the chain had been, they stopped as though they'd run into an invisible wall, and all turning together, swept downstream. With the current in his favor, the otter sped downstream. Again I thought he was lost, but while some of the pack followed the scent in the river, the rest clambered up on the banks and raced ahead. A hundred feet below were shallows, and here the otter had to surface. The next moment the surface of the water was whipped into foam by the furious pack as they caught up to him. For the last hour, no one had seen the otter. It was only after Wadsworth waded into the stream and held up the dead animal that we could be sure we hadn't been chasing a ghost.

It was dark by the time we reached the inn where we'd left the car. Although it was August, I was chilled through. The landlord had a fire going so the field could dry off, and soon everyone had a glass of port, stout, beer, or whiskey in his hand. Knowing I was a poor, weak American not used to the English climate, the field gave me the best place by the fire, and I didn't argue with them. The inn walls were decorated with otter masks, rudders, and pads (paws), some of them a hundred years old. The landlord and his two daughters, who served as barmaids, joined in the conversation, which naturally dealt almost exclusively with otter hunting.

"Ah, if you're writing about otter hunting, you should have been here fifty years ago," the landlord assured me. "The people today don't take it seriously enough. When I was a boy, they hunted three times a week, winter and summer. I recall once seeing the old master one November afternoon turn to three women and say, 'Wade in there and form a sickle' [a blockade across the stream to stop the otter]. In they went, although the water was freezing, and stood there up to waists for four hours. When the hunt was over, they couldn't use their legs, and had to be lifted out. The women wore long skirts in those days, and that made for a better sickle. Things aren't what they used to be."

Ever since the Middle Ages, the king of hunts has always been the stag hunt. In France, the traditional stag hunt, with all the ancient pomp and ceremony, is still preserved. One of the oldest and most famous packs of staghounds is maintained by the Count de Vergie at his home, the Château Touffou near Vienne in the east-central part of France. The count most kindly invited my wife and me to take part in a stag hunt, and so we traveled to Touffou. The walls of the château were covered with horns and heads of game killed on the estate: stag, wild boar, roebuck, and fallow deer. Below the trophies were racks hung with the great curved French hunting horns, riding crops, coats and capes. Some of the trophies are several hundred years old, for the château dates back to the eleventh century.

"In our part of France, the stag is never shot, but killed by the dagger," the count told me as we sat that evening in front of the carved marble fireplace in the living room of the castle. "When the hounds bay the stag, the first member of the hunt to come up goes in with his hunting knife and dispatches the animal. I would not call it dangerous, but as our stags reach a weight of six hundred pounds and have a four-foot spread of antlers, it requires skill.

"I remember one occasion when my brother-in-law went in to kill a stag that the hounds were holding at bay. I was with him and stood in front of the animal to distract his attention. My brother-in-law came in on the stag's flank and thrust for the heart—a most effective blow but one difficult to deliver. He missed, and the stag charged me as the most obvious target. I went down with the tines of the animal's antlers against my chest. Unfortunately, my dagger was knocked out of my hand, but I managed to grab a heavy stick and fought the animal off. My brother-in-law hamstrung the stag and, as he fell, finished him with a blow through the heart."

"Don't you take along a gun so you can shoot a stag in case of an emergency?" I asked.

"Never!" said the count firmly. "I was on a hunt once—not my own, I assure you—when a stag was bayed on a railway track. The master was afraid a train would come along and kill the hounds, so he had the stag shot to save time. The farmers who were following the hunt were so indignant that they refused to accept the meat. The venison is always distributed to the local people. We hunt only for the sport. This was winter, and many of the people needed the meat badly, but they left it to rot rather than touch it."

The count is a big, cheerful man who walks with a slight limp as the result of a hunting accident. French poachers occasionally snare deer by spreading an open noose across a trail attached to a bent sapling. If a deer steps into the noose, the sapling springs up, jerking the deer off his feet. While riding hard after the hounds, the count's horse stepped into one of these snares. The count suffered a bad fall, breaking his hip, and has not been able to ride since. However, the count continues to follow the hunt in an American jeep while his brother-in-law, who has the title of First Button (principal member of the hunt), acts as huntsman.

"Stag hunting is the most complicated of all hunts," explained the count, pouring us some *suze,* a drink made of gentian roots for which Touffou is famous. "We do not hunt simply any deer. We hunt only one specific stag. For example, some of the farmers have been complaining that a certain *daguet* [spiked buck] has been doing a great deal of damage to their melon patches. So tomorrow we will hunt that daguet. As deer live in herds, he will be with other deer. The hounds must cut that particular animal out from the rest, and hunt only him."

Anyone who has hunted with hounds can imagine how hard it would be to make forty hounds pick up a single deer track among a herd and stay on it no matter how the hunted animal tries to mix his trail with others. "How do the hounds know which animal you want them to hunt?" I asked.

"That will be the work of the *valet de limier*," the count explained. "He will come to the château tonight, and I will tell him that we plan to hunt this daguet tomorrow. The valet de limier knows every deer in the forest. Tomorrow, before dawn, he will go out with his limier and discover where this daguet is lying up so we can find him with the pack."

The count explained that his limier is a special hound trained by the valet de limier for this difficult job. As the man's title means "the limier's servant," that gives you an idea of how important this hound is considered to be. The limier is usually a very experienced old staghound. He works mute, and is never allowed to run a deer. He must have an excellent nose, stop instantly on command, and never change on a scent. The count told me: "A good limier can tell instantly from the scent whether a deer is a stag or a hind. I believe that they can also tell the age of the animal, although this is difficult to prove."

Later that evening, one of the footmen brought in the valet de limier. He was an old man in his late sixties, with grizzled white hair, dressed in leggings, and wearing the uniform of one of the count's forest guards (private game wardens), which consisted of white breeches and a brown coat with gold hunting horns embroidered on the lapels. The count told me that the old man had once been a famous huntsman and had hunted 1,783 stags, as well as many wild boars and even wolves. When the count told him about the daguet, he merely nodded and said, "Oui, Monsieur le Comte." But when the count said that I wanted to go with him, the old man's attitude promptly changed.

"It is very cold and wet in the forest at that hour, and I'm sure the American gentleman would prefer to stay comfortably in bed like the other ladies and gentlemen," he said decidedly. "Also, my limier doesn't like strangers. The American is sure to talk when my hound is finding, or move about and disturb him."

I swore to be on my good behavior, and the old man finally yielded, although he still obviously had his doubts.

I slept that night in a great double bed in a room high in one of the château's towers. One of the servants awoke me before dawn the next morning with a steaming cup of black coffee. It was damp and cold, and there was a thick mist outside the leaded glass windows. I pulled on my clothes, and the servant, with a flashlight, led me down the winding staircase in the tower to a small room where a fire was going and breakfast was laid out. I was told that the valet de limier and his hound had already arrived, so I ate fast and went out to join them.

Château Touffou is set in the Chitré forest, and stags have been killed within sight of its towers. The old man and I walked along a little path under the magnificent trees, the limier trotting behind us, regarding me suspiciously. He was obviously unused to strangers. After we had been walking an hour, the blood-red sun began to show through the mist. Birds started whistling to each other from the trees, and a woodpecker scolded at us. We left the path and cut through the woods. The trees abruptly thinned out, and before us was a cleared field, polka-dotted with big green melons. We walked along the edge of the field, the valet de limier going first to look for signs.

We came on some hoofmarks, and the old man stopped to study them. The hound moved up and began to run back and forth, his tail going madly, whining softly to himself. The old man spoke to him, and the hound instantly relaxed.

"Now see," he said to me in a whisper, for we did not know how far away the herd might be. "Most of these tracks were made by hinds, for the prints are long and narrow. But here is a stag. His prints are almost square. But he is not the daguet, for the marks of his dewclaws show, which means he must have been at least three or four years old." He picked up some droppings. "These came from him, for a stag's droppings are heavier than a hind's. But these are not very big, so he is probably not more than four years. Yes, here are more of his tracks. See, he does not walk with his hind legs far apart as a big stag must do because of the size of his testicles. The hinds belong to him, and the daguet won't be with this bunch for it is close to the rutting season and this stag would drive a younger male away."

We worked our way slowly along the edge of the field until we came to a place where the melons had been eaten, the fresh bite marks showing up on the green skins like raw scabs. "Here is our daguet," said the old man, after studying the marks. "The rear and front prints are almost on top of each other . . . the sign of a young animal that does not take long strides. He was out last night feeding and has gone into cover to lie-up for the day."

He put a fourteen-foot leash on the limier and pointed to the trail. The hound took the scent instantly and, after casting about for a few minutes, started off confidently. The old man explained that he had to work the hound on such a long leash to allow him more freedom to move

ABOVE: Harpooning sharks in the surf, like this native Mexican fisherman, is a dangerous business. BELOW: A harpooned shark is finally beached

ABOVE: A manta ray after being struck with a harpoon off the Pacific coast of Mexico. (Photo by Daniel P. Mannix, © 1952 National Geographic Society)

LEFT: Mexican fisherman with daggerfish speared at night with the aid of a torch

Bee Adkins and some of his hounds

ABOVE: "The coyote whirled and began to lead the hounds away from his home." Bee Adkins' famous Copper in action. BELOW: A wildcat is held at bay by Adkins' hounds

about in case he had trouble with the trail. "I do not dare to let him go free, for even the best limier may start running if we stumble on a deer lying up in the broom, and that would spoil everything."

We trailed the daguet to a thick bit of cover. Here the old man pulled the limier in. "I am sure our daguet is lying-up in there," he explained. "But we will check to make sure." We made a complete circle of the area, the man watching for tracks and the hound checking for scent. "Yes, he is in there," said the valet. "There are the tracks of several other deer, all hinds, going in to join him, but none coming out. My limier and I work together, and we cannot both be wrong."

The valet broke off a piece of the green broom that grows like bracken over the forest floor and laid it beside the tracks, the broken end pointing in the direction that the stag had gone. "That is to guide the huntsman," he explained. "Now my work is done for the day, except to report to the count."

We cut back through the forest until we came to a glade where the hunt was to meet. Already there were twenty or thirty horses there under the care of grooms, and a big van, containing the forty-odd hounds that made up the pack. The count drove up in his jeep, wearing his hunting costume with his great horn slung over one shoulder. He introduced me to the other members of the hunt who had begun to arrive. I was soon lost in a series of Monsieur That and Madame This. The men wore green jackets with gold buttons, white breeches, and black caps. Most of them carried horns and wore daggers at their belts. The women wore three-cornered hats and, because they rode sidesaddle, divided skirts. Only young girls are permitted to ride astride. The French stag hunt is as much a pageant as it is a hunt, and the formalities are rigidly observed. I heard one woman say angrily: "Celeste is now a married woman, yet she is still riding astride. How shocking! She should not be asked again."

The valet de limier made his report to the count, while the First Button rode over and listened carefully. "The valet de limier says there are three hinds with the daguet," said the count to me. "The *rapprocheurs* will have to cut him out."

The rapprocheurs are reliable old hounds that are sent in to separate the chosen stag from other deer. The count gave an order, and one of the huntsmen opened a door in the van. As he called the rapprocheurs by name, each hound jumped out of the van. The First Button called them over to him. They gathered behind his horse, staying so close together that a blanket could have covered them.

These staghounds were somewhat bigger than foxhounds, weighing about a hundred pounds, and standing some twenty-eight inches at the shoulder. They cannot wear collars, as the collars might catch in brush, so in order to identify them as part of the de Vergie pack, each hound has a big *V* clipped in the hair on his side that stood out like a brand. The count told me that the pack had originally been developed for wolf hunting, over a hundred years ago, and at that time had a strong admixture of wolf blood to enable them to stand up to their quarry. However, the last wolf in France was killed in 1902 and the pack was converted into staghounds. The present pack is fifteen generations removed from the old wolf strain.

The First Button rode off with the rapprocheurs following at his horse's heels. After him came two hunt servants with whips, and then the rest of the field. The main pack was released from the dog van but held in the glade until the rapprocheurs had cut out the daguets from the hinds.

I complimented the count on how perfectly trained the hounds were. "Yes, but they do not lack spirit," he said proudly. "Once when a stag went over a cliff, five of the hounds went over after him. Unfortunately, they were killed just as the stag was. Sometimes a stag will swim out into the middle of a lake. The pack will follow him. Unless there is a boat available, several will drown rather than give up."

The little procession disappeared among the trees, the men's silver horns flashing in the dark forest like searchlights when patches of sun, filtering down through the foliage, struck them.

"We will go in the jeep," said the count. The jeep had to take a longer way around, but as the count drove at top speed, dodging through places I wouldn't have thought wide enough for a pregnant goat, we arrived at the place where the valet de limier had left the broken piece of broom shortly after the others.

The rapprocheurs had already been put on the trail and were vanishing into the thicket. The field spread out to watch for the daguet when he was bolted. The First Button sat immovable on his horse near us. A few yards on either side of him were the hunt servants, also perfectly still. For a long time the only sound was an angry jay scolding from a tree.

Suddenly one of the hounds gave an eager yelp. A pause. Then two more hounds spoke. I could hear crashing in the broom as the other hounds ran to them. One hound passed me, bounding high above the broom to see what was going on. Then several hounds broke into full cry.

Suddenly a deer burst out of the thicket and fled past us. The hound that had been jumping through the broom swung around with an excited yell, but the deer was a hind, and as he hit her scent he turned away again. Two more deer flashed past us, one of them nearly running into the First Button. When she saw the horse and rider, she gave an enormous bound and vanished into the forest.

"The stag is driving out the hinds first, hoping the hounds will follow them . . . an old trick," said the count to me. Three of the rapprocheurs were speaking together now. "They have him," said the First Button, without looking away from the thicket. "He will break cover in a moment."

The cries of the hounds went up in pitch. Abruptly, one of the horns rang out . . . sounding *Vue* (Seen). Almost instantly another horn sounded and then another, the fanfares mingling with the wild baying of the hounds. Suddenly the stag shot out of the thicket almost beside me, two hounds crashing through the underbrush behind him. The stag paused for a moment, looking around for the hinds. As he did so, the hounds caught up and snapped at his heels. The stag kicked out, swerved for an instant to toss at them with his foot-long spikes, and then gave a leap that carried him past us and into the forest.

The First Button galloped in front of the furious hounds, shouting to stop them. Then he stood up in his stirrups and blew a long call to summon the main pack. After sounding the call twice, he stopped to listen. After a moment, I heard the answering call, coming far away and very faint through the trees. At intervals the First Button repeated the call, and the answer continued to come, each time louder than before. Then I saw the main pack come trotting eagerly through the forest under the care of several mounted hunt servants. The First Button pointed out the trail, and the pack were put on. A few seconds' anxious seeking, and then the whole pack burst into chorus and streamed away through the woods. The First Button sounded the *Bien aller* (Everything all right) on his horn and, putting spurs to his horse, charged into the forest after the pack. Everyone followed him, the horses crashing through the underbrush and their riders lying low along their necks to avoid the branches. The women maintained themselves on their sidesaddles at full gallop by what seemed to me to be a miracle of balancing.

Not even the count's jeep could keep up with the hunt, and we had to follow as best we could, cutting down side roads, going straight across country where the trees permitted it, and stopping at intervals to listen for the sound of the pack and the horns. I had regarded these great horns as mainly ornamental, but I soon realized that they had a real use. In the forests, the only way members of the hunt can keep in touch with each other is with the horns. There are dozens of calls, showing when the hounds are at fault, if the stag has taken to water, and so on. A blind man could follow the complete course of the hunt by listening to them.

For two hours the stag ran almost straight. Then, as he began to be winded, he started to circle. "He is looking for the hinds," the count told me. "If he finds a hind lying-up, he'll prod her out of her bed with his antlers and make her run, while he lies down in the same place. If the hounds are not alert, they'll take off after the fresh scent."

That is exactly what happened. The hounds, who had been speaking only occasionally on the trail, suddenly burst into wild cries. The *Bien aller* sounded, but the count shook his head. He was right, for a moment later we heard another call. "They were on a hind, and the First Button is calling them off," said the count.

We had stopped by the edge of an open field. Suddenly the count touched my shoulder, and pointed. I saw the stag trotting across the field. His tongue was out, but I knew from previous conversations with the count that a stag runs with his mouth open naturally. It is only when he's exhausted that he closes his mouth. The count said softly to me: "Don't frighten him. If a deer is frightened, he loses his scent for some time."

The stag passed within fifty yards of us. He was going at a deceptively slow lope, but I noticed that he covered the ground amazingly fast. At the far end of the field was a hedge some six feet high. Without breaking his stride, the stag cleared it as easily as a horse would clear a two-foot fence. Then he was gone.

The count lifted his horn and blew the *Vue*. The hounds recognized the call, for I heard them begin to yelp in answer. A few minutes later, the whole pack broke cover and came pouring across the field. At almost the same instant, members of the hunt began appearing in all directions along the edges of the forest. The First Button passed us at full gallop, his face running sweat and his horse white with lather. As the hounds ran toward us, they crossed the stag's scent. Instantly they broke into full cry and, swerving together like a school of fish, took the trail. The *Bien aller* rang out, and men and women raced across the field after them. It was really something to hear and see: the cry of the pack, the silver horns flashing in the sun, the brilliant green of the hunting costumes mixed with a few even more colorful uniforms of cavalry officers who were guests of the hunt, and the women looking like Dresden china pieces in their long skirts and jaunty three-cornered hats trimmed with gold braid. In a few minutes they had swept across the field and were gone.

I was astonished at the ease with which the stag had cleared the hedge, but the count said a stag can jump a ten-foot fence easily. "Once I saw a stag jump over a huntsman's horse," he told me. "The stag passed between the mounted man and the horse's head."

The count switched on the jeep's engine and we tore across the field after them. "The stag should turn at bay soon," said the count. "But just where, I have no idea. Once a stag bayed in a wine cellar. The hounds went in after him and between them they broke nearly every bottle in the place. That was the most expensive hunt I ever attended. I remember another time when a stag bayed in the middle of a herd of domestic pigs. The pigs attacked the hounds, and the stag escaped."

Word that a hunt was going on had got around the countryside, and a number of hunt followers had joined up. We passed a number of young boys and girls on motorcycles, several of the local farmers riding their plow horses, and dozens of people on foot. The count pointed out to me one old fellow wearing carpet slippers and riding a bicycle. "He hasn't missed a hunt for years," he told me.

In some places, the stag had kept along the paved road, and here the scent was almost impossible to follow. Several times he mixed his trail with that of other deer, but the experienced rapprocheurs refused to change. "We do not always get the stag, by any means," the count assured me. "I should say we average about 70 percent. We have hunted some old stags in this forest a dozen times. Then, too, occasionally a stag will save himself by some unusual means. Once a stag burst into a church and bayed in front of the altar. The priest threw himself in front of the animal and claimed sanctuary for him. You know it is an old law that a fugitive cannot be arrested as long as he is touching the altar. We respected the priest's wishes, and called off the hounds."

The stag had left the farming country and taken to the woods again. Under the trees, the scent improved. The cry of the pack came almost continuously, for the stag was doubling, running along his back trail to confuse the hounds, and not making long spurts. I left the jeep to follow on foot. While I was going through a patch of waist-high broom, I nearly stepped on him. He bounded up in front of me, dashed through the pack, and vanished with the hounds screaming after him. He had been lying beside his back trail with his antlers pressed along his back while the pack ran past within fifteen feet of him.

The sun was setting, and by now it was hard to tell which was the most exhausted—hounds, horses, riders, or the stag. "The First Button will keep on until it's too dark to see," the count assured me. "He's a deter-mined man. Once he followed a stag into a nudist camp and suddenly found himself confronted with two stark-naked women. The First Button hung his horn over one girl's shoulder, tossed his reins to the other, and killed the stag with his dagger. Then he removed his cap and thanked the ladies for their cooperation. . . . We still have another hour or so of daylight. I should like to get this daguet, as he has done a great deal of damage to the local farmers and they have asked that he be put out of the way."

While he spoke, we heard the horns sound at *Hallali,* which meant that the stag had turned at bay.

I left the jeep and ran on toward the sound of the pack. The whole pitch of their cries had changed. They were snarling, barking, and yell-ing instead of the steady "Hoo-hoo-hoo" of a pack in full cry. The First Button was forcing his heavy hunter through the cover. I saw him jerk off his horn and toss it back to one of the hunt servants. Then he slid off his horse, drawing his dagger as he did so.

I could see the hounds now, thrashing about in a patch of the waist-high broom. Then I saw the stag. He had taken his stand with his hind-quarters in a patch of scrub, but as I watched he charged into the pack with his head down, scattering them left and right. I heard a hound or two yelp, and I guessed those sharp, spiked antlers had gone home. The rest of the pack rushed in to help their friends. The broom was so high it was impossible to see much . . . just a tangle of brown and white, with an occasional flash of the stag. The First Button stood waiting his chance. Then he stepped in among the hounds and struck hard with his dagger, putting the full weight of his body behind the blow. The stag must have died instantly, for when I came up he was motionless and the huntsmen were already whipping off the pack.

The horns, whose shrill cries carry for miles, announced the death. The stag was loaded on the hood of the jeep and we drove back to the glade. The members of the hunt came in by twos and threes, together with the weary hounds. It was after sunset before everyone arrived.

The *curée* (cutting up) was quite a ceremony. The stag was drawn and the venison put aside to be divided later among the local farmers. Then the entrails and inferior parts were covered by the hide with the stag's head still attached to it. The pack lined up, and men blew a series of fanfares on their horns. The first was in memory of a member of the hunt who had been killed the year before. Then the personal calls of several famous former masters of the hunt were blown, followed by some of the calls most frequently used that day. Finally the hounds, who had been waiting patiently, were told to go ahead. They fell on the remains, and in an amazingly short time, nothing was left.

The stag's foot was awarded to an honored guest of the hunt . . . in this case, to my wife. She hadn't been able to ride, having injured her knee the week before while fox hunting in England. However, she had followed the hunt in a car and, as she was a foreign guest, she was awarded this distinction.

Although the French stag hunt is admittedly a pageant as much as a hunt, it's a good deal more than simply an excuse for people to wear picturesque costumes and go through a lot of forms and ceremonies. The members of the hunt ride hard and well. Broken bones are not uncommon, and to kill a big stag with a dagger requires a considerable amount of courage and dexterity. The most important feature of the hunt is the work of the hounds. The organization and direction of the pack are considerably more complicated than in any other form of hunting, and most stag hunters are far more interested in watching the hounds in action than in making a successful kill. As the count told me: "In England, people hunt in order to ride. In France, we ride in order to hunt."

The most popular of the formal hunts in the United States is beagling—occasionally condescendingly called "the poor man's fox hunt." Beagles are the smallest hounds used for hunting in America (dachshunds are somewhat smaller, but I have yet to see anyone go out for an afternoon's sport with a pack of dachshunds in this country, although in Germany and Holland they are used to bolt wild boars from thick cover), and correspondingly easier to feed and house. Beagles are divided into two classes: under thirteen inches and under fifteen, but the smallest generally used are about ten inches at the shoulder. There are twenty-three registered packs in the United States, and their quarry is either the cottontail rabbit or the hare. The hares are nearly always the western jack rabbit, though in a few areas European hares have been imported. The European hare is bigger, faster, and smarter than even the best jack rabbit, but as far as I'm concerned, trying to run one down with beagles is like trying to catch a kangaroo with a pack of Pekingese. Only nineteen-inch harriers can overtake them, and then the field must be mounted. With beagles, the field is always on foot, and trying to stay up with even thirteen-inch beagles is enough of a workout for the average week-end sportsman.

For many years now I have been a member of the Ardrossan Beagles, a hunt near Philadelphia, Pennsylvania, who assemble on Sunday afternoons during the winter to give members of the club, the hounds, and the local jack rabbits a little light exercise. The jack rabbits are all imported, as they are not native to Pennsylvania. They are released in the spring so they will get to know the country by autumn, as hunting a hare that does not know where he is going is no sport at all. Some clubs hunt cottontails, but the bunnies generally stay in cover or go down holes, whereas the jacks go straight across country, seldom resort to cover, and never go down holes.

One of the great appeals in beagling is that the whole family can take part in the hunt. Small children and the older members usually "hill-top," take up a position on a hill where they can watch the hunt from a distance, and as a hare generally doubles they can often watch the whole spectacle without too much exertion. The more energetic members try to stay up with the hounds—often too close to the hounds to suit the master—and as a hare will sometimes give you a four-mile point straight across country at top speed, this takes some doing.

Hares are remarkably clever; there are few tricks even a fox will use that are unknown to an experienced old jack. A hare's basic trick is to turn and run back on her own line and then jump off to the side. The hounds run on to the dead end and then spread out to find the new line, which is actually some one hundred feet behind them. A standard rule in beagling when the hounds check is that "the scent is always behind you." Hares will also run up the bed of a stream, along the top of a wall, or along a fallen log. They quickly learn that scent will not lie on a hard-top road, and take to road-running, a particularly dangerous trick, as the hounds, intent on trying to find the scent, pay no attention to cars. Hares have been known to swim out to the middle of a stream, climb on a floating log, and lie there quietly while the hounds run futilely up and down the banks on both sides trying to find the line.

Our hunt meets at three o'clock on a Sunday afternoon at some agreed-on spot where hare have been observed. The pack arrives in the hound-van and moves off under the direction of the master and the whips while the field follows at a respectful distance. The first question is what section to draw—tall grass, close-cropped pasture, stubble, or hillsides. Hares will lie-up in different areas, depending on weather conditions and their individual habits. Today, the master decides to draw a pasture first. The pack spreads out, but not so far apart that they are out of the master's control. The whips running along the sides keep them together. Behind the pack, the field also spreads out, for with a hundred or so followers they have almost as much chance of putting up a hare by blind chance as do the hounds with their educated noses. A hare crouching in her form has very little scent.

Nothing in the pasture. The master decides to draw the hill slopes. It is a bitter cold day, and the hares may like the warm hillsides. A single blast on the horn brings the pack together except for a few stragglers who need the attention of the whips, and following the master, the pack moves off, to be cast again on the side of a hill. Immediately Warrior gives tongue and the others rush to him, but it is only a pheasant. The whips crack, and Warrior, looking ashamed of himself, turns away. Now there is a "So-ho!" the beagler's "Tallyho!" from a member of the field. Everyone turns, and the hounds run toward the man who is holding his cap over his head and pointing. Another false alarm. A cottontail, not a hare, is racing across the slope. Again the whips rush in and turn the pack while the beagler looks quite as ashamed of himself as did Warrior.

Nothing on the hillside, so the master starts for a field of stubble corn. As the hounds lope toward it, half a dozen voices shout "So-ho!" From the edge of the field a gray shape has started up, dashed straight through the field, and is heading for the hill. The hounds have not seen her, and the master's horn calls them with a series of quick, commanding notes. Now their heads are down, casting about. One hound begins to speak with eager yelps. "Hark to Driver!" Another hound speaks, then two more, then a dozen. For a few seconds the pack sweeps back and forth, uncertain in which direction the hare has run. Then comes the full crash of the hound music as the pack streams away in full cry.

Everyone starts running. Ahead is a post-and-rail fence, and the field master shouts anxiously, "Climb by the posts, please!" If any of the rails are old, they will break in the middle when a sudden weight is thrown on them. The hounds are tearing up the hill. "They're headed for the cross-roads!" someone gasps. If the hare cuts across a highway the hounds, running with their heads down, stand a good chance of being killed by cars. The whips have already seen the danger and are running all out to head the pack. But a watcher on a distant hilltop has his cap up and is pointing. The hare has turned. She ducked through a hedge, turned sharply to the right, and using the hedge as a screen, is running toward a swamp she knows well. The excited pack burst through the hedge and kept on into the middle of the next field. Here they stop, amazed that the scent has vanished.

The master refuses to lift them and put them directly on the new line. He has several young entries, pups that are only learning the game, and he wants them to realize that they can't overrun the line. He waits while the pack spreads out, noses down, tails waving wildly, and the field master calls, "Hold hard, please!" to keep the field from jumping hedge and fouling the scent.

An old bitch turns and goes back to the gap in the hedge. Slowly and systematically she begins to work out the line. Still without speaking she follows it down the side of the hedge; she isn't quite sure as yet. The master watches her, his horn ready. "Matchless has it!" shouts someone, but the master ignores him. Then Matchless speaks. Instantly the rest race to her. Echo speaks, and then Bugler and Restless. They are off again. Now everyone can start running, trying to keep up with the pack, who are going downhill with a breast-high scent.

At the swamp, the pack comes to a real check. The hare has doubled back and forth through the tall reeds and is lying quietly on a little hummock in the middle of the bog. The hounds splash through the water, testing every bit of dry ground with their noses, but it is no use. The whips spread out, cracking their long thongs in the hopes of making the hare bolt. She lies too close. Then Rouser speaks. He has found some scent floating on a puddle. There are crashes in the dry reeds as the others run to him, bounding as high as they can to see over the cover. The hare leaves her hummock and steals away. She gets clear of the swamp without being seen and runs quietly to a path she knows through the woods. Gypsy, skirting the swamp, happens on her line by accident, and after one amazed sniff gives tongue. The master is doubtful, as Gypsy has been known to make mistakes. He splashes through the swamp and studies the soft mud. There are hare's prints. He sounds the horn, and the running starts again.

Two hours and several miles later, probably only the master and the whips are still with the pack. The majority of the field is stretched in a long, scraggling line across country, pulling small children out of mud-holes, trotting along paths that they hope will take them in the same direction the hounds have gone, or openly and unashamedly hilltopping. The hare will almost surely escape, but the purpose of the hunt is the chase and not a kill. By sunset, the master blows off, and a tired field wonders just how far away they are from their cars. They start back, the senior members of the hunt explaining how the master should have cast the hounds at that check near Sugartown, and assuring everyone that the hares these days are a poor lot compared with those of twenty years ago. Also, these modern hounds have lost their noses ("Remember old Chancellor? There was a hound!"), the whips don't know their business, and the hills are definitely getting steeper every year.

It's a great sport, and until the whole country is converted into a solid concrete superhighway, a few people will still practice it. Watching the pack sweep and wheel like swallows on a hillside as the scent shifts, hearing the full burst of hound music as the scent reaches them, the rare glimpses of the hare as she turns, doubles, and then departs in a burst of speed, leaving the bewildered pack to unravel the mixed trail—these are worth many blisters, nettle stings, and wet feet. In spite of the encroachments of developments and highways, people love the jolly little hounds—for five years the beagle was voted the most popular of all breeds in America, and has always ranked among the top ten—and as long as there is even a cottontail to chase, there'll be a beagle to chase him.

CHAPTER 14

Snake Catching

I'm no crazier than anyone else—anyone else in this case refers to the Reverend Mr. Lewis Ford, who stuck live water moccasins in his mouth—but I've always liked to have a few rattlesnakes around. Except for the Indian cobra, a rattlesnake is the most dramatic of all poisonous snakes. You can talk about your kraits, mambas and moccasins, but they don't seem dangerous until after they've bitten you, and your friends congratulate the undertaker on how natural he's made the corpse look. A rattler looks and sounds just as dangerous as he is. Neither man nor beast can hear the dry buzz of the rattle without knowing the owner isn't any Little Lord Fauntleroy, and a rattler reared up in his fighting S-shaped coil is as sinister an object as the human mind can conceive. Man has always feared and admired the rattlesnake. In the form of Quetzalcoatl, the Feathered Serpent, the Aztecs worshiped him as divine. A prehistoric people erected the great snake mounds in Ohio to his honor, and when the Eastern Indians wanted to show that they really meant business, they sent their neighbors a collection of arrows wrapped in a rattlesnake skin. Even today, the Hopi Indians bring rain by dancing with rattlesnakes in their mouths, reasoning that the snakes' rattles resemble thunder and the snakes' quick stroke symbolizes the lightning. White men feel the same fascination. Our first national flag showed a rattler in "fighting coil" with the motto "Don't tread on me." Today the Holiness Faith Healers have built a cult around handling rattlesnakes, and in some parts of the country motorists refuse to buy a tank of gas unless the station is equipped with a first-rate rattlesnake pit.

I first became interested in rattlesnakes when I learned during a cocktail party that there is a rattlesnake boom sweeping the country. My informant was a gentleman who had opened a country club in a hitherto untrammeled section of the Poconos, renowned for its magnificent scenery, invigorating climate, and giant rattlesnakes. As the average golfer shows a certain reluctance to argue possession of the ninth tee with an infuriated rattler, the board of directors was at a loss as to how to proceed, but the problem was quickly solved.

"The country is full of rattlesnake clubs," my informant assured me excitedly. "All you have to do is tell these fellows where there's a good den, and they'll clean it out in no time. They use the hides for leather, have the meat canned as a delicacy, sell live snakes to zoos, carnivals, and snake shows. But the big money comes from selling the venom. They get $350 an ounce for it."

At my age, Elizabeth Taylor could dance around me in her birthday suit and I would only stifle a bored yawn, but any mention of a fast buck brings out the beast in me. By shrewd questioning, I extracted the information that a Mr. Robert Bates of Analomink, Pennsylvania, is a recognized authority on catching rattlesnakes, so as soon as I could get to a phone I called Mr. Bates and asked if I could go along on one of his hunts.

Like all other recreations, rattlesnake hunting has definite seasons—spring and autumn. The only time you can find rattlesnakes in any numbers is when they are either just leaving the dens or returning to them in the fall. During the summer, the snakes spread out through the woods, sleeping by day and hunting at night. In winter, they hibernate below the frost level in dens where no one can get at them. It was April when I called Mr. Bates, and he said the rattlers wouldn't be out until May. "But the first warm weekend, I'll give you a ring," he promised. "You have to hit it at just the right time, for they don't stay around the den more than a few days once the weather gets warm."

The first warm weekend turned out to be Mother's Day and Mr. Bates refused to go rattlesnaking, arguing with charming sentiment that even a rattlesnake may be somebody's mother. But the following weekend was even warmer, so my son, Danny, and I drove north to Marshall Creek where we were to meet Mr. Bates. Mr. Bates turned out to be a quiet man in his seventies who, when he isn't rattlesnaking, operates a lumber mill. He had two friends with him whom he introduced as Wayne Metzgar, a local machinist, and Herbert Kramer, a tool and die maker. Although much younger than Mr. Bates, they were both expert outdoorsmen and all three went hunting together every winter for deer and bear. We all piled into Mr. Bates's truck and started out for the dens.

"Shoulda been last week," Mr. Bates told me sadly as we headed down a back country road. "A party got seventy snakes at one den. Now they'll be spread all over, and picking them up won't be so easy. I hope you aren't a nervous type like the last fellow I took out. He went stumbling all around without looking where he was going, and every time a snake struck at him he'd fall down. Can't catch snakes behaving like that."

I assured Mr. Bates I had every intention of looking where I was going. I also suggested that as he and his friends were experienced snake hunters, I'd let them go first, following well behind.

"It's plenty spunky of you to suggest that," said Mr. Bates, throwing me an approving look. "That's what we call 'dead man's place.' Snakes are pretty sluggish this time of year, and often they won't strike the first two or three men who go past them. It's the fourth guy who always seems to get it. I just hope you get a good clean bite and the snake doesn't get hung up in you the way one did last week with that poor fellow from Leighton."

"What happened to him?" asked Danny.

"Frankly, I think you'd be happier if you didn't know. But I'll say this much. When a snake plunges his fangs in you, he discharges only enough venom to give you a lesson. Snakes can control exactly how much venom they discharge, and they don't like to waste it. Then he pulls out his fangs and goes back into coil. But sometimes his fangs get caught and he can't get them loose. That annoys him, and he keeps pumping venom into you all the time he's trying to get free. That's what happened to the Leighton man. We all went to the funeral."

I began to wonder if rattlesnake hunting was as easy a way to make money as I supposed. I asked if Mr. Bates had ever been bitten. "No, or I wouldn't be here. We never carry snakebite outfits or antivenom or anything like that. Seems unsportsmanlike, somehow. Our motto is 'Give the snakes a fighting chance.' Beats me why people spend all that money to go to Africa to hunt big game when with a forked stick and a bag, they can get all the thrills they want right here at home."

I should add right here and now that the majority of experienced snake handlers most certainly do not agree with Mr. Bates's theory that carrying a snakebite kit is a waste of time. However, I'd like to add that in my opinion a snakebite outfit in inexperienced hands, especially if the operator has just been bitten and is inclined to be panicky, may well do more damage than using no kit at all. Anyone carrying a snakebit kit should make himself thoroughly conversant with its use and if possible receive lessons from an experienced herpetologist.

Meanwhile we had left the paved road and turned off on a dirt track that I would have thought not even a jeep could have navigated. Probably a jeep couldn't have, but Bates's old truck inched along in first gear over rocks, potholes, and high centers while the trail writhed between columns of tall trees.

Used to the Philadelphia suburbs, I couldn't believe that any part of Pennsylvania was this wild. This was the way the country had looked before the coming of the white man. Among the swamp huckleberries and scrub oaks, the ferns were beginning to unfold, their still unopened ends curled like the scrolls of violins. Sandstone slabs exploded through the black earth, held back by their restraining masses of lichens. Here and there gleamed young pines, so vividly green in their fresh spring growth they seemed like Christmas tinsel. Towhees, catbirds, and blue-jays flickered through the still bare branches of the trees, and once we saw a scarlet tanager dart across the road—the first I'd seen since I was a small boy. Occasionally the truck labored through mountain streams, the water as brown and frothy as beer, while brown-red chipmunks sat on stones to watch us.

We went on for hours, seldom reaching a speed of more than a mile an hour. Several times we came to where trees, unable to bear their winter burdens of snow, had crashed down across the track; but the snake hunters had brought not only axes but even a power saw, and soon cleared the way. Finally we came to where a broad stream had carried so much sediment across the road that not even the indomitable truck could continue. "From here on, we walk," Bates explained.

From the back of the truck, the men took a pile of sticks with snubby forks on the ends. Dan and I were each given one, and everyone took a bag. Thus equipped, we started on, our boots crunching on the dried leaves as though we were walking on popcorn. After a couple of miles' hike, Bates pointed through the trees with his stick. "The den is on that ridge ahead," he explained. "But the snakes will probably be spread all over the slope below it. We'll spread out here and start looking."

Everyone started out on his own. It was eleven o'clock, still a little early in the day for the rattlers, who at this time of year require the full heat of the midday sun to warm their cold blood and make them active. We moved from rock to rock and from log to log, looking carefully to see if a snake was coiled up beside it. I was picking my way gingerly up the slope when I saw Herbert Kramer ahead of me suddenly pirouette like a ballet dancer and begin to jab at the ground with his stick.

"Herb's got one," shouted Bates, hurrying forward. "Or maybe one's got Herb," he added as an afterthought.

But it turned out that Herb had seen the black, banded body just before the snake had lunged for him. Herb was lucky, for nothing on earth can dodge the blow of a rattlesnake; the stroke is literally quicker than the eye can follow. A mongoose can kill a cobra but would stand no chance at all against the lightning-quick blow of a rattler. As soon as the snake had struck, he went back into "fighting coil." Before, he had been lying in the warm sun coiled round and round in flat loops like a garden hose. From this coil, a snake can bite but cannot strike out more than a few inches. Now he was reared up, the upper half of his body forming an S. In this position, a rattlesnake is like a coiled spring. He can lunge forward a third—some snake experts say one-half—of his own length, stab with his extended fangs, and return to coil in a fraction of a second.

It was many years since I had seen a rattler in the wild and I had almost forgotten what a wonderful creature he is. I was looking at 200 million years of reptile evolution that produced the most perfect mechanism for striking and injecting venom ever devised. True, the poison of a cobra, drop for drop, is more deadly than that of the vipers, and the rattlesnake is a viper. Cobra poison is mainly neurotoxic; that is, it affects the nervous system and kills by paralyzing the heart and lung action. Viper venom is basically hemotoxic; it destroys the blood cells and ruptures the small blood vessels. However, all snake venoms possess both characteristics, and it would be better to be bitten by a small cobra than by a large rattlesnake.

But when it comes to injecting the venom, a rattlesnake is as superior to a cobra as a modern rifle is to an arquebus. A cobra can open his mouth only about 45 degrees, and then must not only bite but even chew the wound to make the poison run down his fangs and into the cut. The cobra's fangs are simply modified teeth and are short; otherwise the snake could not shut its mouth. A rattler's fangs are much longer, perhaps as much as three-quarters of an inch, and fold back against the roof of his

Bee Adkins' "catch dogs" fighting with a young black bear in the Low
Sierras of north-central California. The white dog is a wire-haired fox ter-
rier, used by Bee to hold the bear after the hounds have run him down.
The darker dog is a mongrel

ABOVE: Otter hunting near Salisbury, England. BELOW: English otter hunters have been following the sport for nearly a thousand years

One of France's most famous packs of staghounds is maintained by the Count de Vergie at Château Touffou

Riding hard after the staghounds

Hunting a jack rabbit with the Ardrossan Beagles near Philadelphia

ABOVE: An expert rattlesnake hunter pins his quarry down with a forked stick . . .

LEFT: . . . before seizing it carefully and throwing it into a stout sack

ABOVE: Giant toads don't look it, but they can move like lightning

LEFT: Most mantraps used in early nineteenth-century England were "improved" by riveting curved metal hooks onto the pan

ABOVE: This print
of a poacher caught
in a mantrap was
published in
London in 1816

RIGHT: Old spring
gun from the
Mill Street Museum,
Ludlow, England

Tracking bloodhounds in action

mouth. When the rattler strikes, he opens his mouth a good 180 degrees, and the fangs snap down into place as he lunges forward. He does not need to bite; he simply stabs with them. As he feels the fangs go home, the snake instantly discharges the venom through them, for the fangs are hollow and operate as miniature hypodermic needles. Because of the length of the fangs, the venom is injected deep into the bloodstream. Unlike a cobra, who can strike only downward, a rattlesnake can strike in any direction, including straight upward. His S-shaped coil enables him to strike with great speed and accuracy, while the strike of a cobra is slow and clumsy.

Gingerly, Herb extended his ten-foot stick and touched the snake. So far, the snake had not rattled. Rattlers often strike without sounding their death warning, especially if they are surprised or sluggish. But this snake was thoroughly aroused by now, and for the first time we heard the dull drone of the rattle. The rattle of a rattlesnake is not like a child's rattle. The tip of the tail is covered by a series of bony cup-shaped segments fitting over each other. When the snake is nervous, the end of the tail vibrates rapidly and makes these segments rub together. The noise sounds like an electric buzzer rather than like a rattle.

"He's only a little fellow, not more than a couple of feet long," said Bob Bates. "Hardly worth bothering with."

But Dan and I wanted a couple of rattlesnakes to take home and keep as pets. Young snakes are usually easier to keep in captivity than adults, so this fellow was just the right size. Obligingly, Bob pinned the snake's head down with the fork of his stick. Luckily for snake collectors, a rattler's head is considerably wider than its body to hold the poison sacs on either side. This is true of all the American vipers, but not of our only other poisonous snake, the coral snake, who is more closely related to the cobras. Bob took care to get his fingers well up against the fork so that when the stick was taken away a space wouldn't be left for the snake to turn and strike his hand. Then he dropped the stick, instantly using his other hand to steady the thrashing coils.

"Hold a bag open," he told Wayne Metzgar, "and I'll drop him in."

Wayne opened the mouth of a sack, and Bob threaded the body into the opening. As he was doing so, the snake opened its mouth. I could see the curved fangs, as white and translucent as fingernail parings, slowly slip out of their protecting sheaths of flesh. At the tiny opening near the tip of one, a yellowish dewdrop of liquid venom slowly formed, the stuff that turns blood to water. That snake would have given all his rattles and six years of his life to get that venom into Bob, and Bob knew it. When he let go, he flung the snake down into the bag, for sometimes a snake, as he is released, can get in a single backlash at the man holding him and sink at least one of his fangs into the flesh. But this snake hit the bottom of the bag before he knew what had happened to him.

"You carry the bag," said Bob, handing it to Dan. "Just don't get it mixed up with your lunch bag and reach for a ham sandwich. That's happened too. Believe me."

Dan took the bag, holding it well away from him. "No holes in this bag, are there?" he asked anxiously.

"Absolutely not. One year Herb and I were driving back with a bagful of rattlers in the back seat of our car. When we got home, I lifted up the bag, and darned if it wasn't empty. Those snakes had found a little bit of a hole and worked on it with their noses until they'd gotten out. Herb's wife came out just then, and Herb said to her, 'Dear, don't use the car for a few hours—it's full of rattlesnakes.' She promised she wouldn't. Then we had to catch the snakes. They were up in the springs and twisted around under the seats and everywhere. After that, we always make sure every bag we use hasn't even the smallest hole."

For some time we poked around without luck. Then Wayne heard a dry little sound among the leaves, and there was another rattler crawling away. There's something fascinating in watching a snake pour itself along the ground. First comes the coffin-shaped head, preceded by the flickering black flame of the tongue. Then follows the ever-moving current of the body, each coil moving in a different direction but all with the same intent and directed by the same calm intelligence. They follow a constantly changing pattern, curve flowing after curve, each ventral scale a miniature oar pushing the snake along. Proverbs lists the movement of a serpent as one of the four great mysteries no mortal can understand, and watching that snake sway along the ground I could understand why.

Wayne, being less romantically minded, reached out with his forked stick, but before he could pin down the snake's head it had gotten under a flat slab of limestone, rosetted with green-yellow lichens. It took all five of us half an hour to pry the slab over so Bob Bates could flick the snake out with his stick. According to experts, a rattlesnake can only crawl about three miles per hour; but this one was headed toward me, and I'll swear he was doing at least fifteen mph. I leaned forward to take a picture, and this snake did something else no snake is supposed to do. He struck at me so hard he went clear off the ground. Knowing no rattler can leave the ground on his strike, I wasn't worried a bit, and the malicious story that I went over flat on my back I brand as a half truth, a calculated misrepresentation, and Hitler's technique of the Big Lie. I just tripped—that was all. Could have happened to anybody.

As this snake was nearly four feet, we didn't want him, so Bob Bates killed him. Bob made rattlesnake oil out of the fat for his friends. This is great stuff, and a sure cure for stiff joints, sprains, rheumatism, sciatica, toothache, sore throat, colds, frostbite, chilblains, and corns, but most of Bob's friends use it for earache. Bob says it seems to help them.

We got four more rattlers, including another little fellow whom Dan and I added to our collection. Then we went on to the main den. It was a deep crack under a great sandstone slab, wide enough for a man to crawl down. "But don't try it," Bob warned. "The snakes are apt to lie up in cracks along the sides, and they'll nip in you in the back of the neck as you go by." Being fearless, this threat wouldn't have stopped me for a moment, but I reflected it would be a nuisance for Bob and his friends to have to carry my corpse back to the truck, so I forebore.

This started a discussion on just how fatal the bite of a rattler is. In the United States, rattlers are responsible for 80 percent of deaths by snakebite, but although about a thousand people a year are bitten, only about thirty die, thanks to modern medical techniques. All sorts of cures have been invented for snakebite, the best known being whisky taken internally. The late W. C. Fields claimed that he always traveled with two suitcases, one full of whisky in case of snakebite and the other full of rattlesnakes. In Kansas, where prohibition is still in force, whisky can only be obtained by a doctor's certificate for snakebite. In one town, the story goes, the snake population is down to a single tired old rattler, and he has ten people on his waiting list. Unfortunately, doctors now claim all alcohol does is to speed up the circulation of blood and distribute the poison that much faster through the system. How those fellows expect to stay in business with such ideas, I can't imagine.

Our three rattlesnake hunters agreed that in case of a bite, about the best thing to do was get as quickly as possible to a hospital, where you could receive antivenom injections and expert medical care. "The bloodstream carries the poison through your system so fast, cutting open the wound or using a tourniquet doesn't do much good," was the consensus of opinion. As it would take six Sonny Listons to hold me down while somebody cut open my leg with a razor blade, I was relieved to know this treatment was no longer considered essential. However, as I've explained, most snake hunters do carry kits, and consider them invaluable.

As far as I can make out, the whole business of snakebite treatment is still a pretty mysterious affair. No one knows exactly the chemical composition of snake venom or how the venom works. Individuals vary considerably in their susceptibility to animal venoms—some people have died of a single beesting, while others have survived the bite of an eight-foot diamondback rattler. Then there are the questions of how much venom the snake actually discharged into the wound, plus the age, size, and weight of the snake, and if he has fed recently and so used up some of his venom on his quarry. Our friends agreed the best treatment is just not to get bitten. "Don't worry about it," Bob advised me cheerfully. "With us, you're as safe as if you were in your coffin."

We got a few more snakes among the rocks near the den, including one big fellow over four feet. Bob Bates told me that although six-foot timber rattlers have been reported, the biggest he ever found was fifty-two inches. "The greatest number of rattles we ever found on a snake was seventeen," he added. "Guess you know a snake gets a new rattle every time he sheds his skin, and as they shed two or three times a year, the number of rattles isn't any real guide to their age. Anyhow, they keep breaking off their rattles crawling around the rocks."

We'd missed the big spring rattlesnake exodus from the dens by about a week, and Mr. Bates felt sorry about it. "They are not too far from the den right now," he assured us. "Professor Martin at State Teachers' College got us to dye some rattlers different colors when they came out of the dens, and then he kept a record of anyone who saw a painted rattlesnake during the summer. If you were walking in the woods and ran across a purple rattlesnake with lavender spots, it's the sort of thing that would linger in your mind, so the professor was able to keep pretty good track of them. He says they never wander more than a few miles from the dens, but it's still tough to locate them."

"How do they find their way back to the dens in autumn?"

"That's hard to say. One guess is that the experienced old ones go first and the youngsters follow them by scent. Some sure stay out late. I've found rattlesnakes here in November."

Bob Bates and his friends had done us a great honor by revealing the location of one of their private rattlesnake dens. So many groups have taken up rattlesnake catching as a hobby, the supply is getting depleted. As a result, the clubs keep the location of their dens a secret. But although rattlesnake catching is a fast-growing fad in the East, we have a long way to go to catch up with our western brothers. Five tons of rattlers are shipped annually from Texas alone, mainly to carnivals and circuses, but the headquarters of the business would seem to be the International Association of Rattlesnake Hunters in Okeene, Oklahoma. They stage an annual rattlesnake hunt every year. The snakes they get are the western diamondback rather than our timber rattlesnake.

There's a lot of question as to whether the western diamondback is more deadly than the eastern timber rattlesnake. I shall content myself with pointing out some recognized historical cases that illustrate the potency of a timber rattler's venom. Cotton Mather in Salem, Massachusetts, back in 1714, couldn't raise cherries because rattlers kept biting his trees, waiting until birds ate the poisoned fruit, and then eating the birds as they dropped dead. On another occasion, a timber rattler bit the tongue of Mather's wagon. The tongue began to swell so fast that only by hurriedly uncoupling it was Mather able to save the wagon. Mather also observed that a certain species of blacksnake served as a pilot to guide the rattler to his prey, and the snake had been called a pilot blacksnake ever since. Let any Westerner try to top those stories.

After thanking our kind friends, Dan and I started back with our two captives. At $350 an ounce, our rattlers were worth at a conservative estimate at least a thousand dollars, and we couldn't understand why Mr. Bates and his friends had never cashed in on this bonanza. Still, their loss was our gain, and we looked forward to operating a lucrative rattlesnake dairy with some slogan like "Venom from contented rattlers."

Dan had constructed a fine snake cage during his manual training classes at school, and it was installed in our living room. We carried the bag containing the snakes into the house, and then I tried to hook them out of the bag with a long-handled poker. I promptly made the interesting discovery that there is no possible way to keep a snake on the end of a poker if he decides to get off. A snake's backbone is composed of some two hundred ball-and-socket joints. You can tie a snake in a knot and he can untie himself, simply gliding through the knot. Trying to hold one on a stick is like trying to lasso a yard of oil. When one of our snakes hit the floor, instead of going into "fighting coil" he promptly started to pour himself off under the davenport.

After a few minutes, both our captives got extremely deft at dodging the poker, swaying their heads around the *L*-shaped end and keeping on going. Before starting the process, we had carefully thrown all other livestock out of the room, including Tilly, our Cairn terrier; Tiba, the ocelot; a couple of ferrets, and a pet 'coon. The whole collection were now lined up on the other side of the glass doors that separate our living room from the rest of the house, positive they could fix those two burr-tails in a minute. Jule, my wife, added considerably to the excitement of the occasion by opening the doors periodically to ask, "Haven't you gotten those things put away yet?" and thereby letting the entire menagerie loose on us. It was due entirely to my magnificent flow of profanity that we finally got both snakes in the cage.

I must say that at first glance—and at second, third, and fourth glance too—the two rattlers didn't seem like prime material for domestication. They lay coiled up on the floor of the cage, regarding us with malignant pride, and even the vibration of our footsteps was enough to start them rattling. In the confined space the hum of the rattles sounded like a hive of bees. But in a few days they began to settle down. They no longer struck furiously at the glass when we passed and didn't rattle even when lifted out of their box with the poker so the cage could be cleaned. As one had seven rattles and the other eleven, we named them Seven and Eleven. Eleven was a few inches longer than Seven, and not as active.

Our next job was to feed them. Rattlesnakes eat only live food, usually rats and other small rodents. As one thing we have plenty of is rats in our barn, we caught one in a box trap and turned him loose in the cage.

We had provided the snakes with a hollow log as a home, and both were inside with only their heads showing, each head shaped like the club pip on a playing card. The rat ran around and then passed too close to the log. Suddenly Seven moved like a flicker of light. He struck the rat and returned to position so fast his coils seemed barely to twitch. The rat went straight up in the air. When he came down he ran wildly for a few seconds, then fell on his side, twitching spasmodically. He was dead in less than a quarter of a minute.

Seven was obviously in no hurry. I'd about decided that he had forgotten about the rat when he started to flow out from under the log. His forked tongue was busy, flickering over the bottom of the cage as he followed the rat's trail. In a sense, snakes "smell" with their tongues. The tongue picks up tiny particles of scent that cling to the forked end. When the snake retracts his tongue, he puts the forked tip into two tiny holes in the roof of his mouth known as Jacobson's organs. These organs enable him to tell if he's on the right track.

Seven behaved as though he had nothing but time, as indeed he did.

He knew well his prey wasn't going anywhere; it was dead and waiting for him. Poisonous snakes have their venom primarily as a means of catching prey rather than for defense. A mink, squirrel, gopher, or even a large rat can give a nonpoisonous snake several bad bites before the snake overpowers it. But a poisonous snake doesn't have to worry. He strikes, gets out of the way, and simply waits for his prey to die.

Eventually Seven came to where the rat was lying. Even now, he didn't seem in any hurry. Seven examined the rat carefully, touching it lightly with his tongue, apparently to make sure it was dead. He reminded me of a hunter who has just shot a potentially dangerous animal and prods it carefully with a stick before starting to skin it out. At last, convinced that the rat couldn't bite him, he made his way around to the head and began to work his jaws over the rat with a chewing motion. Although snakes do not chew their food, always swallowing it whole, they force one side of their jaws forward at a time, inching the prey slowly down their gullets.

During the feeding process, Eleven got interested and came out to investigate. He started on the dead rat from the other end. What would have happened when they met in the middle I didn't know, but I didn't want to find out. Using the poker, I made Eleven disgorge the tail of the rat, and took him out of the cage until Seven had finished eating. After that, I always put in two rats at the same time.

Although both our snakes grew perfectly tame, that is, never rattled or offered to strike at us, we didn't try picking them up with our bare hands. The pit vipers—rattlesnakes, copperheads, and water moccasins —hunt mainly at night, and detect the presence of their prey by means of their pits, two small holes between the eye and the mouth that look like misplaced nostrils. These pits are equipped with miniature thermostats, and by them the snake can tell the presence of warm-blooded prey—or in the case of a moccasin, of cold-blooded frogs—by the difference in temperature. As snakes are more inclined to trust to their pits than their eyes, they are liable to strike at anything warm, even electric light bulbs. Granted, the snake doesn't mean any harm and will regret his mistake if he bites you, but that doesn't do the party of the second part much good.

Some rattlesnake fanciers think I'm too cautious in this respect. When the word was eased around that we'd joined the rattlesnake set, several people from various snake clubs dropped in to see us. No matter what crazy idea you have nowadays, there always seem to be plenty of other fruitcakes in the same league, and they all form clubs. One fifteen-year-old kid told us he not only freely handled his own rattlers but eve picked up wild ones with his bare hands. "Watch the snake's tongue" he told us. "If he holds the tongue out in a rigid position and keeps it out a long time he's nervous, because he's trying to get a lot of scent particles. If he doesn't use it at all, or only moves it slowly in and out, he's quiet and you can pick him up as long as you do it gently." Maybe so, but I'm too young and beautiful to die. The kid told us he was saving up to buy a cobra. I don't know about him, but I'm darned sure his parents ought to have their heads shrunk.

Now that Seven and Eleven were recognized members of the household, I decided to start operating my rattlesnake dairy. Milking a snake is simple enough; you just grab him back of the head, force him to open his mouth, hang the fangs over the edge of a cup, and press the venom glands on either side of the head until the venom runs into the cup. There's some risk attached to the process, but at $350 an ounce I was willing to take it.

Fortunately, I decided to check with the laboratories first. There are several laboratories who buy venom and pay a high price for it, but they will buy only from regular agencies. The snakes have to be carefully identified for species, and, as there are something like twenty-three species of rattlesnakes in the United States, this requires expert knowledge. The venom is then rotated in a centrifuge for five to six hours, put in an electric incubator, dehydrated, quick frozen, and stored in a dark place. Every step of the process can be done only by a trained laboratory staff with the proper equipment.

So our plan to make a fortune out of Seven and Eleven petered out, but they still make interesting pets. As every man's hand is against the poisonous snakes, probably there won't be any left in a few years. That's a pity. You never know when something may come in handy. The venom of certain pit vipers is used in the treatment of various illnesses, especially hemophilia. Hemophilia can also be controlled to a certain extent by hypnosis, and this was virtually the only known way of controlling it thirty years ago. It was through hypnosis that Rasputin could keep the little Czarevitch alive, and so gained control of the Russian court. Rasputin was one of the main causes of the Russian Revolution, which has brought down all this trouble on the world. I'd settle for a few rattlesnakes myself.

Ever since, as a small boy, I thrilled to the adventures of Rikki-Tikki-Tavi, I've been fascinated by cobras. Although cobras do not have the highly developed striking mechanism of rattlesnakes, their venom is far more deadly, drop for drop, and the great king cobra reaches a length of twenty feet—longer than a boa constrictor. A snake that size carries enough poison to kill a hundred men. Even the common spectacled cobra, which rarely grows to be more than six feet long, kills twenty-five thousand people a year in India alone. I had heard amazing tales of the strange powers of the Oriental fakirs who are able to tame these terrible reptiles and make them dance to the music of a flute. So when I went to India on a writing assignment, I looked up a prominent Indian writer named Suresh Vaidya, to whom I had a letter of introduction. Suresh was the soul of cooperation.

"To learn the secret of the fakirs' strange power over these deadly animals, you will have to handle the snakes yourself, wrap them about your neck, put their heads in your mouth—hey, where are you going? You can't run all the way back to the Imperial Hotel in the midday sun without a topi. I'll take you to the village of Badarpur, some twelve miles north of here, where lives the hereditary caste of snake charmers known as the Kom-Jogi. Ten minutes after we reach Badarpur, you'll be up to your colon in cobras."

No one could remain indifferent to such an offer. We hailed a taxi and soon were headed north past the Dewan-I-Khas, the Jamma Musjid, the American Express Company, and other exotic spots.

At last we came to a community of about a hundred mud huts lying against the ruins of an ancient mud fort. At one time Badarpur had been a thriving community, but with the coming of the English the fort had been abandoned, and the gypsy Kom-Jogi took over the ruins. The Kom-Jogi wander as far north as China and as far west as Arabia with their baskets of snakes, often being away from Badarpur two or three years.

"The Indian government would like them to adopt some other way of life, but they cling to their snakes and their ancient ways," Suresh explained.

I was afraid that these strange people would be loath to allow a visiting American to pry into their deepest mysteries, but I needn't have worried. When Suresh explained what was wanted, the headman shouted to the attentive crowd some strange words in Kom-Jogi that translated would be, "Boys, here's a prime American sucker loaded with moola! Let's give him the works!"

Never, not even on the midway of the old Krinko Combined Shows, which was the crookedest ragbag east of the Mississippi, have I ever seen so instant a reaction. From every hut came pouring hordes of men, women, children, and dogs all carrying snakes. (I'm not sure about the dogs, but that was my impression at the time.) At least thirty people were playing on gourd flutes; others were beating on drums, tambourines, and tin cans. They had brown cobras, greenish cobras, black cobras, spectacled cobras, king cobras, kraits, rock pythons, grass snakes, and rat snakes. Naked children, scarcely able to stand, came toddling toward me, dragging furious cobras by their tails and yelling, "Backshesh, Sahib!" Old, toothless women hobbled across the compound plastered with pythons, and decrepit men left what must have been their deathbeds to crawl out of the huts, dangling kraits. Badarpur is an ideal place to have your DT's: everything is provided.

I asked the headman if the snakes were defanged. He replied frankly, "Of course they are, Sahib. What do you think we are, crazy?"

A defanged snake, although not entirely harmless, is most reluctant to bite, as his mouth is sore and swollen. Even if he does, so little venom would be discharged that simply sucking out the wound would probably be enough to keep you from having more than a sore arm. Next I asked about the flute playing.

"Snakes are completely deaf," the headman explained. "The flute isn't to charm the snake; it's to draw a crowd."

He gave me a demonstration. If you put a cobra in a basket and then suddenly take the lid off, the cobra will rear up (especially if you give the side of the basket a kick at the same time) and stay reared up watching you. If you move to the right or left, the cobra will turn also, never taking his eyes off you and always ready to strike. If you sway your body, the cobra will sway with you, sparring for a blow. This swaying suggests the undulating motions of a nautch girl, and so it can be said that the cobra is dancing. So the performer plays some musical instrument, usually the gourd flute, swaying his body at the same time. The cobra sways with him, thus "dancing to the music." The performer can also accomplish the same effect by playing on a tambourine if he keeps swaying.

Although I was not especially impressed by the Kom-Jogi, there have been some outstanding Oriental snake charmers. Perhaps the most famous was Ma Hae, a Burmese woman, who put on a most dangerous and dramatic act with hamadryads, the giant king cobras. Ma Hae's cobras were definitely not defanged; when angered they would open their mouths, and not only could the fangs be seen but also droplets of venom oozing out of them. Ma Hae climaxed her routine by bending over and kissing one of the cobras on top of his head. A motion picture of her going through this routine was made, the narrator claiming she was the high priestess of a secret sect that once a year had to go to a cave in the hills to worship the snake god. It still turns up every now and then on TV, and it's a remarkable show. Ma Hae isn't around anymore; I was told she was finally killed by one of her snakes.

Working with cobras that still have their fangs depends basically on the way a cobra strikes. Instead of going into an S-shaped coil like a rattler, the cobra rears straight up. If you put your elbow on a table, cup your hand to represent the open hood, and sway your forearm back and forth, you have a good idea of the fighting stance of a cobra. Your index finger represents the tiny mouselike head that does the business. You will see at once that your range is limited to the length of your forearm.

Because of the deceptively coiled S, no one can tell exactly how far a rattler can strike, but with a little practice you can tell a cobra's range to the inch. As the blow of a cobra is comparatively slow, a man with steady nerves can jerk away in time to avoid being bitten. That is exactly what a mongoose does. The mongoose keeps just outside the cobra's range, and when he does dart in for a bite, he can jump clear of the blow. A mongoose would stand no chance against a rattler. As the cobra must bite, not just stab with his fangs, if the snake charmer advances his flat palm held straight up and down, the cobra will hit the palm. He cannot get a hold on the flat palm, and is baffled. Of course, if he manages to get a finger or fold of skin, that's different. I am sorry to say that I was present when Grace Wiley, the Los Angeles herpetologist who was the most remarkable person with snakes I ever expect to see, was trying this technique with a newly imported cobra. The cobra got her by the finger. She died in twenty minutes.

All snakes, including poisonous ones, often become extremely "tame" in that they become used to being handled and make no attempt to bite. Grace had two enormous king cobras over fourteen feet long that she handled with complete impunity and even took to bed with her. I read a clipping in an Indian newspaper about a family who kept a pet king cobra named Rakheval that slept with the baby. One night, bandits entered the house, and Rakheval charged them, striking one man in the leg. The rest fled. The dead bandit was found in the front yard of the house the next morning. He had been able to run only about fifty feet before he collapsed. I'll bet that was the last time bandits entered that house; but even so, I'd hate to be that baby. Snakes are highly temperamental and unpredictable creatures.

Probably the most remarkable snake handler in the world today is Bill Haast, who operates the Serpentarium, about twelve miles south of Miami, Florida. Bill not only exhibits poisonous snakes; he also captures them. He spent four months in South Africa collecting cobras. "I had native helpers who were able to track the cobras to their holes by following the snake's spoor in the sand," Bill told me. "Then we'd dig them out and bag 'em. One of my helpers was bitten in the leg. He died in about an hour, although I gave him injections of serum. The poison works very fast."

Bill also collected mambas—a long, thin, whiplike snake that many experts regard as more dangerous than a cobra because of their astonishing speed. "Mambas are full of curiosity," Bill explained. "They live mainly in trees, and often they'd glide down to the lower branches to examine me. I wore a fencing mask when catching them so they couldn't get me in the face. They're amazingly quick. When I got back to camp with my first mamba, I opened the bag to shake him out so I could transfer him to a cage. Before I knew what was happening, the bag was empty and the snake across the room. I hadn't even seen him move."

Bill milks his snakes of their venom, which he sells for $18 a gram. It is used largely as an analgesic (painkiller), although some is used for the manufacture of serums. Bill handles all snakes with his bare hands, including the cobras. No gloves have yet been devised thick enough to keep out a snake's fangs and yet pliable enough to allow a man wearing them to perform the delicate operation of milking a snake. When handling cobras, Bill first distracts the snake's attention with his left hand and then gently lifts the snake with his right. When the snake finds himself being carried toward the extracting table, he rears up in Bill's hands, spreads his hood, and prepares to strike. By slightly shifting the position of his hands, Bill keeps the snake off balance so the cobra is more interested in steadying himself than in striking . . . much as a boxer would find it difficult to deliver a blow if the ground under his feet were constantly moving. Watching his chance, Bill runs his free hand up behind the cobra's extended hood and grabs him by his tiny mouselike head. Meanwhile his wife has rolled the extracting table up to the snake's cage. On the table is a V-shaped glass cup covered with a rubber cap. The cobra is induced to bite through this cap, and the venom runs down into the cup. After the venom has been extracted, the snake is fed by putting a rubber tube into his mouth, and a special "snake formula" is pumped into him. Captive snakes, especially ones that are constantly milked of their venom, often refuse to eat, and Bill takes no chances. The rubber cap is then sterilized; the snake's mouth is washed to make sure he didn't pick up any germs; and the cobra is returned to his cage. That's all there is to it.

"Of course, the big king cobras aren't so easy to handle as these little five-foot fellows," Bill explained to me after milking an ordinary Indian spectacled cobra. "Some of my kings are fifteen feet long, and very powerful. I usually lift out a king with my snake hook (a short pole with a hook on the end of it) and put him on the grass. The king will rear up some three feet high and then charge me. I can put one hand against his upraised body and hold him off. Reared up like that, he can't get his head down far enough to bite my hand. While he's trying it, I grab him by the back of the neck with my other hand. But even after I've grabbed him, handling a snake that big and strong is a hard job."

Handling poisonous snakes with your bare hands is the most sporting of all hunting, for your opponent has as much chance to kill you as you have to kill him. For that reason, I don't expect it ever to become too popular, although I don't know. So many people have become interested in keeping poisonous snakes that some countries have passed laws prohibiting it, as there's always a chance the snakes may escape. Youngsters, both boys and girls, seem especially fascinated by the snakes and the danger. I have received dozens of letters from teen-agers who have started snake clubs, and all I can say is that the accounts of their activities scare me to death. I don't suppose handling any kind of snake is more dangerous than driving a high-speed sports car, but even so I consider it a very risky hobby. No one knows what a snake may do next—especially the snake.

CHAPTER 15

The Joint Is Jumping

You haven't lived until you've heard the music of a pack of toads in full cry after their elusive quarry. Many's the morning when the simple yeomanry of Chester County, Pennsylvania, are roused from their slumbers by the melodious sound of a hunting horn, followed by the full crash of the chorus as the Treweryn Toads (as my pack is named) give tongue. Oft a farmer will nudge his sleeping wife in the sweetbreads and mutter, "Ain't that guy Mannix the beatenist feller? Certainly we'll miss him when the game warden shoots the S.O.B."—this last being a colloquial expression for Sweet Old Boy. Then the unsuspecting hayseed will sink back into innocent slumber, little dreaming that the Treweryn Toads are at that moment probably battening on his chicks, ducklings, or young turkeys, for the toads do riot a bit now that my whipper-in (a chap named Murph the Surf) has taken up other hobbies.

If you've gotten this far, you are doubtless wondering what in hell's name I'm talking about. To fill you in, a few years ago, while in Paris, I stopped by a quaint little bookstore on the Left Bank that specializes in obscure sporting books and has taken me for more travelers' checks than most tourists spend in Le Pigall or the Scheherazade. Glancing through the shelves, I encountered a book by Abel Boyer and Maurice Planiol dealing with training animals for the chase. After discussing such routine sports as hunting with shrikes, cormorants, cheetahs, and caracals, the gentlemen buckled down to business. I read:

"The historian Abou el Fadhel (sixteenth century) says that in India the sportsmen train toads to catch small birds. El Fadhel never grew tired of watching this unusual sight."

Well, I should think he wouldn't. I'd been under the illusion that I'd trained some pretty unusual animals to do some queer things in my time, but this one had me kissed off against the cushion. I knew that big bull-frogs will occasionally catch small ducklings, but these sepia John Peels obviously went out with a pack of toads to clean up on the local bird population. Either those Indian toads were part goshawk or El Fadhel ought to be called El Fakir.

However, I decided to look into the subject. Reference libraries proved of no help, although according to the experts toads did about everything else except catch birds. Toads, unlike frogs, are not aquatic, and spend their lives prowling around the woods looking for prey, going into the water only to breed. There are some weird specimens hopping around the world, such as a South American horned toad (no relation to our Western "horned toad," which is really a lizard) that is green with chocolate markings and has elongated, pointed teeth. It attacks with open mouth and can give a nasty bite. The seven-inch-long Colorado River toad lives on scorpions and is so poisonous it has killed dogs. The Surinam toad has pockets on its back to carry its eggs and newly hatched young, and a flap of skin under its jaw that it wiggles like a worm to attract quarry. But my own favorite is the Brazilian flying tree toad, who flies like a flying squirrel and can go ninety feet. I contemplated investing in a few of these; but unfortunately we have several developments around us, and I had an idea that if, while the honest burghers were supping their martinis on the back porch of an evening, they saw a flight of flying toads winging their way back to Chez Mannix the results might be catastrophic. So I reluctantly gave up the idea.

About this time my wife figured I needed a vacation to rest what for want of a better word I'll call my mind, so we took a trip to Florida. While in Miami, we dropped in to see Bill Haas at the Serpentarium. On Bill's desk, where most people have a photo of the wife and kiddies, Bill had a shot of the biggest, ugliest, meanest-looking toad I'd ever seen. Toads have never been famous for their girlish beauty, but this one had Frankenstein, Quasimodo, and the Phantom of the Opera looking like Shirley Temple.

"That's a *Bufo marinus*," Bill told me. "The world's largest toad. We have several on exhibition in the snake pens because a lot of people would rather see them than the snakes."

"Don't the snakes eat them?"

"Do you think a snake is crazy?" asked Bill, and looking at the picture of *Bufo m.*, I could see what he meant.

"Our only trouble with them is that they keep eating the young chickens we put in for the snakes," remarked Mrs. Haas.

I was off again. If these giant toads could eat a chicken, by golly, they could go bird hunting. I asked for a demonstration.

The Haases gave it to me. They dropped several chicks in one of the pens, and we waited. We didn't have long to wait. There was a miniature explosion from under some ferns, and out bounded a huge toad, easily nine inches from the tip of his nose to his sternum. He made one jump into the middle of the chickens and sat for a minute while making his choice, turning slowly as the birds ran around him. When he made his grab, the blow was so quick I couldn't follow it. One moment, there was the toad eyeing his quarry; the next second there was the chick in his mouth. The toad sat back on his haunches and used his hands to stuff the bird into his throat, virtually capsizing his eyeballs as he did it. In a flash the chick was gone, and the toad was all ready for the next course.

"You can get the chick back again if you want to," remarked Bill. "All you have to do is press the toad and the chick will pop out uninjured."

The Haases gave me a couple of giant toads, and I took them back on the plane. As there is some curious ruling against taking live animals on passenger planes, I smuggled these aboard in the pockets of my raincoat. I had to use a raincoat, since the toads needed to be kept moist, and the pockets of an ordinary coat won't hold water. At one point in my colorful career, I had to smuggle tarantulas from Patagonia onto a plane, but these toads were tougher. They were a lot bigger than the tarantulas, kicked more, and riding from Miami to Philadelphia with two pocketsful of water isn't as easy as it sounds. But we made the journey all right, and I put them in the living-room aquarium. Then I started to read up on giant toads.

I thought that all I had were a couple of big toads—instead, I soon found I'd kidnapped two of Florida's most important natural resources. The giant toad was first discovered in 1758 in southern Texas when someone noticed them collecting around campfires to eat the insects attracted by the light. They not only ate insects; they were so big they could also handle roaches, centipedes, and even mice. When the British heard about them, they imported hundreds of the toads to the West Indies to keep down the roaches and other pests. In 1844, they were shipped to Jamaica to eat young rats, and did such a good job of it they virtually freed the island from the cane rats that did thousands of dollars' worth of damage each year. We shipped them in 1932 to Hawaii, where they proved to be so beneficial that they are now raised there commercially and have been introduced into Formosa, the Philippines, New Guinea, and Australia.

Unlike many predators that have been introduced to destroy some pest, the toads seem to be entirely beneficial. The only objection to them is that the males are noisy in spring; they're so big that cars hitting one on a road at night have gone into a skid, and dog owners object to them because they exude a fairly potent poison from glands in their warts that can make a dog very sick if he tries to bite one. The poison is harmless to humans unless you try to bite a toad (which few people do), although there was one case in Florida of a small child sitting in a rubber pool who started playing with a toad and broke out in a bad case of hives; the toad's milky-white poison got in the water and coated the child's naked body. Although frogs' legs are a great delicacy, the toads' poison makes them unfit to eat—which is perfectly all right with the toads. About the only animal that can eat a toad is a skunk. He rolls the toad around in wet grass first to get the poison off. One curious effect of the poison is to seal off the sweat glands.

Toads seem to be more intelligent than frogs. If carried off from their pond, they can return to it from a mile away, seemingly by some sort of homing instinct. They can be tamed, and even taught to come to a whistle. When catching large prey, toads are smart enough to grab it by the head first, which frogs don't. On the other hand, they can't jump nearly as far or as fast as can a frog, and their range of vision is limited to about three feet. Frogs can see objects ten feet away.

I expected toads to be difficult to tame, but I had no problem. When picked up, instead of trying to escape they'd give a little chirping note of irritation, turning their heads to look at me. Feeding them was no problem. I started them out on night crawlers, which they grabbed at once. Within a few days they'd learned to take bits of meat dangled on the ends of thread, although they usually ate the thread too. After a week or so I could dispense with the thread and they'd eat the meat from a tray.

However, this was clearly an artificially induced trait. Ordinarily something had to move before they showed any interest in it. According to their simple code, anything that moved was alive and they'd make a try for it. If, while picking up the meat, a pebble dropped from it and rolled, the toads would make a grab for it. Once they had the pebble in their mouths, they'd realize they'd made a mistake and spit it out, but they'd grab another in the same way. Once I heard a lot of commotion in the tank, and went over to see what the trouble was. The window was open and the breeze was blowing some ferns in a wall holder. Their shadows were moving on the floor of the aquarium, and the toads were trying to eat the shadows.

The toads had definite personalities. The biggest we called Cal (short for Caliban). The smaller, being somewhat hunchbacked, we named after Aesop, who, incidentally, was very fond of writing about frogs and toads. Aesop, being livelier, would jump away when I reached in to pick him up, but Cal preferred to play dead. Cal would roll his eyes inward, turn over on his back, and go limp. In this position he was the deadest-looking article I ever hope to see, and the first time he pulled this trick on me I thought he'd died of heart failure. It turned out, however, that Cal liked to have his belly rubbed. Even when playing dead he would put his head back, arch what little neck he had, and chirp contentedly to himself. Aesop never seemed to enjoy being handled, but he got used to it after a time.

Once when I was handling Aesop a little too roughly, he released the milky poison from the glands in his shoulders. It didn't hurt me in any way, although I washed it off as soon as I could. Even ordinary toads possess this poison to a limited extent, and if it gets into an open cut it can be irritating and possibly cause a mild infection. Hence the legend that toads give you warts. If someone has a highly sensitive skin, possibly they can.

My next job was training them for the hunt. We have plenty of mice in the barn feedbins, so I began by collecting a few in a catch-alive trap, and dropped them in the aquarium. The tank was half water and half land, and the toads were in the water with only their eyes showing, looking like sawed-off hippopotamuses. When the mice landed on the gravel they sat still for a few seconds, and the toads paid no attention to them. Then the mice began to move.

Instantly the toads' heads popped up. They watched the mice intently, and then Aesop started for the bank. Without turning his head, Cal gave

Aesop a kick in the face with one of his webbed hind legs that stopped the smaller toad cold. Then Cal gave a bound and alighted on the gravel among the mice.

When catching insects, toads use their tongues. As with frogs, the toad's tongue is hinged to the front of his mouth, with the tip reaching back down his throat. When he's within four inches or so of a bug, the toad flips out his tongue, snares the insect, and jerks it into his mouth. The motion is so fast only high-speed photography can see it.

I'm positive Cal couldn't have caught as large an animal as a mouse with his tongue, but I couldn't see what happened. One moment Cal was beside a mouse, and the next instant the mouse's tail was hanging out of Cal's mouth. Swallowing the mouse completely was a tougher job. Cal's eyes turned inside out while he was doing it. That gave Aesop his chance. He hit the beach, and another mouse disappeared.

Cal soon learned not to bother chasing the mice. He let Aesop do that for him. Cal would take up his position in one corner of the tank and wait while Aesop jumped around. Cal would wait with quiet dignity until a mouse dashed past him. As the mouse went by, there was a sudden flicker of his head. That was all, but the mouse's tail would be waving frantically from Cal's huge mouth. Aesop, on the other hand, chased the mice until he caught up with them; and as the toad could cover a foot with every bound, that didn't take long. Then he'd suddenly stop and start collapsing his eyes. Only after looking around would I notice that another mouse had disappeared.

I was afraid the toads were getting too highly specialized at mouse catching in the confinement of the tank where the mice couldn't get away. I noticed the first few times they'd moved very fast, watched their quarry carefully, and were showing real skill in the hunt. Now Cal simply sat and waited until a mouse practically ran into his mouth, and Aesop was getting wilder and wilder in his jumps. He knew he'd get the mouse eventually.

So I decided the time had come for the field trials. As Cal and Aesop couldn't jump nearly as far or as fast as frogs, I felt reasonably safe about taking them outside. Also, they'd be easy to catch, for their skin was dry and warty instead of being smooth and slimy. I decided to start them off on mice; but the problem was how to get the mice into the open, as the toads didn't have the figures for going down holes.

In England, a friend of mine showed me how to bolt field mice out of

their burrows by putting bumblebees down the holes. However, Cal especially took a long time to make up his mind, and I had an idea that a
field mouse coming out of a burrow with a bee on his tail wasn't going to
waste any time. I had another idea. There are plenty of mouse holes in
our tackroom. I stopped them all up except one. Then I told Danny, my
son, to pour some water down the hole.

I climbed on top of the feedbin, and waited. The toads sat quietly
contemplating the infinite. I wondered what they'd do when the mice
appeared.

I'd taken for granted the mice would pop out of the holes as rats do,
but the first mouse stuck his head out and looked carefully around, his
whiskers twitching nervously. Instantly the toads stiffened almost imper-
ceptibly, but made no other move. To my surprise, I saw they had
changed color. On the white gravel of the aquarium they had been
almost white or a very light shade of gray. Now they had turned almost
black to match the color of the dark hardwood floor. They were almost
invisible. A crouching cat, no matter how still she is, looks like a cat. The
toads looked like lumps of dark earth. Squat, perfectly motionless, it was
incredible they were actually alive.

The mouse stole out. He stopped exactly midway between the toads.
Aesop made a jump for him. For the first time I saw the toad try to grab a
mouse. He lifted his head, let his lower jaw drop, and grabbed. The
mouse shied sideways, turning to stare at this suddenly animated lump of
clay. As he did so, Cal made one quick motion. The mouse was gone. I
couldn't even see the tail.

Another mouse ran out. Aesop promptly took after him. He was faster
than the mouse—for a few jumps at least—but he couldn't turn as
quickly. The mouse dodged and ran for the hole again with Aesop after
him. He made the mistake of letting Aesop get him in a corner. He tried
to dodge again, but Aesop was too quick for him. He caught the mouse
by the head and shoved him down with his amazingly versatile forepaws,
which were almost as nimble as a monkey's hands.

Cal grabbed the next mouse the instant he came out of the hole, and
Aesop went over to help him. Cal shoved him away with one hand, and
Aesop retired. There was only one more mouse, and Cal got that one too.

In a wild state, toads undoubtedly catch a certain number of mice and
small rats, but they do it by a different system. The toad hops around
until he finds some place where game is plentiful, and then just sits

down. Sooner or later a mouse will run by, and toads have nothing but time. They can go weeks without food if necessary, and there are always insects.

Catching birds was something else again. As toads are largely nocturnal and birds don't get around much at night, I didn't see how it could be managed. We have plenty of English sparrows on the place that are a pest, and I was perfectly willing to sacrifice a few of them. However, I noticed that the sparrows went to roost in an old privet hedge around the paddock, and they were particularly lively in the evening when the toads would be up and around. This gave me an idea.

I built a couple of small caves for the toads under the hedge. The caves were nothing but hollows under a flat stone where the toads could sit. Toads like to hide under things until after dark, mainly because they dehydrate easily and have to be where it's cool and damp. They can't drink with their mouths, and have to absorb water through their skins. In dry weather, toads will keep out of sight for weeks and then go jumping around after the first rain. Hence the legend of "rains of toads." People used to think they came down from the sky with the water.

I poured some water in the caves and put Cal and Aesop inside. I was sure they'd stay there until after dark. Then I scattered some scratch feed around and settled back to watch.

The first couple of evenings didn't bring any results because the sparrows didn't see the scratch. Then they discovered the free handouts. Right away they started fighting over it, as English sparrows always do.

A few seconds later I saw Aesop cautiously stick his head out and look the situation over. Then he crawled slowly out and, to my surprise, began to stalk the sparrows. Instead of hopping, he crawled toward them, extending one hand and pushing himself along with his webbed hind foot. He crept closer and closer to the fighting sparrows. He stopped, gathered his legs under him, and gave one bound. The sparrows scattered in all directions except one. That was in Aesop's mouth. He rubbed his belly with his hands, turned his eyes inside out to help his swallowing, and gulped. Then he settled down again.

It took a long time before a second batch of sparrows came along and settled on the scratch. This time Cal tried it. He also made a long, slow stalk and then jumped, but Cal missed. The sparrows flew off—all except one that stayed on the ground motionless. Whether it was too scared to move or whether Cal had hit it and temporarily stunned the bird, I couldn't tell. This was Cal's chance, and he hastily crawled over to the bird with legs so extended he seemed to be walking on tiptoes like a giant spider. Instead of grabbing the sparrow, Cal stood there and stared at it with his huge golden eyes. As long as the sparrow didn't move, he wouldn't touch it. Maybe the sparrow realized that.

The two animals stood there for what seemed to me at least five minutes. The sparrow couldn't stand the strain, and took off. As he left the ground, Cal leaped after him. He got the sparrow by the tail and tried to stuff him in his mouth with his forepaws, but the sparrow was bigger than a mouse, and struggling. As toads have no teeth, Cal had to get the bird in his mouth whole. There were a few seconds of struggle, and then the sparrow flew off, leaving his tail in Cal's mouth.

I've since found out how bird catchers who use toads operate. They have a couple of dozen toads and tie them by one hind leg under little palm-leaf sheds. Then they pour a cup of water under the toad, scatter some birdseed around, and stake out the next one. When a toad gets a bird, the trapper makes him disgorge, puts the bird in a cage, and waits for the next.

The giant toad has turned out to be important in scientific research. His poison is a rich source of serotonin, which formerly could be produced only by using tons of beef blood. Serotonin is produced by cells in the brain, and its lack causes certain forms of insanity. Too much produces asthma and, in extreme cases, shock. Doctors now believe that lack of serotonin may be the underlying cause behind many cases of cancer, heart disease, and allergies. The toads are "milked" of their poison in laboratories, and the poison, produced by their paratoid glands, is collected and purified. So it may turn out that old *Bufo marinus* is one of our most valuable citizens.

Probably the world's leading frog-and-toad man is the French scientist Jean Rostand, the son of Edmond Rostand who wrote *Cyrano de Bergerac*. Mr. Rostand lives contentedly surrounded by thousands of frogs and toads, and wants no other friends. "In my pets I see the entire universe" he has said. I'm not quite up to that, but I got Cal and Aesop a couple of lady toads, and maybe next spring we'll have some tadpoles. I'll admit my pack is rather small now, but a toad lays about twenty thousand eggs, so perhaps in a few years toad hunting may replace fox hunting as the great Main Line sport. It's the only sport I know of where you can sit and smoke a pipe while watching the hunt in progress.

CHAPTER 16

The Most Dangerous Game

Man is the greatest of all predators; but, unlike other predators, he preys largely on his own kind. Like any other animal, man can be trapped, shot, or run down with hounds. As with so many exotic sports, the most ancient ways of hunting human beings now seem to be the most modern. Apparently man reaches a point of technical skill in killing that defeats itself; he becomes so highly specialized and so dependent on mechanical techniques that he suddenly finds himself helpless before the most primitive means of killing. He must then revert to the old ways of hunting or be destroyed.

Trapping humans was a highly developed mechanical skill that reached its perfection in the early part of the last century. Owing to the Industrial Revolution, which threw thousands of people out of work, the highways were full of wanderers desperate for food. The great estates stocked with pheasant and rabbits proved to be an irresistible temptation to them. Poaching became a way of life, and the keepers could not patrol the woods, fields, and hedgerows day and night. The answer was man-traps.

The first traps, introduced in the middle of the eighteenth century, were simply bear traps imported from Canada. By strapping flat pieces of board to their legs, the poachers could protect themselves from the jaws and then open the trap by pressing down on the spring. So spikes were introduced, and more powerful springs. I saw one of these traps at the Norwich Museum. It was 6 feet long and weighed 88 pounds. The jaws were 19 inches long, and the teeth 2½ inches. The pressure was over 600 pounds. It was constructed with a double spring. To open the jaws, a man had to put a foot on each spring and press down simultaneously while forcing open the jaws with his hands. If he had one foot in the trap, he was helpless unless he had friends with him. As the poachers often worked in gangs, an improved trap was later introduced that could be opened only by special clamps that fitted over the springs and were then screwed down by a lever. No one could escape from this trap unless he had the special clamps.

Most of the traps had small metal hooks riveted onto the pan, or metal plate on which a man stepped to spring the device. Still later, curved hooks were set into the jaws, as some men in their agony would manage to tear their leg out even with the two-inch teeth.

Catching someone in a mantrap was regarded as a joke. On March 23, 1827, suit was brought against a big landholder named Sir J. Shelly who had caught two innocent individuals in mantraps while they were taking a short cut through his property. Shelly answered the charge by pointing out that the two men were lawyers. "I agree it was a melancholy occurrence, but then it is so rare an event for a lawyer to be caught in a trap that I hope not to be reprimanded for it," he said in court. The judge and jury rocked with laughter, and the case was dismissed.

Many of the traps were astonishingly well made. Although mantraps with teeth or jaws strong enough to crush the leg were made illegal in 1827, on January 27, 1916, an English curate named Lawson was caught by a mantrap while taking a walk along a deserted path in some woods. The trap had three-inch curved teeth, and the Reverend Mr. Lawson was held helpless for several hours until some passerby heard his cries for help. Although the trap had presumably been set over a hundred years before, it still worked perfectly. It had simply been set and then forgotten about. As with all trappers running a trapline, the keepers seldom took the trouble to check their traps daily and often forgot about traps set in isolated areas.

Traps were occasionally employed long after their use had been made illegal. I talked to an old keeper in Essex who remembered his grandfather setting out traps after a poaching gang had taken a shot at him and blown off the muscles of his left arm. He told me: "Grandfather never buried his traps, just covered them with leaves. A good keeper never set one along a main path. There was too much chance of catching a child going berrying or even a fox or deer. They were usually set along trails known only to the keepers and the poachers. I remember one keeper said he once put out a dummy deer and then set the trap where a man stalking the deer would step in it. A good place to set them was alongside a log where a man would naturally bring his foot down while stepping across. They were also set in holes through a hedge or by a gate in a fence. If you could find a hide (blind) where the poachers had been shooting ducks, you set the trap there. Sometimes you'd see where poachers had been jumping across a narrow place in a stream. You set the trap where they'd land. Must have surprised them no end."

When the bone-crushing type of trap was made illegal, a "humane" trap was introduced. These traps were perfectly square, and the jaws were composed of two iron bars. The jaws did not come completely together. They stopped when they were about two inches apart, and locked into place. This trap was designed to catch a man around the ankle and hold him.

I tried out one of these traps at the Horniman Museum at Forest Hill on the outskirts of London. Though the trap was over one hundred years old, it worked perfectly. Luckily, I had the sense to wrap a piece of cloth around my ankle, for the jaws hit the side of my leg hard enough to bruise the flesh, although not to break the bone. The springs of this "humane" trap were very weak compared to the old type, and a man could easily have freed himself if it hadn't been for a neat little device that automatically locked the jaws in place after the trap had been sprung. The locks (there was one for each jaw) had to be opened with a key before the jaws could be forced apart.

All mechanical mantraps of whatever design were prohibited in 1861, but landowners showed quite a lot of ingenuity in thinking up traps that weren't technically mechanical but still made their grounds unhealthy places to wander around in. In Surrey, a gamekeeper used a rope with a sliding noose at one end. He spread the noose open across a path and then attached the other end of the rope to a bent-over sapling. If a man stepped in the open noose, he disturbed a trigger arrangement that released the sapling, and the victim was jerked into the air to dangle by his foot. The first day the keeper set this device, he caught his master, the squire, in it. The keeper didn't find him for several hours. However, the squire took it in good part. When the apologetic keeper released him, the squire said briskly, "Good job, Hawkins. Must keep these damn' poachers down."

The most elaborate trap of this period was constructed by a Lord Spencer. It was a pit twelve feet deep and eight feet across, with sloping sides so no one who fell in could climb out. The top was a pair of doors covered with growing grass to make them invisible, and so delicately hinged that a rabbit could open them. After the victim had fallen through, the doors flew shut again to be ready for the next customer.

Lord Spencer's best haul came one night when he caught a fox, two rabbits, a pheasant, a wild boar, and a young couple who had wandered hand in hand into the woods looking for a quiet nook. A few days later, he caught a whole family, consisting of a father, mother, and two children who had gone picnicking. Spencer remarked, "I felt inclined to have a certain amount of sympathy for this family, trespassers though they were, as they had spent twelve hours lying in the mud at the bottom of the trap, but the shocking language the man employed when my keepers brought him out the next morning caused me the deepest revulsion."

The trap was finally filled in after it caught a prominent local businessman named Kinder who spent the night holding up one of the doors with his cane while screaming for help. Mr. Kinder sued Lord Spencer but didn't collect anything. As the trap never did catch any poachers, it was not considered a success.

Mantraps were abandoned not only for humanitarian reasons but also because the invention of the spring gun provided a far more efficient method of dealing with trespassers. I was allowed to rig up one of these guns by the Mill Street Museum in Ludlow, Shropshire. It was a flintlock pistol, capable of carrying a heavy charge. The gun was mounted on a swivel so it could swing in all directions. An iron rod, about a foot and a half long, was fastened to the trigger, and projected an inch or so in front of the barrel. At the end of this bar was welded a ring, and three other rings were threaded on it. Wires were attached to each of these three rings and led down separate paths. If a man touched one of these wires, the pressure caused the gun to swing around and point down that wire. The instant the gun pointed directly along the wire, the wire pulled the trigger and the gun fired.

I made some experiments with this gun, thanks to the kind cooperation of the museum authorities, cocking the gun and then touching a wire leading out from one of the rings. The gun swung around and the hammer fell almost instantly, depending, of course, on how much pressure was exerted on the wire. The wires were usually strung a foot or so above the ground so a man would stumble over them. If the wires had been waist-high, a man might have had time to leap back before the gun went off.

However, there was a delay of a second or so before the gun could bear and fire. On at least one occasion this saved a man's life. A Mr. Charles Barclay had a spring gun set in his woods, and his keeper, while chasing a winged woodcock, forgot about the gun and stumbled over the wire. The keeper instantly knew what he'd done, and flung himself face downward. The gun fired over him. Poachers gradually learned to dodge the shot in the same way, so landowners often pointed the muzzle of the guns downward in order to hit the man as he landed on his face.

Spring guns are still legal in England if they are set inside a house between the hours of sunset and sunrise. Outdoors, the only guns permissible are alarm guns that fire a blank cartridge. Even these can be dangerous. During the last war, Sir Malcolm Campbell, the racing-car enthusiast, grew so tired of having people shoot the ornamental waterfowl on his estate that he set up a number of alarm guns. One of his gardeners stumbled over the trip wire, and the discharge from the blank cartridge hit him in the leg. The wound became infected and he lost the leg. Sir Malcolm was fined five pounds.

During World War II, mantraps (called antipersonnel devices) reached their highest point of mechanical perfection. In general, they were of three types—the "pull" type (such as a wire attached to the pin of a hand grenade); the "pressure" type, which exploded when someone stepped on a button in the top; and the "release" type, which exploded when a weight lying on it was removed. This last device was often put under a book. If a man lifted the book, the device went off.

These mantraps were usually left behind by retreating troops. Rommel's engineers delayed the Allied forces for weeks by planting thousands of Teller mines, which exploded if a man stepped on them, and S mines, called "bouncing babies," which bounced into the air, at the same time discharging three hundred steel ball bearings in all directions. The Italians helped by scattering fountain pens from planes. If you pulled the cap off the pen, it exploded in your hands. Some unfortunate people are still finding these pens along the North African coast.

Booby-trapping houses reached a high degree of development. Pictures were booby-trapped with "pull" devices—usually a picture of Hitler, since the Germans knew the Allied troops would jerk it off the wall. Pressure-type traps were installed in the seats of chairs. Bombs were set into the walls of fireplaces so that if a fire were started, the house would blow up. It got so bad troops would sleep in the rain rather than risk entering a house.

Now that mantrapping had attained refinements undreamed of by the simple eighteenth-century landholders, suddenly the whole trend has gone into reverse. One of the most serious problems faced by our troops in Vietnam is mantraps, but mantraps of the most primitive type. How to outwit these devices is more than our best military experts can solve.

The simplest but also the most effective device is sharpened bamboo stakes, coated with dung or vegetable poisons, and hidden in leaves along a jungle trail. These stakes are sharp enough to go through a man's boot, and the wounds they cause almost invariably become infected. Another device is a deadfall made of two-hundred-pound wooden blocks studded with bamboo spikes, hung from branches, and released by a trip rope made of vines. There are also spring bows. The bow is braced crossways against two stakes, bent, and a poisoned arrow set in place. The bowstring is held in place by an elaborate trigger arrangement that connects to a vine stretched across a trail. If a man touches the vine, the bowstring is released.

In Africa, still other contrivances are being used, the most common being a pit, covered with dry leaves laid across twigs, with a sharpened stake in the bottom. In the Congo, an arrangement called the "cartwheel" is employed. This trap is made by cutting down a sapling, tying it into a hoop, and laying the hoop flat on a trail. Fastened around the circumference of the hoop, and pointed inward, are a series of sharp, flexible sticks dipped in poison. If a man steps in the center of the hoop, his foot forces the sticks down. They then spring up around his ankle. If one of the poisoned sticks breaks the skin, only very quick medical help can save him.

A far more interesting way of manhunting is tracking. During the Mau Mau rebellion in Kenya, I attended a tracking school for British officers near Nanyuki, some one hundred miles north of Nairobi. The school was held in a stockade, surrounded by barbed wire and a moat studded with sharp bamboo spikes. I reported to Major R. T. Elliott, head of the school and formerly game warden of the district. He was a tall, slender man with a close-clipped military mustache. Here I met my fellow students. They ranged in age from youngsters of eighteen, fresh from

English schools, to a grizzled old sergeant who had spent thirty-odd years in the service. They were all very polite to me, although I soon discovered everyone took for granted that as an American journalist I had come to do an article exposing the horrors of British colonial rule. But no one seemed to mind. As one young fellow said, "It's quite all right. We're used to it." It is interesting today to read similar accounts by British and French journalists of the atrocities perpetrated by our troops in Vietnam.

The first day of the course was blackboard work and a lecture by Major Elliott. "Your first problem is where to look for tracks. The Mau Mau generally walk near the crest of ridges—not along the crests themselves, as they'd show up on the skyline—but along the side, so they can look over the top. They also follow game trails. Game moves mainly at night, so if you find tracks with spore [animal tracks] over it, you can be reasonably sure the tracks were made the day before. When you find tracks, the next problem is to age them. If they're in soft grass, it's good to remember that grass trodden on straightens up in from one to six hours, depending on the weather and the type of grass." Here the major went into a discussion of the different types of Kenya grasses and their resiliency in dry or wet weather. "If the tracks are in damp earth, they'll change color as the sun hits them. Because the pressure of a man's foot squeezes some of the moisture out of the ground, the print will go from gray to a slaty white, again depending on weather conditions and the type of earth. Make a scratch mark in the earth and compare its color with the color of the print. Now, if the man has walked over leaves, remember that the underside of a fallen leaf turns yellow, and a leaf that has been stepped on tends to curl. By getting low and at an angle to the trail you can see the yellow edges of the trodden leaves among the others, and the degree of curl tells the age of the track. Look out for spiderwebs across the trail. A complete web usually takes from six to eight hours to spin—depending on the type of spider." The major then described the various species of spiders and how long each one took to spin a web. "Keep an eye out for broken twigs. If the ends of the twigs are clean and white, they're freshly broken. Don't confuse twigs broken by game with twigs broken by humans. The hard hooves of antelope and gazelles usually make a sharp break; a man tends to bend and crack a twig. The gangs will automatically wade along all streams they cross to throw off tracking dogs. Look for water splashed on stones and on the banks to see where they came out."

Another former game warden, Fred Bartlett, described a tracking case he'd been called in on recently. An Italian resident in Kenya had been killed, together with his wife and family. "For the first fourteen miles, the trail of the gang was easy to follow. It was the dry season, and the earth was too hard to show tracks, but the ground was covered with knee-high dead grass. When a man walks through this grass, he bends it at a slightly different angle than the grass around it. If you look directly down, you don't notice the difference, but by looking ahead and moving about until you get the right angle, you can see the trail as clearly as a footpath.

"After the raiders had crossed the open bush country and reached the forest, the tracking was harder, but we could still follow them by lifting bushes and finding tracks under the branches. The branches spring back after a man has gone through and don't leave any sign, but often you can find tracks in the soft earth under them. We camped that night in the brush and went on at dawn. One hour in the early morning is worth four at any other time of day, for we could see where they'd knocked dew off the bushes.

"At two o'clock that afternoon, our tracker pointed to the tracks with his chin—natives don't use their fingers to point. Bent blades of grass were still oozing juice. Then we came on a bit of saliva where a man had spat. It was still damp, and although strong breezes were blowing, no dust had settled on it. The raiders were just ahead.

"We caught up with them in some thick stuff. One man was still wearing the dead Italian's coat. We started shooting, and the MMs bolted. We got two but the rest escaped. Today, we know more about the business and wouldn't have been so keen to rush it—we'd have spread out and surrounded them."

That afternoon, Major Elliott took the school out in the bush country for some practical examples of the points he'd made in the lecture. "We probably won't find any Mau Mau tracks, but we should find some signs of carriers," he explained. "Carriers" are the village natives, often women, who carry food from their *shambas* (small vegetable patches) to the gangs hiding out in the forests.

Kenya bush country somewhat resembles the semiarid areas of the Southwest. The ground is generally covered by yellow knee-high grass, with occasional patches of sandy soil. Unless the quarry being tracked has walked over these sandy patches, there is seldom any regular series of tracks. There is only part of an imprint in a patch of dust, ten feet farther on a little crushed grass, then some disturbed leaves fifteen feet along the trail, and so on. Whenever possible, three trackers are used. The man doing the actual tracking watches the trail ahead. The other two follow him, one watching to the left and the other to the right to make sure that the gang hasn't turned off suddenly. The men were rotated every two hours to give the main tracker a rest. Tracking is hard work and a strain on the eyes, especially under bright sun.

Often a tracker is merely following the "drift" of the trail rather than systematically going from sign to sign. If a tracker sees from the direction of a trail that a gang is obviously heading for a saddle in the hills or a ford across a river, he goes ahead at a trot, simply keeping a lookout for occasional signs as a check.

We came to a waterhole—a big, muddy depression with a puddle of greenish water in the center. There was a line of human footprints through the mud, almost obliterated by the spore of game animals that had come down to drink.

"Good," said the major. He turned to me. "Now you listened to the lecture this morning. What can you tell about those tracks?"

I was able to say that the tracks had been made before midnight, as there had been a sprinkle of rain then and there were marks of raindrops in the imprints. The major nodded. "Now look at those little balls of mud that come up between the toes." He picked one up and crumbled it between his fingers. "Hard, but not baked out. Mud like that will dry out in two hours but won't get baked until it's had at least ten hours of sun. We had a sunny day yesterday and sun today. Those tracks were made after sunset last night and, as you say, before midnight. What else?"

Knowing that the tracks were probably made by a carrier and that most carriers were women, I studied the tracks for size. They looked small so I guessed a woman.

"Right," said the major. "From the size it could be either a woman or a boy, but the feet are splayed. Because native women carry heavy loads on their backs, their feet are usually splayed. Now, was the woman carrying a load?"

I asked one of our native trackers to walk beside the tracks so I could compare the marks. The woman's imprints were deeper, so I guessed that she was carrying a heavy load.

"Wrong," said the major. "Her tracks are deeper because she was running. See how the toes spread out? Also, notice the length of her stride. Now, why was she running? Let's see if we can find out."

All twelve of the native trackers, each with an armed guard to protect him in case of ambush, spread out to look for signs. I waited with the major. In a few minutes, there was a whistle from one of the trackers. He had found where a group of men had walked through the grass, obviously the night before. We followed the trail until we came to some soft earth that showed the imprint of part of a boot heel.

"A military patrol," said the major, glancing at the mark. "She was coming back after leaving food for the Mau Mau, and bumped the patrol in the dark. She bolted off, and they probably didn't even see her. No use following her. We'll cross dozens of these food-carrier tracks. All right, now we'll divide the school into two groups. Fred, you take one group and I'll take the other. We'll start off, and then you start tracking us. We'll try to throw you off."

When I left the school, Major Elliott saw me off. "I hope you found it interesting," he said rather apologetically. "Of course, you Americans won't have any need for tracking. It's only used in guerrilla warfare, the sort of thing you'll never be involved in. The next war, if one comes, will definitely be a push-button affair and there'll be no need for these old skills."

"Of course," I answered sincerely. I was watching the last stand of colonialism with white men fighting primitive natives and forced to use equally primitive techniques. As the United States was not a colonial power, nothing like this could happen with us.

The most dramatic method of manhunting is with hounds. Traditionally the hounds used for this purpose are bloodhounds. There is considerable question as to what constitutes a "bloodhound." Roughly speaking, I would say there are three general types. Several hundred years ago, a special breed of tracking dog (I think it would be more correct to speak of them as "dogs" rather than "hounds") was developed to track fugitive slaves and then hold them at bay until the horsemen could come up. Apparently these tracking dogs were first developed in Cuba, as they are usually referred to as "Cuban bloodhounds." They were fast, very aggressive dogs, and probably did not have especially good powers of scent. The "true" bloodhound is much bigger, much slower, and has amazing powers of scent—possibly the best scenting powers of any animal. They are extremely docile and never attempt to attack their quarry. Purebred bloodhounds exhibited in dog shows have become so intensely bred for show points that they are not (to the best of my knowledge) used for actual tracking work. Men who use bloodhounds professionally employ a "working bloodhound" that is not as heavy as the show hounds. They have straighter legs, lack the exaggerated haws and very long, drooping ears, and are faster.

Tracking bloodhounds are never, or hardly ever, worked free. They are always kept on a lead. This is partly because they would quickly outdistance the handler (except in open country where the handler can be mounted), and as they do not give tongue (which would alert the fugitive) cannot be traced. As they are not aggressive, when they overtake the fugitive, they do not bay him and could easily be killed by a man with a knife or even a club. Also, even the best hound will sometimes be at fault, especially when tracking such an elusive quarry as man, and needs the handler to put him on the right trail if the fugitive wades down a stream or breaks the trail by running over hot sand or rocks that do not hold the scent.

One of the most experienced bloodhound handlers I've ever met was Lew Proudfoot. Lew was a wiry little man with enormous powers of endurance. He and his wife, Rose, exercised their hounds daily, rain or shine, over the most varied and difficult terrain they could find—dense woods, rocky country, and swamps. In addition, Lew practiced constantly with a rifle and a .38 revolver. "The dogs and I are always out in front, so if any shooting starts we're the first ones to get it," he explained.

Lew outlined his philosophy of working the hounds like this: "The dogs and I are skilled technicians, and we work for anyone who'll pay us. If I had to figure out the rights and wrongs of every case I'm called in on, I'd starve to death." Within three years, Lew and his hounds traveled to Nicaragua, Guatemala, Mexico, Alaska, Japan, and Canada, often on jobs when Lew didn't know who his employers were or whom he was trailing. He was paid to do a job, and that was that.

Once Lew was called out of bed just before dawn at his home near Elverson, Pennsylvania, by two hard-faced men in a black automobile. They began shooting questions at him about his hounds, his experience, and whether the hounds if allowed to run free could be counted on to attack and hold a fugitive. Lew answered all the questions and then said, "Now I've got some questions to ask you."

One of the men pulled out a roll of bills and counted $1,000 into Lew's hand. "Does that answer your questions?"

"It sure does," said Lew. "Let's go."

The men drove Lew and his hounds to Pennsylvania Station in Philadelphia. There they took the Silver Meteor to Miami. One compartment had been reserved for Lew and another for the hounds. In Miami, a magnificent limousine was waiting for them. They were whisked to an airfield where a private plane stood ready on the runway. Not until the plane was in the air was Lew told his destination.

Lew had been hired by Rafael Trujillo then president of the Dominican Republic, to help break up a revolution that had already cost four thousand lives. Two days before, Dominican soldiers had found some revolutionists hiding in a native village some sixty miles from the Haitian border. The men had escaped into the jungle. There was no way of tracking the fugitives except by bloodhounds. Through the speed of modern transportation, President Trujillo had been able to send for Lew Proudfoot and have him on the spot before the trail grew too old for tracking. Lew never found out how the Dominican government got his name.

As soon as the plane landed, Lew was met by a Dominican Army officer with a company of soldiers. "You must put the dogs on the trail immediately," he ordered. Lew insisted that the hounds have a few hours' rest and some water. He had brought six hounds. He selected two of the best, Duke and Tojo. Leaving the rest of the hounds at the plane, he started off with the officer and his men for the native village.

"I was going to take the dogs into the village and put them on the trail at the house where the fugitives had been sleeping," Lew explained. "But the officer didn't want that. 'If the villagers see the dogs, they'll know what we're doing. They may send a runner ahead to warn the men.' So I told him to send some soldiers into the village and get the men's bedclothes. When they came back with the blankets, I gave the dogs the men's scent. Then we made a big circle around the village through the jungle, walking slow and letting the dogs go first. When we crossed the men's trail, the hounds began to whine. I said 'Get 'em boys,' and we were off."

The trail was nearly three days old but the damp jungle held the scent. The undergrowth was terrible. In places, the hounds were almost crawling on their bellies under the thorn thickets. Lew had to stay with them. After a few miles both hounds were covered with blood from the thorns. Mosquitoes swarmed around the hounds' heads, biting their soft noses and getting under their great hanging ears. Their feet began to bleed, and left red stains in the pad marks. Yet the two bloodhounds never lost the scent and never hesitated in their steady trailing.

Finally the hounds showed signs that the trail was getting hot. They began to tremble with excitement. Occasionally they would stop and freeze, like bird dogs pointing. They were catching wisps of air-borne scent coming, not from the trail ahead, but directly from the fugitives themselves.

Lew saw a tiny shack made of palm leaves. This was the revolutionists' hideout. He stopped the hounds and silently pointed it out to the officer. The man nodded. He gave a whispered command, and his men sprawled out through the jungle to surround the hut.

"My job was finished," said Lew. "I just sat down with the hounds and we watched. The officer shouted to the men inside the hut to surrender. They refused. Then everyone started shooting. After four of the revolutionists had been killed, the rest gave up. We took them back to Ciudad Trujillo. I don't know what happened to them, but I'd be surprised to hear that they died of old age."

Even when not on a job, Lew keeps the hounds in practice by constant trailing. Bloodhounds instinctively track, just as bird dogs will instinctively find and point coveys, but to get the best results from any dog, the animal must be trained.

Two men are needed to train a bloodhound—the handler and someone who plays the part of the fugitive. At first, the fugitive simply calls the hound to him, rewarding him with a bit of liver. Gradually the distance is increased, but for the first two weeks the fugitive never gets out of sight of the hound.

Then, after calling the hound, the fugitive runs behind a building, leaving on the ground a handkerchief heavily impregnated with his scent. A small bit of liver is left with the handkerchief. After the hound has eaten the liver, the handler shows him the handkerchief saying, "Go get 'em, boy." If the hound doesn't take the scent, the fugitive calls to him while still hiding. Eventually the hound learns to follow the trail.

Finally, the fugitive takes short walks through the woods, dragging his feet in order to leave a better trail. When the hound finds him, the dog is always rewarded with a piece of liver. Slowly, the hound gets into the spirit of the game. He lives for nothing but unraveling complicated trails. Then he may be considered trained. Lew believes it takes from a year to sixteen months for a bloodhound to be properly trained.

A bloodhound handler of a somewhat different sort is George Brooks of La Crosse, Wisconsin. When I knew George he was a man of fifty-one, working as a soda clerk at the Bodega Lunch Club, but his real life was with his hounds. He had an understanding with Mr. Bonadurer, the proprietor, that when the police called on him he could leave his job at any time to take out the hounds. George had no interests except his great dogs. He never read a magazine or book, never went to a motion picture, did not drink or smoke, and to keep himself in hard condition lived on a diet of ground round steak.

Perhaps George's most famous case was the capture of Ray Olson, a slot-machine racketeer, stolen-car operator, and suspected kidnapper. A posse had traced Olson to an isolated cabin near Cable, Wisconsin. Olson shot two deputy sheriffs, and escaped. The greatest manhunt in the state's history was launched, and George's bloodhounds were called in.

"To track a man you need two things," George told me. "You must know where the man has walked so you can put the hounds on his trail, and you should have a 'scent guide,' something he has handled so the dogs will know whom they're after. In the Olson case, I hadn't either. By the time I got to the cabin, hundreds of people had walked around it, and there was nothing I could be sure only Olson had touched. Finally I took the dogs out half a mile from the cabin and cut a great circle. They hit a trail and looked at me inquiringly. I said, 'Man gone, boys,' and they struck out. For three days 175 posse men and I followed that trail with no security but the hounds' noses. Then we began to come on the smoldering ruins of cabins. Olson burned down every cabin he slept in, to make sure he wouldn't leave behind a scent guide I could use for the dogs. The hounds would just circle the smoking remains and pick up the trail again on the other side."

Then Olson tried to throw off the dogs by hiding out in the Chippewa Flowage, a great lake region studded with tiny islands. Knowing that scent won't lie on water, Olson built rafts and traveled for miles along the inlets. But sooner or later he had to land, and the hounds picked up the scent again. Then, after two weeks of constant trailing, Olson made a sudden shortcut across country. George could tell by the direction the dogs were working that Olson must be headed for a distant lake. Part of the posse went on by car to cut him off. When they arrived at the lake the posse men sighted Olson running for a boat tied to a wharf. They all opened fire, and Olson dropped riddled by fifty-six slugs. When the hounds arrived they smelled the body and looked up at George with their mournful, floppy-eared faces. No matter what these human beings did to one another, the hounds knew that they had done their job and pleased their master. Being only dogs, they had no other interest.

George never takes the hounds out of their pen except to put them on a trail. As they are exercised daily, he hires schoolchildren to lay trails for the hounds. "Bloodhounds like to trail but they get bored with it," he explained. "If you take them out for a walk, they'll pick up a trail, follow it for a while, then change to another and keep that up. When you take them out on a case, they'll do the same thing. So whenever I take them out, they know they've got a job to do and I make them stay on the one line until they find the quarry."

George thinks the most remarkable feat of trailing that his hounds ever performed occurred in Eitzen, Minnesota, when his big bloodhound King followed a six-day-old trail down the pavement of a busy town. A man had vanished after leaving a suicide note, and a posse of eighty-five men had been looking for him for nearly a week. They found his car, abandoned on a side road, and George put King on the faint scent.

"In all the years I had King, that was the only time I'd ever seen him drop his head on a trail. Always before, he'd worked with his nose in the air, no matter how poor the scent was," said George. The road had been graded, leaving a ridge of dirt along one side. The scent had long ago been blown off the road itself, but apparently some of it was still lodged along the base of the ridge. King followed the ridge, not the road, and took the posse to a little place named Dorchester across the line in Iowa. The hound continued to work up the sidewalk, although thousands of people must have walked over the faint trail. The supposed suicide was finally located in a restaurant having lunch. He was returned to his family.

The Jens Thompson case is a perfect example of the uncanny trailing abilities of bloodhounds and the terrible persistence with which they follow a trail in spite of everything. Jens Thompson was a farmer living near Houston, Minnesota, who got into an argument with some neighbors named Lukes. After brooding over his wrongs, Jens got a rifle and shot four of the Lukeses. Then he took to the woods. The murders occurred during the worst drought in the history of Minnesota. Dry ground makes very poor tracking, and George had nothing to go on. Then a boy reported seeing a man in an apple orchard who might be Jens. The hounds picked up the scent and started off.

For four days the posse followed the hounds through the dense forests with no assurance except the behavior of the hounds that they were on the right trail. Constantly breathing in the hot, dry dust put a heavy strain on the animals. George was using two hounds—a powerful, determined southern hound named Big Ted, and his famous King. King, who was doing most of the trailing, developed a hemorrhage of the lungs, and began to bleed at the mouth. He still kept going. On the fifth day the hounds were going through a cornfield when King stopped and started to dig. He uncovered a corncob with kernels gnawed off. Jens had stopped in the field to get food, and in order to hide his trail had buried the corncob. For the first time the posse knew they were really on the murderer's trail, for no one else would have taken the trouble to bury the cob.

In the next ten days most of the posse men dropped out. George slept on the trail with no covering but his hounds. At one place the desperate fugitive jumped off a thirty-five-foot cliff, hoping the hounds wouldn't dare to follow him. King and Ted slid down the rock face with George hanging onto their leashes. The despairing sheriff offered George $5,000 if he'd turn the hounds loose. George refused. "Jens still has his gun, and he'd shoot my dogs if they caught up to him."

In a last attempt to throw off the hounds, Jens climbed to the top of an almost unscalable hill and then doubled back parallel to his own trail. The climb took him nearly all day. On his way down, it began to rain. As the hounds approached the hill, they were able to air-scent the fresh trail in the cool, moist air. Ignoring the hill, they cut across to the new trail. Suddenly the exhausted fugitive found George and the hounds only a few hundred yards behind him. He could do no more. When the posse finally caught up, Jens surrendered without a struggle.

Later George asked Jens why he hadn't shot the hounds and saved himself. "Why, I haven't anything against those dogs," the big farmer said calmly. "They were just doing their job. I'm only sorry I didn't get old man Lukes as well as his four sons."

Although the use of bloodhounds has always been recognized in police work, employing attack dogs that would not only follow the fugitive but attack him was considered inhuman. When attack dogs were used by police in Alabama against Negro demonstrators, the whole world was shocked. Now the use of attack dogs is a standard practice in nearly all large cities. Subway crimes in New York became so common some solution had to be found. A criminal could run from a policeman, especially as in the crowded subways the officer did not dare to use his gun. Police dogs, trained to follow, attack, and hold a fugitive proved to be the answer. The dog most ideally suited for this work would probably be the now extinct Cuban bloodhound.

Why do human beings want to hunt? It is not a basic desire to kill; no one enjoys wringing a chicken's neck or butchering steers. It is not a desire for food. The most famous hunt of all, immortalized by millions of paintings and dozens of songs and stories, is the fox hunt. Hunting is the thrill of the chase and the satisfaction of outwitting the quarry. If we can believe Robert Ardrey's conclusions in *African Genesis,* man, ever since he first developed from lower anthropoids, has been a hunter. There is not and never was a nonhunting human being—it would be a contradiction of terms. Most people can no more deny their desire to hunt than they can deny the sex drive.

As man grew in ingenuity, he naturally invented more efficient means of hunting—the more efficient, the better. He invented the gun, which still remains the most practical all-around hunting device. But still more efficient methods of killing have been developed: automatic rifles, bombs, the hand grenade, the flamethrower, poison gas. Man was forced to limit himself in the interest of "sport" to conventional firearms, and even to restrict their use to certain seasons. Otherwise he would have exterminated the game, and turned himself from a hunter into a purposeless killer as well.

The time may have now come when man must even further restrict himself, not by laws but by inclination. Every year we are growing more interested in wild animals for themselves alone. For years the only books on African big game were descriptions of how to shoot them. The sensational success of Joy Adamson's books on Elsa, and others, shows that interests are changing. The Adamson books involve killing—it was necessary to shoot game to feed Elsa, and the lioness herself had to be trained to kill—but it was killing with a purpose, not killing for killing's sake. People are interested in Elsa because a lioness is a large, dangerous animal. Mrs. Adamson also had a pet hyrax, a jolly little fellow resembling a woodchuck who never hurt anything, but a hyrax simply does not have the appeal of a predator, for the predator can kill and man is a predator.

In all the sports described in this book, the primary interest lies with the animals. They are not simply targets; they are skillful adversaries. At worst, they always have at least a sporting chance. In some cases they have as much chance of killing the hunter as he has of killing them.

As animals decrease in numbers and sportsmen increase, some limitation on man's powers to kill must be found. For many generations, the gun was the symbol of man's domination over other creatures. That man is dominant no one now doubts. A twelve-year-old girl armed with a powerful enough rifle can kill every sort of African big game—and has. To shoot a deer with a rifle is no longer a proof of one's masculinity. A generation is growing up that no longer has the tradition of Teddy Roosevelt or Ernest Hemingway. These "modern" forms of hunting are now old-fashioned. People want something new. To find it, they go deeper into the past. They are more interested in skills and techniques than in results, for with modern firearms anyone can get results.

This, then, is not a book on ancient sports but a book on the sports of the future. I hope future sportsmen may get some ideas from it.

SELECTED BIBLIOGRAPHY AND SOURCES OF WEAPONS AND ANIMALS

Chapter I The Feral Cats

Two good general books on the feral cats are *Cats of the World,* by Armand Denis (Houghton Mifflin, New York, 1964), and *Wild Cats,* by C. B. Colby (Duell, Sloan & Pearce, New York, 1964). For training the wildcats, see *Traité de fauconnerie et autourserie,* by Abel Boyer and Maurice Planiol (Payot, Paris, 1948). It has a chapter on the cheetah and caracal. See also J. E. Harting, *Essays on Sport and Natural History* (Horace Cox, London, 1883), with a chapter on cheetahs and how to make hoods.

For magazine articles on hunting with cheetahs in India, see the *National Geographic Magazine,* February, 1942, "Life with an Indian Prince," by John and Frank Craighead; and *Natural History,* March, 1938, "World's Fastest Hunt," by Robert Cushman Murphy. For training cheetahs to course hare in Europe, see *Le Saint-Hubert* magazine (official organ of the Saint-Hubert Club of France), August, 1948, "Les Guépards de Course," by V. Marchand.

Anyone contemplating purchasing a feral cat should by all means write to Mrs. Harry G. Cisin, Long Island Ocelot Club, Amagansett, Long Island, New York. Club membership is $5 a year, and for this you receive the club newsletter, with such useful information as descriptions of cat diseases, names of vets who know the feral cats, how to import and train them, and local laws concerning them. Mrs. Cisin also sells pamphlets on the ocelot and the margay. Both are excellent. Club members have everything from lions to margays; they are not confined to ocelots.

Chapter II The Blowgun

The blow gun I used on the deer hunt was made by the Wham-O Manufacturing Company, 835 E. El Monte St., San Gabriel, California 91778. Since then, the

Survival Research Company, 71 Ridge Crescent, Manhasset, New York 11030, has turned out a very superior precision-made blowgun. Cherokee blowguns could formerly be purchased from the Qualla Arts and Crafts Co-op, Cherokee, North Carolina, but I have been unable to get one from them in recent years. Apparently the Cherokees don't use them anymore. A pity, for these big guns with their two-foot wooden darts were excellent for small game.

Chapter III Falconry

A useful introduction to falconry is *A Beginner's Manual of Falconry,* by S. Herman, E. Jameson, Jr., and Hans Peeters, published by the California Hawking Club, Davis, California. This book also has a list of dealers who sell hawking tackle, and a list of bookstores specializing in books on falconry. A handsome and elaborate work is *North American Falconry and Hunting Hawks,* by Frank L. Beebe and Harold M. Webster, privately printed in 1964. An excellent book on accipiters is *A Hawk for the Bush,* by J. Mavrogordato (Witherby, London, 1961). Two of the famous old stand-bys are *The Art and Practice of Hawking,* by E. B. Michell (Methuen, London, 1900), and *Coursing and Falconry,* in the Badminton Library of Sports and Pastimes, by Harding Cox and Gerald Lascelles (Longmans, Green, 1892).

Chapter IV Hunting With the Bow and Arrow

An excellent general work on archery is *New Guide to Better Archery,* by Thomas A. Forbes (Collier Books, New York, 1962). Books on hunting with the bow are *Modern Bowhunting,* by Hiram J. Grogan (Archers Publishing Co., Box 832, Norristown, Pennsylvania), and *Bow Hunting for Deer,* by H. R. "Dutch" Wambold, 322 North 6th St., Emmaus, Pennsylvania. Some of the old classics are *The Witchery of Archery,* by Maurice Thompson (Archers' Co., Pinehurst, North Carolina, 1928); *Hunting with the Bows and Arrows,* by S. T. Pope (James H. Barry Co., San Francisco, 1923); *Hunting the Hard Way,* by Howard Hill (Follett Publishing Co., Chicago, 1953), and *Wild Adventure,* by Howard Hill (Stackpole Co., Harrisburg, Pennsylvania, 1954).

There are several magazines published for archers, including *Bow and Arrow,* Gallant Publishing Co., 550-A S. Citrus Avenue, Covina, California. Articles on big-game hunting in Africa and elsewhere with the bow appear in its issues of July–August, 1963; September–October, 1963; May–June, 1964. Anyone interested in the sport should write to the National Archery Association, 23 East Jackson Blvd., Chicago 4, Illinois.

Chapter V The Crossbow

In *Archery World,* January, 1965, there is a good description of how to make a crossbow. Articles on crossbows and hunting with crossbows appeared in the *Bow and Arrow* magazine for January–February, 1964; November–December, 1965; and July–August, 1963. Crossbows are obtainable from George Stevens, Huntsville, Arkansas; Dave Benedict, 20601 Covello St., Canoga Park, California; and Wham-O Manufacturing Co., 835 E. El Monte St., San Gabriel, California 91778. Anyone interested in the crossbow should write to the *National Crossbowman,*

10 Arlington Road, Cranford, New Jersey 07016.

The definitive book on crossbows is *The Crossbow: Mediaeval and Modern, Military and Sporting,* by Sir Ralph Payne-Gallwey (The Holland Press, 112 Whitfeld St., London, W.1, 1964).

Chapter VI   Ferrets

The magazine *Fur-Fish-Game* in its classified ads usually has ferrets advertised for sale. One dealer who handles ferrets and also makes the copes and harnesses is Allen Latzig, Howard Lake, Minnesota. An excellent book on ferrets is *Ferrets: Facts and Fancies,* by A. R. Harding, obtainable through *Fur-Fish-Game,* 2878 E. Main St., Columbus 9, Ohio. Published in 1944, it deals mainly with the great old days of ferreting.

Chapter VII   Boomerangs

Several companies have put various makes of boomerangs on the market. Often they will discontinue a certain model, so it is hard to say what companies are making what sort of boomerangs for what purpose at any specific time. The companies here listed have been making booms, mostly of the return type, for some years.

Colonel John M. Gerrish, 4409 S.W. Parkview Lane, Portland 1, Oregon, makes the best boomerangs I have found. They can be used on small game if the wingtips are reinforced with copper wire.

Wham-O, 835 E. El Monte St., San Gabriel, California 91778, makes a set of 12 boomerangs from plastic, 10½ inches across. A good, inexpensive outfit for practice.

General Sportcraft, 215 Park Avenue South, New York, N.Y. 1003, also makes servicable practice boomerangs.

Bill Onus, who can be reached through W. & J. Barr, 105–7 Brunswick St., Fitzroy, N.6. Victoria, Australia, makes very handsome painted Australian boomerangs. They are trimmed to approximate the skew twist.

By far the best book on boomerang throwing and making is *Primitive and Pioneer Sports,* by Bernard S. Mason (A. S. Barnes, New York 1937). Unfortunately this book is out of print, but it can occasionally be found in libraries or secondhand bookstores.

The *Encyclopaedia Britannica* (fourteenth edition) has a brief but good article on boomerangs, with a useful bibliography.

Articles on boomerangs have appeared in *Nature,* Vol. 63, 1901, London, pp. 388–340; *Scientific American,* August, 1939, Vol. 161, pp. 90–91; *Sports Afield,* March, 1956; *Sports Illustrated,* August 16, 1954, pp. 66–68; and *L'Aéronaute,* 4ᵉ année, No. 7 (Juin, 1871), pp. 97–102.

Chapter VIII   Badger Digging

A good account of badger digging is in *Hunt and Working Terriers* by Captain Jocelyn Lucas (Chapman & Hall, London, 1931). Also in *Animaux de vénerie et chasse aux chiens courants,* by J. Oberthur (Durel-Editeur, 103 Quai Branly, Paris, 1947), pp. 111–125.

Chapter IX The Bola

I don't know of any place in the United States where bolas can be purchased. I got mine from La Cruz del Sur, Galerías Pacífico, Florida 753 Local F. 17-T.E. 32–0091, Buenos Aires, Argentina. I know of no book in English that gives an account of the bola. The best book I've found is *Trenzas Gauchas, sequido de El Cuarto de la Sogas y Al Tranco,* by Mario A. López Osornio (Artes Gráficas Bartolome U. Cheiesino, Ameghino 838, Avellaneda, Buenos Aires), pp. 193–196. For the Eskimo bolas see *American Ethnology,* Ninth Annual Report, p. 244.

Chapter X Aquatic Hunting

The best account of training cormorants in English is *The Domestication of the Cormorant in China and Japan,* by Bertold Laufer, published in the Anthropological Series, V. 18, No. 3, Natural History Museum, Chicago, Illinois. There is also an account in the *American Naturalist,* January–February, 1926, Vol. 60. There is a brief account in *Les Oiseaux de sport,* by Pierre-Amédée (Librairie ad. Legoupy, Paris, 1903), pp. 27–35. This article includes an account of training pelicans.

There is a chapter devoted to trained cormorants and otters in *Falconry: Its Claims, History and Practice,* by Gage E. Freeman and Francis H. Salvin (Longman and Roberts, London, 1859). This is the only book I know that describes how to train an otter for sport.

Chapter XI Steel in the Surf

I know of nothing on harpooning sharks in the surf, or on manta rays. On catching and keeping saltwater aquarium fish, there are *Capture et acclimatation des poissons exotiques* (Paris, Payot, 1938); *Salt-water Aquarium Fish,* by Herbert R. Axelrod and William Vorderwinkler (Sterling Publishing, New York, 1965); *The Salt-water Aquarium in the Home,* by Robert P. Straugham (A. S. Barnes, New York, 1964). The *National Geographic Magazine,* Vol. 79, 1941, pp. 347–372, has a good account of catching saltwater fish for aquariums.

Chapter XII Hunting American Big Game With Hounds

Two books on native American big-game hounds that I have found helpful are *The American Trail Hound,* by Fred Streever (A. S. Barnes, New York, 1948), and *Hunting Dogs,* by Oliver Hartley (A. R. Harding, Columbus, Ohio, 1937).

Chapter XIII Formal Hunting

There are many books on fox hunting but comparatively few on otter and stag: *Deer, Hare and Otter Hunting* (The Lonsdale Library, Vol. XXII, Seeley, Service & Co., 196 Shaftesburg Avenue, London, no date); *Animaux de venerie et chasse aux chiens courants,* by J. Oberthur (Durel-Editeur, 103 Quai Branly,

Paris, 1947) ; *Beasts of the Chase,* by Lionel Edwards (Putnam, London, 1950) ; *Horn and Hound,* by H. A. Bryden (Methuen, London, 1927). Two interesting books on the general subject of hounds are *Hounds of the World,* by Sir John Buchanan-Jardine (Scribner's, New York, 1937), and *Hounds and Hunting Through the Ages,* by Joseph B. Thomas (Garden City, New York, 1928).

Two excellent books on beagling are *Beagling,* by W. Lovell Hewitt (Faber & Faber, London, 1960), and *American Beagling,* by G. G. Black (Putnam, New York, 1940).

Chapter XIV Snake Catching

A useful book in this field is *Snakes and Snake Hunting,* by Carl F. Kauffeld (Doubleday, Garden City, N.Y., 1957). There are, of course, a number of good general books on snakes, such as *A Field Guide to Reptiles and Amphibians of the United States and Canada East of the 100th Meridian,* by Roger Conant (Boston, Houghton Mifflin, 1958); and *Snakes Alive,* by Clifford H. Hope (The Viking Press, New York, 1949). The best book on rattlesnakes I know is *Rattlesnakes: Their Habits, Life Histories and Influence on Mankind,* by Laurence M. Klauber. University of California Press, Berkeley, California, 1956). *Travel* magazine for May, 1934, has a good article on Ma Hae, "A King Cobra Performs," by Captain Frank Outram. There is a good article on Egyptian fakirs and African cobras in *Travel* for September, 1921, "Moussa Mohammed, Snake Finder of Luxor," by Elizabeth L. McQueen.

Chapter XV Toads

Except for the brief reference in *Traité de fauconnerie et autourserie,* I know of no references to using toads to hunt small game. The *National Geographic Magazine* for April, 1950, has a good article on toads and frogs. There is also the *Handbook of Frogs and Toads of the United States and Canada,* by Anna Wright (Comstock Press, Ithaca, New York, 1933). The best book I know on keeping toads and frogs in captivity is *Frogs and Toads as Pets,* by Herbert R. Axelrod (T.F.H. Publications, 245 Cornelison Ave., Jersey City 2, New Jersey).

Chapter XVI Manhunting

I know of no books on mantraps or man tracking. A good book on bloodhounds is *Bloodhounds,* by Leon F. Whitney (Orange Judd Publishing Co., New York, 1947). There are chapters on using bloodhounds to track man in *Hounds of the World,* by Sir John Buchanan-Jardine (Scribner's, New York, 1937), and *Beasts of the Chase,* by Lionel Edwards (Putnam, London, 1950).